BACK IN THE SADDLE AGAIN

GENE AUTRY
with Mickey Herskowitz

Back
in the Saddle
Again

Doubleday & Company, Inc.
Garden City, New York   1978

Library of Congress Cataloging in Publication Data

Autry, Gene, 1907–
Back in the saddle again.

Discography: p. 191
Filmography: p. 207
Includes index.
1. Autry, Gene, 1907–   2. Moving-picture actors and actresses—United
States—Biography.   3. Singers—United States—Biography.
I. Herskowitz, Mickey, joint author.   II. Title.
PZ2287.A9A32   791.43′028′0924 [B]
ISBN: 0-385-03234-x
Library of Congress Catalog Card Number 76–18332

To my wife Ina, and the memory
of my mother, and to all of Saturday's
children . . .

ACKNOWLEDGMENT

The author wishes to express his thanks to Leslie Adams, Western film historian, whose files provided answers when memory alone could not. My thanks also to Pat Watkowski, for her efficient secretarial services; to Nancy Perez and Davelyn Leister for their research; and to the many friends who contributed to the lifetime described in this book.

Contents

BACK IN THE SADDLE AGAIN

CHAPTER ONE

A Ticket to Ride

I was picking when I should have been tapping, but the customer didn't seem to mind. The opening of the door had startled me. I slid my feet off the counter top and moved to put away my guitar. But he motioned—with the hand that held the copy—for me to continue. Then he sat down at the scarred old writing desk in the waiting room.

I have long since forgotten what song, if any, he interrupted. I might have been just strumming, what they call *improvising* today. You did a lot of that to pass the long nights in the telegraph office; especially if you were in Chelsea, Oklahoma, as I was on that evening in the summer of 1927, working as a relief operator on the Frisco Line.

Near the end of the four-to-midnight shift all interruptions were welcome. When I finished whatever tune I had been playing, the visitor asked me to sing another. I did, with great energy. From time to time he nodded at me, looking up from the pages he was fussing over.

When he dropped his copy on the counter, he said, "You know, with some hard work, young man, you might have something. You ought to think about going to New York and get yourself a job on radio."

I knew who the customer was, even before I read to the bottom of the last page and saw where he had signed it, *Will Rogers*. You couldn't spend any time in Oklahoma, after all, and not recognize that face or that voice, which had the sound of a man chewing on cactus.

His words encouraged me, but not quite to the point of quitting my job and barging off to bring Broadway to its knees. I saw Rogers several times that summer. He was visiting a sister in Chelsea, and he'd drop into the telegraph office to wire his columns back to the newspapers in the East.

A full year passed before I was prepared to take his advice. For one thing, I wasn't certain I wanted to throw away my "career" with the railroad. It paid well, for the times. It made you an important man in town. And for a lot of years I had never thought about being anything other than a telegraph operator.

For those under thirty it must be difficult to understand what the railroad once meant to this country. Not just in the movement of people, or the territories it opened, but as a romantic symbol of an age that once was and will never be again. Oh, sure, we still have trains today. But AMTRAK doesn't wave as well or toot as loudly when it goes by.

Many of my early memories are of the railroad, of people milling around the platform and dozing on the benches. It was like that in Tioga, Texas, where I was born, and where the tracks ran right through the heart of town. Folks would flock to the station when they heard the whistle of an arriving train, just to see who got off and who was leaving.

That was a more romantic time, a lilac time, just after the First World War and before the Great Depression. It was a time of gaslights and high starched collars and no Social Security. Along the line between Texas and Oklahoma, the twenties didn't roar much. There were few cars and no paved roads and not everyone could afford a radio. News traveled slowly, when it traveled.

And that was what made the telegraph office the center of our universe. Part of the joy of hanging around the railroad depot was watching, and hearing, the operator tap out his messages in Morse Code. We were the first to know about floods and election results and bank robberies. During the World Series we'd post the score by innings on a blackboard. By late afternoon maybe two hundred people would be standing there, watching the numbers go up, *seeing* the game.

I was in my senior year in high school, at Tioga, when I talked my way into a job at the depot. I'd get up every morning at five-thirty and work for an hour before school, sweeping out the station and unloading the baggage and mail. I'd return at noon to practice the Morse Code, and again after school. I'd even hang around the station at night, listening to the train orders, learning to figure the express and freight and ticket rates.

That was what I wanted and what I expected my life to be: a train dispatcher, maybe work my way up someday to superintendent. I earned a little money on the side entertaining at the Rotary Club and the Chamber of Commerce luncheons, but I saw no real future in that. It struck me as good experience, getting up in front of people, but I wasn't sure why. My other part-time job was more practical. It got me into the movies free.

After we moved to Achille, Oklahoma, I ran the projector at the Dark Feather Theater, where the daily fare usually consisted of Tom Mix and William S. Hart and Harry Carey, and all the serials. I got saddle sore just from watching. I taught myself how to thread the machine, an old Vidagraph, and how to run an arc light.

No, I didn't identify with those fantasy figures on the screen, flickering in the light of my own projector. But I could identify with the fellow under the green eyeshade at the railroad depot. And the railroad offered something real. It offered a hundred and fifty dollars a month and a better life. Those tracks led to other places and I planned to ride them out of the small towns that had been the only world I knew.

Let me say right off that there is no point in trying to glorify one's childhood. Growing up is simply one of the debts we must pay to society. It is hard for me, at best, to imagine anyone caring whether I slopped hogs as a kid. But if you are going to tell your story and wrap it between covers, what you came from ought to be included. As they say, a bar of the music that made the man.

The essential facts are these:

I was born Orvon Gene Autry on September 29, 1907, at Tioga, Texas, the son of Delbert and Elnora Ozmont Autry. My grandfather was a Baptist preacher, William T. Autry, a practical man who taught me to sing when I was five in order to use me in his church choir. He was short a soprano. Grandpa's family had crossed the plains in covered wagons, coming to Texas with the early settlers (and adventurers) from Tennessee, the Houstons and the Crocketts. An Autry died at the Alamo.

I was twelve when I ordered my first guitar out of the worn and discolored pages of a Sears, Roebuck catalogue. The story that I bought it on the installment plan is untrue, the invention of a Hollywood press agent. Local color. I paid cash, eight dollars, money I had saved as a hired hand on my uncle Calvin's farm, baling and stacking hay. Prairie hay, used as feed for the cattle in winter. It was mean work for a wiry boy but ambition made me strong.

I was ambitious mainly to get out of baling hay. The guitar would in time make that possible, but I had no sense of it then. By my fifteenth birthday I knew my way around whatever stages the town had. I was in all of the school plays, and when I sang my cousin, Louise, Uncle Cal's daughter, would accompany me on the piano. I began to earn money in a Tioga café where the nightly collections amounted to about fifty cents.

My mother, who had been a beauty in her day, a gentle and dainty and thoughtful lady, always hoped I would be a professional man. But that dream went against the trend of my time and place. No one I knew as a child attended college. Where I grew up, on the line between Texas and Oklahoma, X was not a rating for dirty movies. It was the legal signature for about a third of the adult population.

But the pace was serene, the life pastoral. We were the sons of ranch hands and farmers and drifters. I knew how to ride a horse and milk a cow and drive a buckboard. I guess we were poor. Nearly everyone was. But the Autrys were never Tobacco Road poor. My father earned good money, when he felt like it, which was some of the time.

Father was a livestock dealer, a horse trader, a foot-loose, aimless man who loved people and animals and the smell of the good earth. He was uneducated and a casual provider, but he had a western sense of values. I remember him talking once about his younger brother, Homer, and saying proudly, "You know, son, that Homer is a fine man. He just won't hardly lie to you in a hoss trade."

Most of my early years were spent moving from one small town to another, all less than a thousand people, scratching a living out of the hard scrabble ground. From Tioga we moved across the Red River into southern Oklahoma, where we lived on a farm at a place called Achille. We pronounced it a-SHEEL, and it was so small you could start a crime wave by stealing three chickens.

That America doesn't exist any more, except in our imaginations, which may be the best place. The three most popular spots in town were the country store, the church, and the barbershop. In Tioga the barber was Old Man Anderson. He cut my hair until I was grown. I think of him half a century later and I can still smell the Lilac Rose talcum on my neck. Long after I was established in the movies I went back to see him. He trimmed my hair and I posed in his chair for pictures. The barbershop was as close to a public library as we had. Featured *Whiz Bang* comics and the *Police Gazette*.

The farmers and ranchers looked forward to receiving their copies of *Capper's Weekly*, which contained all the latest livestock news. It was owned by a man who later became a senator from Kansas. The big-city dailies from Tulsa and St. Louis arrived two or three times a week and it did not take a great deal of news to cause a stir.

The year I was seventeen, in 1924, the headlines told of the brutal murder of a little boy in Chicago named Bobby Franks. Two young men from wealthy families, Nathan Leopold and Richard Loeb, were accused and later convicted of what the press labeled "a thrill killing."

It was in the accounts of the murder trial that my school friends and I puzzled over a reference that was strange to us. None of us had ever before heard of the word "homosexual."

(Ten years later, as a star of the "National Barn Dance" on radio, I did a benefit show at the prison in Joliet, Illinois. One of the inmates was in charge of the entertainment and he went out of his way to put me at ease. He was a quiet, cultured fellow, assigned to the chaplain's office. "Mr. Autry," he said, "I'm Nathan Leopold. I want you to know that while you're here you have nothing to fear. You are probably safer inside these walls than on the streets of Chicago. If anyone made a move at you, the rest of the inmates would gang him on the spot. They know if anything happened, it would be the end of these privileges.")

We lived in a small corner, and we did not always learn in it quickly, but we learned. When radio began to sweep the country, finally reaching Tioga, I taught myself out of a magazine article how to rig my own crystal set. You began by wrapping a copper wire around a salt box. You needed a tuner and a little crystal about the size of a thumbnail. You ran an antenna from the top of your house to the nearest pole, back into the bedroom window and tied it to the "set." Then you'd take a cat whisker, turn it until you found a frequency, put on your headphones and listen to the radio.

When the Fields Brothers Marvelous Medicine Show came to town one summer, looking for a local boy to sing with them, I was recommended to Professor Fields. I traveled with them for three months, softening up audiences with mournful ballads before the professor began pitching his wares: liniment and pills and his own product, a patent medicine called "Fields' Pain Annihilator." This experience so hardened my instincts that, even today, I am not offended by television commercials that sell remedies for stomach gas and underarm odors. Besides, I earned fifteen dollars a week. For a teen-aged boy, in the 1920s, this was more than money. It was the riches of Arabia.

No one in Tioga ever accused the Autry boy of being lazy. I was up milking the cows before the first light and had done a fair day's work by the time I left for school. Later, when we lived in Achille, I rode a horse five or six miles to class. Along the way I did the addition tables in my head. I was good at math, enjoyed it, and knew it might lead to a job with the railroad.

They had in those days, in small towns, a custom called First Monday. Trade day. The ranchers and farmers would pour into town and trade anything under the sun. It was a big day, a festive day.

Father stayed close to the stockyards, the cattle pens. He was a whittler. I can see him yet, working on a stub of wood, one boot raised on a rail, standing there for hours at a time, talking and whittling and bartering. He dealt mostly with the ranchers but, sometimes, with the drummers. These were the merchants who carried their goods in a trunk. They would come into town on the early train and rent a horse and buggy, then make the rounds, stopping at all the country stores and ranches and farms, drumming up business. Father would trade for chickens, eggs, cloth, leather, or whatever they had.

When I was younger he invited me to come along on some of his trips. We would ride twenty-five or thirty miles across the border into Texas, sleeping at night in our wagon. Other times he and Uncle Homer would buy mules, by the hundreds, and sell them at auction to the plantation owners along the Mississippi Delta. When it came to judging stock no one outsmarted my father. But as a businessman he was not very astute. Some days he would bring home five hundred dollars. Other days he would bring home only the lint in his pockets.

Delbert Autry was a handsome man, whose sandy hair, same color as mine, showed no traces of gray up to the day he died at eighty-five. He was well liked, but rigid in his ways. Every son, at some point, may wish he had known his father better. As I grew older, I found myself drawing closer to my uncle Calvin, on whose farm I had done the chores that paid for my first guitar.

Mother encouraged my interest in music, though she never imagined I could make a living at it. She wanted her first-born son to be a professional man, anything other than a farmhand or a cattle trader. At night she sang to us, hymns and folk ballads mostly, and read psalms. I was practically raised on the Twenty-third Psalm. She played the piano, and a guitar in the Latin style, and on Sunday she was the church organist.

We lost her in 1930 from a disease the family never discussed, but which I suspect was cancer. She had been ill quite a long time and suffered terribly with stomach pains. No one ever heard her complain, but her health was never very robust. She didn't weigh much over one hundred pounds.

My father drifted off soon after Mother died and I became the head of the family. I looked after, and supported, my two sisters, Veda and Wilma, and my brother Dudley, who was ten. Years later, under the name of Doug Autry, he tried mightily to break into show business. He traveled with a circus, sang with small bands, worked country club dates and one-nighters wherever he could find them. Doug chased rainbows but I was a poor one, after all, to discourage him, to tell him the effort would not be worth while. I had caught mine.

I always regarded the death of our mother as a tragedy, because I was then on the verge of making the kind of money that might have prolonged her life or made her last days more bearable. The money came too late. She died old at forty-five.

She had gone years without proper medical care. We didn't know about clinics and specialists in Tioga and couldn't afford them if we had. The family had no savings. At fifteen I had gone to work at the railroad as an apprentice for thirty-five dollars a month. Even in those days that salary would barely keep you alive. As a telegraph operator, moving from town to town, I was able to work my way up to one-fifty, a "steady income," as we referred to it proudly in those Depression times. I was able to send part of my pay home, but not enough to help Mother.

The last time I saw her my first records had been released and were attracting notice. I was on my way to Chicago to start a career in radio. If Mother knew she was dying she didn't let on. I talked about postponing my trip. She insisted I leave. "You go to Chicago, Gene," she said. "There might not be a next time."

The telephone call came a few days after I stepped off the train. She had gone into a coma. Within a week Elnora Ozmont Autry was dead. She never saw me in pictures. She didn't live to see me own a ranch, instead of working on one. She had every mother's nervousness about the future of her son.

The last question she asked me, was I *sure* I ought to give up my job with the railroad?

*   *   *

The railroads were still a link to the Old West. Not that I was especially looking for one. The old outlaws had died off or gone to prison, but tradition dies hard in the Southwest and you still read of an occasional train holdup.

One occurred in the little town of Waleeka, Oklahoma, shortly after I had become a full-fledged telegraph operator on the Frisco Line. The Matt Kimes gang hit my station. They were among the last of a special kind of desperado, bred in Oklahoma, whose imagination was limited to banks and train depots. This was just after midnight and the ticket window was down, as a safety precaution. Worked fine, except that when I heard a knock I raised it. Pointed at my nose was the barrel of a gun.

The man holding it said, "This is a stick-up. Let's have the money." If that sounds no more inspired than the average movie dialogue, I can assure you there is no clearer way of getting across the message. One of the gang held the gun on me and another came around and cleaned out the cash box. It contained only change, at most a hundred dollars.

When they left they locked me inside a meat car standing on the platform, what we called a "reefer," used to refrigerate meat between transfers. I was trapped in there for nearly two hours, until the next train came through and stopped. Luckily for me, the signal was down and no train ever runs a red signal. When the train came in, the crew tried to rouse the operator, meaning me, and I kept kicking against the door, hard as I knew how.

You couldn't yell loud enough to be heard outside those cars. They kept looking around and finally one of the crewmen heard me thumping away and let me out. It was so cold in there I thought my ears would fall off.

Of course, this was one scene you would never find in a Gene Autry movie, unless Smiley Burnette or Pat Buttram played it.

I never carried a gun, even though we were in the middle of the Oklahoma oil fields, mean country, and robberies were a part of the job. The railroad instructed us to turn over the money without resistance if we were held up.

Later, when I was working in Bristow, the Kimes gang struck the bank. A crowd gathered outside while they were emptying the safe, and about that time I sauntered out of my office to see what was going on. It was just a few blocks from the station and the word spread fast. I joined the crowd just as one of the robbers, holding a shotgun, backed through the door. I heard him yell inside, "Matt, they're ganging up pretty heavy out here. You better get that loot and get the hell out."

They all started pouring out then and one of them shouted, "Stand back, or some son-of-a-bitch is going to get hurt." Then he fired the shotgun straight up and blew out a window upstairs, over the bank. Four of them piled into a car and drove off.

I had seen Matt Kimes only twice, but I was getting mighty tired of running into him like that. I was reminded of him years later, in 1934, when I arrived in Hollywood to make motion pictures. I met a fellow who was then playing character parts in Westerns, who had actually held up a train in Oklahoma, back in the days when it was still Indian Territory.

His name was Al Jennings. He had gone to prison, served five years of a life sentence, and settled in California, a fine place for a man with stories to spin. He claimed, among other things, that he had run for governor of Oklahoma. There is no record that he did, but it is possible Jennings ran without letting Oklahoma know.

He was an entertaining cuss whose career as an outlaw was brief and somewhat comic. Along with his three brothers, Al failed in his first two attempts to rob a train. The first time he stood on the tracks and tried to flag down the engineer, who ignored him. Al was nearly run over. The next time they rode alongside a roaring locomotive and fired their pistols in the air as a warning. The engineer waved and kept going. They finally robbed a small passenger train of sixty dollars, and Al and one brother were captured a day later. The other two rode into a nearby town and tried to pick a fight with Temple Houston, the son of Sam Houston and a famous lawman of his day. Houston shot them both, killing one.

Al Jennings was a little bitty fellow, dried up like a prune. Kimes was short and stocky and homely. I don't know if there is a conclusion to be drawn from that about bandits as a type, except that the ones I met were not very pretty. Off the screen, either.

When I was a young boy in Achille, listening to the stories of the old-timers, I understood that there was a kind of glory attached to that life. Oklahoma was not what you would call well policed in those days. Three of the popular pastimes of the young rogues of that day were drilling for oil, drinking moonshine whiskey, and cheating Indians.

They were mostly Choctaw and Cherokee. In Oklahoma, each of the Indians was given a portion of land, maybe a hundred acres or so. But they were never trained or prepared for the business dealings that would be coming at them. When the automobile came in, many sold off their land at a fraction of its worth, just to buy a big car they didn't know how to drive.

I had seen the Indians exploited and considered it then, as now, a tragedy. It was no protest on my part, but later when I made my own pictures, I had no taste for the stock cowboy-and-Indian scripts and we avoided them.

From my desk in the telegraph office, I could see the changes taking place all around me. As I say, sooner or later everyone in town dropped by to send a message, or receive one, or watch the trains pull out.

Will Rogers had dropped by and, after a year had rolled on, I had reason to think seriously about what he had said to me. The Depression had given me a reason. It had grown more severe, business had fallen off, and the Frisco Line was cutting back. I didn't know if my singing talent had improved, but I was quite sure that my prospects with the railroad had not. I knew it wouldn't be much longer before I'd be unemployed.

So one morning when the eastbound train pulled out I was on it. I was nineteen, riding free on my railroad pass, and with a hundred and fifty dollars tucked in a sock in my one suitcase. I slept in a chair car for the three days and nights it took us to reach New York. They didn't serve meals on the train out of Chelsea. There was a chain of Fred Harvey restaurants along the route of the Frisco Line, and when the train stopped you'd dash in for a quick meal.

Actually, I didn't take the train directly into New York. I stopped off in Chicago and saw the second Dempsey-Tunney fight on September 22, 1927, under the lights at Soldier Field. While I was in Chicago I looked up Jack Capp, later the president of Brunswick Records, then in charge of the division that made their "race" records—what we call soul music today. I told Capp I had a railroad pass and was going on to New York. He gave me the name of a friend of his at Okeh Records, Tommy Rockwell.

I had no appointments and no clear idea of what I would find when I got there. But I had a few names to call and a pure heart. I didn't know enough to be discouraged.

The train went into Newark and you rode the ferry across the Hudson River. That was when I had my first look at the New York skyline. It was purely a shock for someone from the flatlands of Texas and Oklahoma. I thought to myself, "My God, if I ever get in there I wonder if I can find my way back?"

When the ferry docked, they herded you onto a bus and dropped you at a station across the street from Grand Central. For a dime I checked my suitcase and guitar in a locker and walked outside. I looked around, found a policeman, and asked him, "Where's Times Square?"

He pointed west and said, "Over there about five blocks."

So I walked over to Times Square. It was early on a Sunday morning and the streets were absolutely deserted. The buildings, the empty shops, the whole scene, had the look of a woman the morning after a party, when she wakes up in her flannel night-gown, her hair a mess and no make-up. I had seen Times Square and Broadway in newsreels, always at night with the lights on and the people thick as syrup. This wasn't the way I had pictured it.

But I went back later that evening and the place had sprung to life. It was just an explosion of neon lights and milling crowds. I had on boots and a cowboy hat and western clothes, and a few people shot me a curious look, but most of them were dressed funnier than I was.

I had checked into a hotel on Forty-fifth Street, near Broadway, called the Riley Hall. It wasn't exactly a New York landmark, but the price was right. I planned to stay three weeks to a month. I figured that was how long my bankroll would last me, and that's how much leave the railroad had granted me. See, I hadn't yet quit my job. I had confidence in myself, but no one had ever accused ol' Autry of being *reckless*.

Will Rogers had told me to try radio, but I had another idea. I planned to call on the record companies. It seemed to me that the quickest way to get on radio was to cut a record.

I had met the mother of Johnny Marvin, then a recording artist of some popularity at Victor. I stopped off one day in Butler, Oklahoma, where the family owned a café. Mrs. Marvin told me to look up Johnny if I ever got to New York, and I took the precaution of getting his address and phone number.

When I reached Johnny, he told me his younger brother, Frankie, had just gotten into town and we had a lot in common. Like me, Frankie was broke and trying to get started. I moved into his room at the Manger Hotel, which later became the Taft. We'd both make our separate rounds during the day, and play pool at night. It wasn't much of a social life, but neither one of us had any money to blow on women.

As the weather grew colder, we took turns wearing Frankie's topcoat. It was the only coat we had between us.

The days turned into weeks as I lugged my guitar up and down Broadway, to the rhythm of the record company doors slamming in my face. At the time, there were only a handful of companies—Victor, Columbia, Brunswick, Edison—and I tried them all, day after day, hoping for an audition. My first problem was to get past the reception desk.

I had been waiting for hours in the anteroom at Victor one day, guitar across my lap, when the thought must have struck the receptionist that I might not ever leave. She glanced up, smiled nervously, and asked what kind of songs I did.

"Cowboy stuff, mostly," I said, "and some hillbilly. When I can get anyone to listen."

"I'll listen," she said. "Go ahead, play something."

That was all the encouragement I needed. An audience of one. I was halfway through "Jeannine, I Dream of Lilac Time," when Nat Shilkret, the man who wrote it, by then working for Victor, strolled into the room. He stopped for a moment, then ducked into another office and reappeared with a fellow named Leonard Joy. I now had an audience of three. Joy turned out to be the Number Two man at the company, in charge of promoting new artists and their records.

Joy asked me to come back the next morning. "We're recording a band," he said, "and if you'll be here then we'll cut a test and see what you sound like." There were no tapes then, of course. It was all on wax.

To me the whole process was magic. I didn't sleep much that night. Stayed up for hours, practicing.

When they opened the offices the next morning I was waiting on the doorstep like a bottle of milk. I sang "The Prisoner's Song," a weepy tune, and a Jolson hit, "Climb Upon My Knee, Sonny Boy," probably not the smartest choice on my part, and we cut the test record. After everyone listened to the playback, Nat Shilkret asked me to step into his office.

"You got a nice voice for records," he said, "but you need experience. My advice is go home. Take six months, a year. Get a job on a radio station. Learn to work in front of a microphone."

I didn't feel like a failure. But time had run out on me. I had been in New York a month and had stretched my money as far as it would go, living on five- or ten-cent hamburgers and all the coffee I could hold for a nickel.

When I said good-by to the Marvin boys, Frankie offered a piece of advice. "Forget that Jolson stuff," he said. "Learn to sing some yodel songs. That's more to your style."

With that I rode my railroad pass back home to Oklahoma. Shilkret had given me a to-whom-it-may-concern letter, saying I had potential, and I used it to wangle a radio show over KVOO in Tulsa. I was billed as the Oklahoma Yodeling Cowboy, backed up by Jimmy Wilson's Catfish String Band. Meanwhile, I had gone back to my job as a relief operator working up and down the Frisco Line. The idea of paying for radio talent had not yet caught on in the Southwest.

For the next six months I traveled more back roads than a bootlegger, singing at Kiwanis clubs and high schools and private parties all over the state. And it was during those last days on the railroad that I began to write my own songs, with Jimmy Long, who worked with me as a dispatcher. Jimmy was older, settled, a good influence. Together we came up with one called, "That Silver-haired Daddy of Mine." I sang it on the air in Tulsa and the response delighted us.

Now, for the first time, I read about myself in a daily newspaper. As a favor to a friend, George Goodale, a reporter for the Tulsa *World*, interviewed me. The story made light reading, about a struggling young telegrapher who wanted to be a big-time singer, and we had to buy the managing editor a half gallon of corn whiskey to get it published. Cost three bucks, as I recall. Years later, George became my press agent.

I was ready to try New York again. I had gained experience and exposure and the next step, I thought, was a record contract.

On October 9, 1929, backed up by the guitars of Frankie and Johnny Marvin, I cut my first record for Victor. Johnny had written one of the sides, "My Dreaming of You." Jimmy Long had composed the other, "My Alabama Home."

The rules of the record business were a little loose then. It was not uncommon for an artist to do the same song for more than one company under various labels. So two weeks later I made a test record for Columbia, which released it on the Velvatone label. One of the songs was "Left My Gal in the Mountains," written by a friend of mine named Carson Robinson.

Two other young singers were in the studio that day cutting records. One was Rudy Vallee and, yes, he had his megaphone with him. I consider Vallee one of the great performers of all time, still going strong, still popular, in his seventies. One of my first guest appearances on network radio would come on Rudy's show, "The Fleischmann Yeast Hour."

The other singer was an ample, sweet-faced girl named Kate Smith. The general sales manager at Velvatone was then Ted Collins, who resigned later to manage Kate's career. It proved to be a shrewd move. By the 1940s, Collins was wealthy enough, and foolhardy enough, to buy a pro football team, the Boston Yanks. Eventually, the team went broke, but whenever Ted needed to raise money to meet his payroll all he had to do was book Kate somewhere to sing "When the Moon Comes Over the Mountain."

But I remember that recording session best for the way we did it. I walked into the studio with nothing but my guitar and my own courage. Our equipment consisted of two old-fashioned horns. I sang into one and the engineer, an old-timer named Clyde Emerson, placed the other on the chair in front of my guitar. They did it that way to avoid having to pay a royalty to RCA, which owned the rights to the microphone and other electronic recording gear.

We had no arrangements. I just kept singing until Clyde Emerson was satisfied, and that was it.

I was under some pressure by then to sign an exclusive contract with Victor, but I wanted a few days to think about it. I had been given the name of Arthur Sattherly, the new head man at American Record Corporation, a division of Columbia. American had put together a series of chain store deals that meant big numbers. Under separate labels, it would produce records for such companies as Sears and W. T. Grant and Kresge's. Tin Pan Alley was impressed.

Sattherly had just taken over and he was looking for a new artist to launch his own drive. "Victor is big," he said, "but they have lots of stars. You can get lost over there. With us, you can be Number One." That sold me.

The next day I called and gave my regrets to Loren Watson, the boss at Victor. Then I walked over to the American offices at 1776 Broadway—a nice, patriotic address—and signed a contract with Art Sattherly. I was to be paid an advance of fifty dollars a side for each record I cut, against royalties.

My first recording date under that contract was set for early December. Six sides. That came to three hundred dollars. It meant I could coast for a while. But more than that, signing with American meant a turning point in my career. On the Conqueror label, I would soon crank out several records for Sears, and it was through this connection that I was invited to appear on the "National Barn Dance," on station WLS (World's Largest Store).

Sometimes you can yank on one stitch and an entire sweater will unravel. Well, this was my stitch. Hit records, a movie career, a happy marriage, goodies and groceries all came to pass. I was en route to Chicago in 1932 when I stopped off in Springfield, Missouri, to visit my friend, Jimmy Long.

And there I met the girl I was to marry, a coed with blue eyes and skin like rose petals. She was Jimmy's niece, Ina Mae Spivey —eighteen, an Oklahoma girl, living with the Longs while she attended music college in Springfield. We had only a few dates in the next month or so, but I was a frequent guest in Jimmy Long's parlor.

I was now a regular on the "National Barn Dance," and making thirty-five dollars a week singing on radio for Sears. By night I played the tank towns of southern Illinois. Three months after I met Ina Mae Spivey, I was booked into St. Louis, and Jimmy joined me for the show. The next day, his wife and niece came over on the train to go shopping.

I went off with Ina and we agreed to meet the Longs for dinner in a little café on the city's south side. We arrived early. As we sat there, I suddenly blurted out, "Honey, let's get married."

She said, "Gene Autry, are you out of your mind? We hardly know each other. This is only our fourth date. Besides"—fine feminine logic—"I just brought enough clothes for the weekend."

I convinced her we could overcome that problem. The next thing I knew, we had rushed off to get a license and find a wedding chapel or a justice of the peace. A Lutheran minister married us and his wife witnessed the ceremony. When we rejoined the Longs—by now a couple of hours had passed—Jimmy was not very happy with us. "Where have you two been?" he demanded. "Jessie and I were starting to worry."

Ina said, "Uncle Jim, Gene and I got married."

Jimmy said, "I don't believe it. Gene would have told me. I know he would." He looked at me sharply. I sort of ducked my head.

Then Jessie said, "Jimmy Long, today is April Fool's Day. Don't you know a joke when you hear one?"

And for the first time I realized the date *was* April 1, 1932. I turned to Ina and said, "I hope you weren't fooling, honey. I wasn't." She reassured me, with a kiss, and the snug little booth in the corner of a short order restaurant became the scene of our wedding reception. She was only eighteen. I was twenty-two.

I now had steady work, a wife, and a hit record. "That Silver-haired Daddy of Mine," the song Jimmy Long and I had spun off one night in a railroad depot, was off and running. A month after its release, thirty thousand copies had been sold.

A year later, Art Satterly met with Bev Barnett, my first press agent, and an idea was born: a gold-plated copy of "Silver-haired Daddy" to celebrate the half-millionth record sold. When the sales hit a million, they gave me another one. And that was the start of the gold record tradition.

There was a touch of irony in all this. The early thirties marked the heyday of Al Jolson, the era of Mammy songs. I thought back to that first, fumbling audition in New York, when I had sung a Jolson hit. Now I had one of my own, and it went against the trend. Equal time for daddies.

CHAPTER TWO

The Most Famous Reindeer of All

At a time when the "National Barn Dance" was gaining listeners all over the South and Midwest, I found myself receiving love letters from a lady in Iowa. I mean, mash notes. She had developed the notion that I was singing to her, just to her, and the letters, reeking with Gypsy Rose perfume, would begin: "Gene, darling, I heard the song you sang to me last night and I *understood*."

You get a stream of letters, all in that vein, and you begin to feel a mite nervous. It had nothing to do with protecting my image. I don't know if they had groupies in my day, but they had crazy women and suspicious husbands and I tried to avoid both.

Finally, her doctor wrote and asked if I would reply to the lady and tell her, firmly, that I was not in love with her and not singing to her. He said I would be doing a great service. She was going through the change of life, he said, and her mind had grown a little *fuzzy*.

I could never bring myself to do that but, in time, her letters stopped. In the last one I received, she described being alone that night. After hearing me sing she walked outside, stood on the porch, and gazed at the evening sky. "I looked at the stars in the heavens," she wrote. "I saw millions of them. But *you* are the only star in my blue heaven."

And that was where I got the idea, and the title, for one of my early hits: "You're the Only Star in My Blue Heaven." It was released in December 1935.

Music has been the better part of my career. Movies are wonderful fun and they give you a famous face. But how the words and melody are joined, how they come together out of air and enter the mind, this is art. Songs are forever. We carry them with us, at work or play.

I recorded more than three hundred tunes, helped write a third of them, mostly with Fred Rose, had *nine* that sold a million or more, and can't read a note of music. This always confounded the people around me. It sorely tested Carl Cotner, who did most of my arrangements. I would *know,* I would feel it, when a song needed . . . something. But I didn't know what, or how to tell Carl, and those sessions were wild.

I would stop in the middle of a song and say, "Right there, that's the place. We need . . . Carl, you know what it is. We ought to put it in right there."

And Carl wouldn't know. He would fiddle around until he stumbled onto what I wanted, trying out combinations of chords and finger exercises, until my ear told me it was right. In time, after years of working closely, and Carl having to read my mind, he developed an instinct for it. We'd hit a spot that struck me wrong, and Carl would punch it up or give it some kind of run, and I'd be happy.

How Carl Cotner came to work for me is, in itself, a story worth retelling. In the 1930s I was constantly looking for musical talent. Anyone who ever tried to keep a group together knows that it is like traveling with gypsies. You wake up in the morning and someone else has left, gone into business for himself.

Over the years I brought in the Jimmy Wakely Trio from Oklahoma, with Johnny Bond, and I hired Merle Travis, Don Weston, and Whitey Ford, who was better known as the Duke of Paducah. I gave Steve Allen his start on radio, in 1942, over KOY in Phoenix. I did my shows from there while I was stationed at Luke Air Force Base, and Steve was hired to do minor acting parts. We would have a script about shooting down Japanese planes, and Steve would say something like, "Zero coming in at four o'clock, sir."

But this day I was on the highway to Cincinnati, and I was desperate for a lead fiddle player to round out our stage show. Frankie Marvin was driving. It was nearly dusk, and along the side of the road I spotted a couple of hitchhikers. One of them was carrying a fiddle case. I shouted at Frankie to pull the car over. We spun gravel, braked to a stop, and I jumped out.

"Can you play that thing?" I said to the one holding the fiddle case. "I'm Gene Autry and I'm looking for a fiddle player."

"It's a guitar," he said. "I got a guitar in there, and I haven't been playing long."

I auditioned him anyway, right there by the side of the road, just so the stop wouldn't be a total waste. He wasn't very good. But when he finished he said, "I know just the guy you want. Lives in Logansport, Indiana. Name is Cotner, Carl Cotner. Best fiddle player in these parts."

Carl Cotner was a young fellow with a kind of kewpie face and dark blond hair. He had been barnstorming all over Indiana with his own jazz band, playing the fiddle, saxophone, clarinet, and piano. I hired him over the phone, and he finished that first Midwestern tour with us. He was a willing, pliable, unselfish type who did whatever you asked.

We were about the same size, build, and description. It occurred to me that we could use Carl as a stand-in for some of my movie scenes. At the end of the tour I asked him if he could ride a horse.

"Sure," he said. "Rode all the time on our farm."

"Did you use a saddle?"

"Hell, we couldn't afford a saddle."

I told him to get one, and practice with it, and I would use him in my pictures. He rode his rear off, and a few months later I wired him to come on out to Hollywood. It was the first time Carl ever had been away from the Midwest. He rode the Super Chief out and I sent George Goodale, who had just succeeded Bev Barnett as my press agent, to meet him at Union Station. When Carl stepped off, George could not believe his eyes. He had been caught in a rainstorm boarding the train, and his new cotton suit had shrunk four inches in every direction. He was carrying his fiddle case, the bare skin showed above his white socks, and all he needed was a little straw in his hair. Goodale loved to describe that scene, sometimes getting through it with only one glass of water and several deep breaths.

That was in 1935 and Carl is still with me, all these years later, on a handshake. In 1936 we picked up another young musician out of a coal mining camp in Graceburg, Kentucky. He walked in backstage one night and said, "I'm Merle Travis and I'd like to play some guitar for you." He was carrying it in one hand, no case, no strap. He was seventeen and he sang in a voice that made the room seem small. What he really wanted was to write music, and one of his tunes, "Sixteen Tons," launched the career of Tennessee Ernie Ford. Another one, called "Smoke, Smoke, Smoke That Cigarette," didn't hurt Phil Harris any.

But he was young then and raw, and the fellows found a number of creative ways to agitate him. One of our bass players had the kind of huge case, almost a trunk, in which he carried his fiddle. It was open this night in the dressing room, before a show in a little town in Canada, and Merle just crawled in there, stretched out, and went to sleep.

When he started to snore, I walked over, closed the lid, and we all started singing, "Nearer My God to Thee." We could hear Travis screaming through the cover, "Hey, fellas, no, let me out . . ." Eventually, we did.

I have been devoured by this business for thirty-five years, from the prime of Al Jolson to the arrival and ascent of the Beatles. I am still involved, in an occasional way. An album of my old songs was re-released in early 1975 by Republic Records, and Carl Cotner dropped one off at the office of Dick Clark, whose "American Bandstand" show on television was one of the pop symbols of the 1950s. A few days later, Dick called and asked if he could send over for another one. He had a fellow in his office, he said, whose boyhood hero was Gene Autry. Said he had my photograph over his mantel at home, and he'd love to have the record. Said his name was Ringo Starr, and he was a lad when I made my second tour of England in 1953.

Over the years I have heard any number of my friends try to explain whatever success I had. I don't try, on the theory that success is meant to be enjoyed, not analyzed. But I like what I heard a sound engineer say once. He said, "Autry loves the feel of a microphone in his hand. He knows how to work it, when to turn away from it, or into it, how to control it."

I accept that as a compliment from one technician to another.

It was a craft and I worked at it. You hear all the time about performers, whatever their personality, who were simply *transformed* when they hit that stage and felt the glow of the lights and the warmth of the crowd. But I never experienced that. So many singers would go on, like Jolson, and not only sing *at* the audience and down their throats, they had to have a runway so they could get closer. They just overpowered you. I could never do that. I just laid back and let the audience come to me. It was like listening to the boy next door sing. I thought of myself as a showman, not a great entertainer. I never tried to be more or less than Gene Autry.

I had an advantage over many of the old-timers. I not only liked music, I liked the people who made the music. There are songs I sang, and helped write, songs that sold in great numbers and made me richer, whose words I can't remember. But the ideas and the people behind them, I can recall clearly.

Remember the line from "Naked City"? "There are eight million stories in the city." It's that way in the record industry. There must be at least eight million songs—at times I feel as if I recorded that many by myself—and each one has a story.

Three times in my life I picked up songs in prison, from inmates, that became hits. Showfolk are very good about doing prison benefits. It probably has to do with that there-but-for-the-grace-of-God syndrome. Hard times and poverty breed crime. You can go through the history of this country, through the Depression years, and you'll see what I mean. Of course, many are just bad apples and deserve no compassion. But whatever lopes through your mind, you find yourself not turning down many requests to perform behind those grim, gray walls.

So I did a show in 1937 at McAlester, Oklahoma, and during lunch with the warden a group of convicts came in to entertain us. One of them sang a ballad he had written himself and I liked it.

"How long you going to be in here?" I asked.

"Forever," he said.

I didn't worry that thought any longer. But I couldn't get the song out of my head, and a few weeks later I wrote him and obtained his permission to record it. The title was "I Want a Pardon for Daddy."

Music brought better fortune to a young black man named Johnny Bragg. I appeared at the Tennessee State Penitentiary in Nashville in early 1953, and one of the guards asked me if I would look at a song written by one of the inmates. It turned out to be "Just Walkin' in the Rain."

The song had been recorded inside the walls, on the Sun label, by a group calling itself The Prisonnaires. Sun was then a small Memphis company, not yet known for having produced the first works of a local boy named Elvis Presley.

I was under contract to Columbia Records. Although I never recorded the song myself, I talked them into buying the rights to it. "Just Walkin' in the Rain" became a million seller for a new Columbia artist, Johnny Ray.

But the big winner was Johnny Bragg. The royalties he received from the record, and the fact that he had a new career waiting, helped him win an early parole.

The next year, when I appeared at the prison in Nashville again, the word had gotten around. The *composers* were lined up to see me. One of them, a fellow named Jack Toombs, had roughed out a song on lined schoolbook paper. I decided it was worth recording and wound up with another hit: "You're the Only Good Thing That Happened to Me."

One final jailhouse story. In the summer of 1932, I did a benefit at the women's penitentiary in Huntsville, Texas, and prisoners were bussed in from jails in nearby counties. All through the show a thin young woman, with a pinched face and dark hair parted down the middle, kept sobbing. If I sang anything half sad, such as "There's an Empty Cot in the Bunkhouse Tonight," she bawled her eyes out. It was, I have to tell you, a little distracting.

Later, I said to one of the prison guards, "That was a mighty sentimental lady sitting out front."

"Which one you mean?" he asked.

"That ole gal in the first row," I said, "doing all the crying."

"Oh, that," he said. "That's Bonnie Parker."

Those tears were hardly in character with what I had read about Bonnie Parker, and would keep on reading in the months— and years—to come. She had been captured by deputies after a wild chase, which ended when Clyde Barrow crashed their car into a tree. Clyde escaped. Released after three months in jail, Bonnie rejoined Clyde in August 1932. They had less than two years to live.

She was twenty-three when she and Clyde were ambushed at a roadblock near Gibland, Louisiana. She looked much older— cold, almost spinsterish. She died with a sandwich in her mouth and a gun in her hand. On her tombstone, in a cemetery in Dallas, is written this verse:

> As the flowers are all made sweeter,
> by the sunshine and the dew,
> So this old world is made brighter
> by the lives of folks like you.

Many a hit record has been inspired by thoughts less tender than those.

It occurs to me that music, with the possible exception of riding a bull, is the most uncertain way to make a living I know. In either case, you can get bucked off, thrown, stepped on, trampled—if you get on at all. At best, it is a short and bumpy ride. It isn't easy to explain why you keep coming back. But you do.

After I was established as a recording artist, and doing my weekly radio show, I started dropping by a little night club in Hollywood to hear a singer, not yet known, whose style I enjoyed. One night, after a set, he joined me for a drink. He seemed depressed.

"You know, Gene," he said, "I don't think I'll ever get anywhere in this business. In the first place, I'm bald, I talk like a black, look like a Jew, and I'm a dago. What *chance* have I got?"

That was Frankie Laine.

A year or two later he struck it rich with "Mule Train," the title song from a movie of mine, a song that I didn't even get around to recording myself until Laine had made it a hit.

There is no science, you understand, that can explain why

some singers make it, and when, and with which song. As a talent scout, I would have to say my record is mixed.

The first time I ever heard Francis Albert Sinatra sing was in 1940, in Minneapolis, where I was one of the headliners for the Aquatennial Celebration. The Tommy Dorsey band was appearing there with young Sinatra as the male vocalist. He was thin as a nine iron and he wore these polka dot bow ties that sort of nestled under his Adam's Apple.

Tommy introduced us. Frank had just scored with a hit record, "I'll Never Smile Again," and his effect on women was already a sight to behold. The ladies just melted and the teeny boppers were into their squealing, swooning act.

When I returned to California, a friend asked me what I thought of Sinatra, and I remember saying with great confidence, "He'll never be a Crosby."

I thought he was a fad and wouldn't last. But he became one of the classic entertainers of his time. And when his career did flounder, he came back bigger than ever, starting with a part in a movie called *From Here to Eternity*, in which he did not sing a note.

My admiration for Frank grew over the years. I caught his shows wherever he might be working, and I would spot him in my audiences at Madison Square Garden. After I bought a hotel in Palm Springs, one of his favorite playgrounds, he would drop by one or two nights a week, reserving a table for twelve or more. He always called me *Gino*. I guess Frank thinks I'm Italian.

I envy Sinatra as an artist. What a warm feeling it must be, to know that the young people of three generations made love to your music—on the porch swing, in the front seat of a car with the top down, on a picnic blanket with the transistor playing. I'm not sure what they did to mine—loved a little, danced, stomped, laughed, cried, yodeled, or pitched horseshoes. That's all right. All ways help.

During those two weeks in Minneapolis, we made the Nicollet Hotel our headquarters. A group of us, including Fred Rose, Johnny Marvin, and Jack Van Valkenburg, then a vice president (and later the president) of CBS, often met for dinner in the hotel's supper club. One night we were joined by Dorothy Lewis, the star of the ice show. Dorothy was pretty and unspoiled, and attracted her share of teasing. That night the lines seemed funnier than usual, possibly because the manager of the club had told the waiter to bring us whatever we wanted, and Van Valkenburg, no small thinker, had started off by ordering a case of champagne.

At one point I leaned across the table and said, "Dorothy, I'm going to get you in the movies."

The others groaned and wisecracked, but Dorothy searched my eyes. She didn't want to seem naïve. On the other hand, she had a trusting nature. "Now, look," she said. "Just stop your kidding. Or is this for real? Please, be honest with me."

I knew something no one else at the table knew. Herb Yates was casting a picture to be called "Ice Capades." I recommended Dorothy Lewis to him and she landed one of the leading roles. Fair is fair. I went back to my room that night with a song in my head. The next day, Fred Rose and I put it on paper. The title was, "Be Honest with Me."

Freddie Rose was a gifted composer out of Nashville, who discovered Hank Williams and wrote such favorites as "Your Cheatin' Heart." We worked well together, often sitting down and designing a song for a particular movie scene. We did that in 1942 for a movie called *Home in Wyomin'*. We needed music for a scene in which a little street urchin rolled a cigarette out of corn silk and smoked it. The song we wanted was already a hit, "Small Fry," but the rights were high and the studio wouldn't pay it.

So Freddie said, "Well, hell, let's just take the scene and write our own." And we did. The song became "Tweedle-o-Twill," and over a dozen artists recorded it.

Rose and I even collaborated on one song during the war. I was stationed at Love Field, in Dallas, in the Air Transport Command. One day I read a letter in *Yank* magazine—they ran pages of them from GI's all over the world—and one line caught my eye.

This soldier had written in and said, "My gal jilted me, my castles crumbled, at mail call today." I dropped the magazine, found the nearest phone, and called Rose in Nashville. "Fred," I said, "how soon can you fly out to Dallas? I got a great idea for a song."

He flew in the next day and we drove straight to my apartment at the Stoneleigh Hotel. In one afternoon, we finished the words and music to, "At Mail Call Today." It was perfect for the times, a kind of Dear Abby letter set to music, about a soldier who had been overseas so long that his girl wouldn't wait.

The record did well, and would have done better, except for a problem unique to the war. The supply of wax was limited. Mitch Miller was head of Columbia Records then and he channeled whatever he could get to Sinatra or Perry Como or whoever was popular. In the record business, in those years, the rule of thumb was that whoever had the wax had the hit. I was overseas half the time and that, plus a mild prejudice that prevailed against most western music, kept me from getting a fair share.

Neither a prison in Nashville nor an airfield in Dallas was the oddest place I found a song. That happened during my prewar tour of the British Isles in 1939. Two young Englishmen, Michael Carr and Jimmy Kennedy, visited my dressing room in Dublin between shows. They had written a song with me in mind, they said, and hoped I would record it. The song was "South of the Border."

They had never been in Mexico, and had seen it only in my films (which meant they were probably looking at Arizona). How two Englishmen came to write a song about a country they had never seen, for a movie cowboy they had never met, is a question I wish I could answer. But "South of the Border" sold over a million copies.

As far as I know, years passed before Carr and Kennedy made it to the United States. But their music traveled faster. Their other hits included "Harbor Lights" and "Red Sails in the Sunset."

After the war, the music industry began a massive hunt to find a new Christmas number that would appeal to the kids. "Jingle Bells" was wearing thin. In 1946 I was the grand marshal for the annual Hollywood Christmas parade, an event that combines the spirit of the season with all the trimmings the fantasy factory can muster. It had been a tradition for cowboy stars to appear. I had ridden in my first one with Tom Mix.

The parade route jangled right on down Hollywood Boulevard, leading to what the promoters called Santa Claus Lane. The curbs and sidewalks were lined with kids, thick as chinch bugs, craning their necks, some perched on the shoulders of their dads. Santa was in the big sleigh a few rows back and as I rode past each block I could hear the kids, already looking behind me, shouting to each other, "Here he comes, *here comes Santa Claus.*"

With that as a title, and a few scribbled notes, I went to work with Oakley Haldeman, then the manager of my music publishing company (set up after the war). In August of 1947, well ahead of the holiday season, we recorded "Here Comes Santa Claus." That winter it swept the country, as the first new Christmas song in years.

Now the rush was on. Everyone wanted to do a Christmas novelty. "Here Comes Santa Claus" was an even bigger hit in 1948, with new versions out by Bing Crosby, Doris Day, and the Andrews Sisters, among others.

The next year I was in the market for another Christmas song as a follow-up to "Santa," and I sifted through dozens of lead sheets and demo records that came through the mail, most of them unsolicited. It was decided that we would cut two records, meaning four sides. We quickly agreed on three of the songs: "He's a Chubby Little Fellow," "Santa, Santa, Santa," and one I especially liked, "If It Doesn't Snow on Christmas." But we had no prospects for the fourth side.

Meanwhile, a young New York songwriter named Johnny Marks had mailed me a home recording of a number called "Rudolph the Red-nosed Reindeer." I played it at home that night for my wife. It not only struck me as silly but I took the position that there were already too many reindeer flying around.

"Hell," I said to Ina, "how many kids can get past Dancer and Prancer right now?"

But to my surprise, Ina loved it. There was a line in the song about the other reindeer not letting Rudolph join in any reindeer games, and she was touched by it.

"Oh, Gene," she said, "it reminds me of the story of the Ugly Duckling. I think you ought to give it a try. The kids will love it."

With time running out, I reluctantly gave the demo record of

"Rudolph" to Carl Cotner, and told him to work up an arrangement. "After all," I said, with a shrug, "we still have to do four songs."

The recording session did not go placidly. There was an argument with the A&R man over a point that no longer matters, if it did at the time, and everything seemed to drag. The job of the A&R man—the initials stand for artist and repertoire—is to look for songs and artists and fit the two together. In those days he also acted as the producer—if you let him. We finished the first three numbers and Carl Cotner said, "Gene, we have less than ten minutes left. What do you want to do?"

I looked at the clock. The union allowed you four numbers and three hours of recording time. I said, "It's only that 'Rudolph' thing. Throw it in and let's go."

Up to that moment I wasn't certain I'd even use it. Neither was anyone else. But "Rudolph the Red-nosed Reindeer" was an only take, which was unheard of, even in those days. This was before tape, meaning that you couldn't edit out your mistakes.

When we hit the last note the engineer's voice boomed over the studio speaker: "That's it! Wrap it up. No overtime today."

I always prided myself on the quickness with which I admit I was wrong, especially when it turned out as well as "Rudolph." America fell in love with the red-nosed reindeer. I introduced the song that winter in Madison Square Garden, at the annual rodeo we did there. We had a guy dressed in a reindeer costume with a big bulb of a nose, and when I got to the second verse of the song they threw a blue light on him and he danced. We did a class act.

"Rudolph" sold two and a half million records that first year and they are still counting. By the end of the 1977, my record had passed the ten-million mark in sales. In all versions, by nearly four hundred artists world wide, in almost every language including Chinese, it had sold well over a hundred million copies. It is the second biggest seller, after Bing Crosby's recording of "White Christmas," of all time. It wasn't until years later that I learned, from Johnny Marks, that he had sent out demo records to Dinah Shore, Bing Crosby, and a half dozen other major artists, none of whom showed any interest. He added my name to the list as an afterthought. And, in the end, I recorded it to please my wife. All "Rudolph" did was move me out of the country class and onto the top pop charts for the first time.

The most famous reindeer of all is still going strong today. The song appeared on a new album by John Denver. "They all sound alike to me," Johnny Marks told an interviewer, "but I still like the Gene Autry version best."

Every Christmas since 1949, Johnny calls. We chat about the latest sales figures for "Rudolph," and he wishes Ina and me the best of holiday greetings. He talks about "Rudolph" as though he were real, and to Johnny he is, as our creations often tend to be. Somewhere in my home is a platinum record, which stands for the five-millionth copy sold. Not many singers ever get one of those. Old "Rudolph" is pretty real to me, too.

How that matched up with my cowboy image, I can't say. But as if "Rudolph" wasn't enough, we put our brand on the Easter bunny with a song called "Peter Cottontail." That one sold a million, too.

It is risky, at any age, to reflect on how the times change. Times always do. But every turn in my career was dictated, or pushed along, by forces not always within my control. The war, and a new generation of war babies, brought about the children's songs that kept my popularity as a recording star high, at a moment when it could have waned.

I'm not at all sure I sensed it then, but I know now that I was caught up in the vast changes that were reshaping the country, and the people, as I left the railroad. My goal was to get on radio and make records. To skip lightly now over a span of years, in the space of a few sentences, may give the impression that it all happened easier and faster than was actually the case.

So this is the time to tell you about a dressing-room door from the Tivoli Theatre, in Danville, Illinois. Today that door, framed under glass, is on display in the lobby. Words hand-lettered in white paint are still visible, and below them a plaque which says:

"This is a door taken from a dressing room 'backstage' at the Tivoli Theatre, upon which Gene Autry painted the above inscription when he appeared with Jimmy Long in person on the Tivoli Theatre stage, March 19–20, 1932."

What I had written, in large, flowing letters, was the simple declaration: "GENE AUTRY, AMERICA'S BIGGEST FLOP." No matter how I tug at my memory, I can no longer recall the cause of my frustration. A clumsy act? A small crowd? Or no crowd at all.

It didn't matter. I had no way of knowing then that my career was perfectly aimed. I was just right for those times, those deepening Depression years. When the thirties started I was still tapping out Morse Code and singing to myself. Tom Mix was king of the cowboys and western movies were in trouble. But as the old pulp writers might put it, there really was a silver bullet somewhere with my name on it.

From 1931 to 1934, even as my first hit records were beginning to carry my name beyond the Midwest, I was content—exhilarated would be too strong a word—in my role as a WLS headliner. Sears was now sponsoring the "Gene Autry Program," and I was singing and touring with the "National Barn Dance," and guesting on other shows.

One of the regulars on the "Barn Dance" was a ukelele player named Little Georgie Gobel. He also fancied himself a singer. I'm not sure either one of us ought to admit to this, but in 1933 I backed him on the guitar while George yodeled his way through two records. The songs included "Billy Richardson's Last Ride," and the ever popular "A Cowboy's Best Friend Is His Horse." On the record label appeared the credit: accompanied by G. Autry.

(Years later, when we were appearing not far from Erie, Pennsylvania, Pat Buttram told me there was a great young comic over there we should go see. "What's his name?" I asked. "George Gobel," he said. "Why, I know him from the 'Barn Dance,' " I said. "He's no comedian." But Pat talked me into going, and Gobel had that audience in convulsions. I told him then he *had* to go to Hollywood and, not long after that, he did.)

I realized one of my boyhood dreams in those years when I worked with Al Jolson, on radio. Later, after my first rodeo appearance in New York, I stood in the wings watching Jolson on Broadway, and he brought me out to the stage and introduced me.

Jolson was an incurable horse player, a spirited man, and a genius at what he did. He was the greatest attraction of his era, but today they wouldn't let him on the stage. He did his act in blackface.

In that era the minstrel show was a staple, and Eddie Cantor came along to continue the tradition. In the first talking movie, *The Jazz Singer*, Jolson wore blackface. You couldn't do a minstrel show today and you couldn't go on the air with "Amos 'n Andy," either. Funny though. Flip Wilson or Redd Foxx could do the same scripts, and it would be hilarious.

There is no point in trying to tell those under thirty how big radio once was in this country. It just enveloped everyone. We set our watches by it, woke up and went to bed with it, depended on it for news and advice and wisdom. And the products. If you liked Rudy Vallee, you *loved* Fleischmann's Yeast, because Fleischmann's sponsored his radio show. (The first time in my life I ever wore a tuxedo was for a party honoring Rudy Vallee. For accessories I wore cowboy boots and a white stetson.)

Those were sweet years in Chicago. Ina and I had rented an apartment on the north side of Chicago, near the Edgewater Beach Hotel. My sisters and brother lived with us, part of the time. We had the family together, my records were selling, and I was invited to perform at the Chicago World's Fair in 1933. They knew me around town, at the Aragon, where Wayne King played, and at the Hotel Sherman, where Ben Bernie was filling the College Inn. The Blackhawk had Art Castle. Chicago was a toddling town in those days.

Out in Hollywood, the Western movie was going through a kind of moral spasm in 1934. Mix couldn't make it in the talkies. Hoot Gibson was getting fat. More and more of the old silent Ken Maynard chase sequences were turning up in everyone else's films. The serials were running thin on plot and the popcorn concession was down.

Then came the final blow. The Catholic Legion of Decency was howling about violence and filth on the screen. The public, insisted the Legion, was outraged at the so-called "Flaming Youth" films which had come into fashion. They were no worse, I suppose, than the openly sensual flicks that featured Valentino and Theda Bara and other swains and vamps of the day. But the Legion demanded a crackdown and called on Hollywood to begin producing clean, wholesome (sexless) pictures.

The minor league studios like Monogram and Mascot were

taking a bath. So it happened one day that a man named Nat Levine, the owner of Mascot Pictures, was in New York trying to raise money for a Ken Maynard shoot-em-up. Levine had specialized in Saturday morning serials, such as *Burn 'em Up Barnes*, and one with Clyde Beatty, the wild animal tamer.

Levine met with Herbert J. Yates, who owned American Records and Consolidated Film Labs, a processing plant that later became part of Republic Studios. The way it worked, whenever Yates invested in a movie he got the contract for processing the film. He probably developed the prints of 90 per cent of the pictures then being made in Hollywood.

It seemed clear to Herb Yates that the Western movie needed a shot in the arm. He discussed it with Moe Siegel, then the president of American Records, and they agreed that the straight, action Western was a thing of the past. So they met again with Levine, and Yates said, "Nat, I'll give you the money, but on one condition. We have a fellow who sells a helluva lot of records for us. He's on radio in Chicago, on a national hookup, does the 'Barn Dance.' Nat, it would be worth your while to take a look at Gene Autry."

To get the financing for his picture, Nat Levine would have looked at a singing kangaroo. A day later I received a call from Yates and Siegel, telling me Levine was on his way to Chicago and wanted to meet with me. I had finished my show at WLS when he arrived . . . *blew in*, is the phrase I meant to use.

"They tell me you sell a lot of records," he said.

"Oh, I reckon so."

"I'm going to make this picture with Ken Maynard. Cowboy picture. Low budget. Usually, we try out a new actor, we give you a screen test, read lines, things like that. No need to bother. If you'd like to come out and appear in it, we've written in a barn dance scene. You can call the square dance, do a few songs. That can be your screen test. We'll see what kind of reaction we get when the movie plays."

I didn't know if it was my turn to talk or not.

"Well, Autry, how do you like it?"

"Sounds okay to me."

"Good. Call me before you come." He paused at the door. "You're a nice boy. You may call me collect."

So it was done. The name of the picture was *In Old Santa Fe*. I was to be paid a flat sum of five hundred dollars, but no one told me until I got to Hollywood. That night an odd thought crossed my mind. I'm not a devoutly religious man. But twice the church had been involved in my future. My grandpa, the preacher, taught me to sing at five. And now, at twenty-seven, the Legion of Decency was sending me to the movies.

CHAPTER THREE

Hooray for Hollywood

That year, 1934, in the movie *In Old Santa Fe*, I sang a song or two and no one got sick, and so was born a new Hollywood art form: the horse opera. Gene Autry was soon established as the Original Singing Cowboy.

But, strictly speaking, I was not the first cowhand to warble a song in a Western. Ken Maynard had attempted a few of his own and, about the same time, Lone Star Productions had experimented with a former Southern Cal football player named Marion Morrison. As John Wayne, he went on to somewhat sturdier roles, but in 1933 he was "Singin' Sandy" in a movie called *Riders of Destiny*.

Two factors weighed against Wayne's rise as a Western singer, other than the obvious one of finding a leading lady who wouldn't crack up. To begin with, his songs had to be dubbed by someone else and, in those days, the lip synch was unreliable. But the clincher was the fact that when he appeared in public and his fans pleaded for a ballad, or two, he had to decline.

Over the years a number of well-known Western actors *denied* being the voice of Singin' Sandy, among them Smith Ballew, Bill Bradbury (Bob Steele's twin), and Jack Kirk, who once sang with a group known as the Arizona Wranglers. The old-timers insisted it was Ballew who dubbed Wayne's voice.

Years later, Wayne and I showed up at some Hollywood social function, where the soda water was flowing pretty good. Across the room, cutting through the din of the crowd, came that familiar voice:

"Hey, Autry."

"Hi, Duke."

He was grinning broadly. "I caught one of my old Singin' Sandys on TV the other day," he said. "You know, it wasn't as bad as I thought."

"That so?"

"Well, hell," he said, "if I'd kept on singing, and worked at it, you wouldn't have stood a chance."

"Duke," I said, with as much sincerity as I could, "it wasn't my singing that put me over. It was my *acting*."

Wayne threw back his head and laughed. "Aw, horse bleep," he said, and turned toward the bar.

Naturally, we didn't use language that indelicate in Gene Autry movies. Nor violence, nor excessive gunplay, nor anything that might suggest that men and women sometimes slept in the same room. Today, you see girls doing on the screen what they used to do *off* the screen to get *on* the screen.

I don't approve of the so-called adult movies of the 1970s. If that stamps me as a square by today's standards, I can only plead that my values haven't changed. I was just as square the day I arrived in Hollywood in June of 1934. Nor do I feel it necessary to defend the innocence of the films I made, all those sundowns ago. The times were different then, as times usually are. The country was different. So were the people.

Oh, we had sin and mischief and temptation, and a few other things you wouldn't find in an Autry movie. But there was less meanness, I think. People were not so selfish, so cynical. In those days, movies were a way of getting your mind off real life. Today you can't tell them apart.

We headed for Hollywood that summer the way you would take off for a weekend at the beach. The three of us—my wife, Ina, and Smiley Burnette—piled our bags into my new Buick and pointed it west out of Chicago. I can no longer recall, if I ever knew, what I expected to find when we reached the end of that road. But Hollywood was already the glamor spot of the world, and I never had been farther west than Albuquerque.

We drove through in five days and on the way, rolling through Arizona, Smiley and I wrote a song called "Ridin' Down the Canyon." Smiley scored the music in the back seat. Later, he would tell people, jokingly, it took him three miles to finish it, and I paid him $5.00 for the rights to the song, so he made $1.67 a mile.

I saw more of Hollywood my first month there than in all the years since. We did all the touristy things; even visited Grauman's Chinese Theater and stared at the footprints. We had rooms at the old Hollywood Hotel, on the corner of Hollywood and Highland, one of those California gothic places with a portico and a dimly lighted lobby. It's not there any more. When I realized we were going to stay for six months, we rented a place at the Riviera Apartments. Spanky McFarland, of the Our Gang comedy, and his family lived below us.

My first impression of Hollywood was of all that whiteness. The homes. The buildings. The studios. It was like a Russian winter scene. And there was plenty of land for sale. Not exactly for pennies, but cheap enough. The San Fernando Valley, where I built my home years later, near the Warner Brothers and Universal lots, was almost uninhabited then.

But I had no notion of staying. I wasn't comfortable in California, where the style of living was already casual. A few years later, a friend of mine from Texas came to visit and we entertained him with a barbecue on our patio. "Gene," he said, shaking his head. "You sure have come a long way. I kin remember when you ate indoors and went to the bathroom outdoors."

I had only the one scene to do in Maynard's picture, the barn dance scene, and I was nervous about it. I had worked at fairs, in theaters, in rodeo arenas over much of the South and Midwest. But I had never appeared in front of a camera before, and I knew none of the tricks. In a close-up, you could shake your head just a fraction and it would move across a screen thirty feet wide. I had to learn that you could convey a lot more with the movement of your eyes than with your head.

And my hands worried me. I didn't know what to do with them. So it occurred to me to wear gloves. Then, when I had nothing else to do, I could tug on them. It became my most identifiable screen habit, like Cagney hitching his pants. But later, when I was grinding out eight movies a year, they had a practical use, too. In some of the fight scenes, when you were scuffling and rolling around in the dirt and gravel, the gloves kept my hands from getting scraped and skinned.

It was quite a jolt when I saw myself on the screen for the first time. Everyone had been kind to me, even Ken Maynard, though I had a suspicion that the barn dance scene had been written for him. If he knew it had been pre-empted as a screen test for Gene Autry, he really didn't care. Ken was a crotchety sort, one of the genuine characters in a community famous for them.

Once, while working at Universal, he went on a binge and refused to leave his dressing room. A light in the ceiling kept shining in his face, and he was too stubborn to get up and turn off the switch. He kept a loaded revolver at his bedside. He reached for it, shot out the light, and went to sleep.

In the dressing room directly above Ken was the old character actor, Slim Summerville. The bullet ripped through the floor and missed him by inches. In his bare feet, Slim flew out the door, stomped into the producer's office, and said, "Look, I don't ever want to be over that bastard again. Tomorrow you move my dressing room over to the other side of the studio." And they did.

Any problems I had were of my own making. The scene was as easy as California living. I sang the title song, and called out a square dance, and picked a guitar when I wasn't tugging at my glove. But after I saw the first screening—in the B Western, where you could finish an entire movie in a week, it seems pretentious to call them *rushes*—I was ready to call it quits. I moved like my parts needed oiling, and I didn't like the way I looked or sounded. I went home that night and snapped at Ina, "Look, I don't think this picture business is for us. To hell with it. I think I better stick to radio."

I was eager now to get back to Chicago. California struck me as formless, too sprawling, too far from the rest of the country.

There was no way to know what fate, and Nat Levine, had in mind for us. *In Old Santa Fe* was released with a cast line that read "*and introducing Gene Autry*," to my knowledge the first credit of that kind ever given. Nat persuaded Smiley and me to tour briefly to promote the movie and, in some theaters in the Midwest where I was known through radio and my records, the marquee often read: "Starring Gene Autry and Ken Maynard." Small-town folks take care of their own.

We were not on the road long when Levine called us back to

Hollywood, where he was finishing a serial with Maynard called *Mystery Mountain*. We appeared in two chapters, me as a henchman named Thomas and Smiley as a mine guard. I don't remember what I was paid for this, but knowing Nat Levine's record in matters of thrift, I doubt that it was much above the flat fee of five hundred dollars I received for my first part.

I was more convinced than ever that I had no future as an actor, when Levine asked me to star in a serial entitled *The Phantom Empire*. It was typical Saturday-matinee fare, but this one had a twist. I played the role of a radio entertainer, on a dude ranch, who discovers an underground kingdom, the entrance to which is through a cave on the ranch. The plot was inspired, if that is the word, by the discovery of Carlsbad Caverns.

But during that series we introduced such props as flame throwers and laser beams, years before the Army, or science, made them a part of the public arsenal.

When we finished filming the thirteen episodes of *The Phantom Empire*, I had no reason to think that my movie career was just beginning. Nor was I at all sure that was what I wanted. But, as luck would have it, we returned to Chicago in the middle of December, in time to catch the worst blizzard the city had seen in years. By the time we hit St. Louis, it was nothing but snow, sleet, and ice all the way home. When Nate Levine called, a week later, I had come to think of Los Angeles as the land of milk and honey.

At Mascot Studios, Levine had been trying to sell his producer, Mandy Schaefer, on the idea of starring Gene Autry in a new kind of Western, one with as much music as gunplay. Schaefer threatened to quit. He thought the idea was ridiculous, and so did everyone else. A Western was sixty minutes of furious action. How could it be interrupted four or five times for guitar recitals?

And Autry? Toughness was the trademark of the Western hero. Autry had a soft voice and a shy smile and peaceful looks.

Mandy Schaefer went on to produce dozens of my movies. The songs, instead of interrupting the story, were used to push the plot forward. All Westerns followed a formula, but we had found a new one: 1) A decent story; 2) good music; 3) comedy relief; 4) enough action, with chases and fights; and 5) a little ro-

mance. And always we played it against the sweep of desert scenery, mountains and untamed land and an ocean of sky. When I
made Westerns, that was the cameraman's dream, getting that
panorama of the sky. Years later, when I brought my baseball
team, the California Angels, to Palm Springs to train, that was
the first thing the players complained about: the high sky.

I returned to Hollywood in early 1935, to stay, and to strike
paydirt in a movie called *Tumbling Tumbleweeds*. It was the
first of a genre, the first Western plotted and sold around the
main character's ability to sing. The Autry image was established
in that film almost 100 per cent. It was tinkered with in minor
ways; on occasion I wore a Tim McCoy style neckerchief, three
feet of white silk. But, for the most part, the Autry of *Tumbling
Tumbleweeds* was the Autry of 1947's *Robin Hood of Texas*.

Those years are worth noting because, after the war, the movie
business I knew—my corner of it—was never the same. Westerns
had saved the industry in the 1930s, proof of which was the
emergence of Republic Studios.

The Hollywood trades at the time called it a merger when, in
1935, Mascot, Liberty, Monogram, Majestic, Imperial, and
Chesterfield fell out of sight under the new corporate logo of
Republic Pictures, Inc. What it really amounted to was one Herbert J. Yates, of Consolidated Film Labs, making an early day
offer that couldn't be refused. In short, Yates, the lab processors,
called in the markers on the boys. Such pioneers as W. Ray Johnston and Trem Carr of Monogram, and Nat Levine, at Mascot,
who had headed their own companies since the day Edwin Porter
first turned his cap backward and hollered action, were now having the shots called by an ex-tobacco salesman. Johnston learned
from this, and when he raised enough money a few years later to
reorganize Monogram, he saw to it that the lab bills were paid
ahead of the actors. Who ever heard of an actor foreclosing?

Yates ended up with Mascot's North Hollywood studio, plus
the contracts of Levine's two most valuable properties: Ann
Rutherford and Gene Autry. Levine was left with a producer's
title and a film unit of his own to manage. W. Ray Johnston
fared slightly better. Yates let him keep the title of company
president, but Herbert J. retained control of Monogram's Lone

Star Productions. Its only asset was a contract with John Wayne's signature on it.

Board room politics didn't much interest me then. Hollywood didn't exactly dazzle me, either. I seldom stayed around long after we finished a picture. Whatever weeks we had until the next one, I spent galloping around the circuit with my own Western show, hitting the small- and medium-sized towns, getting around to meet the theater owners who played my films and the salesmen who sold my records. I knew them all by name.

Most of today's stars would probably put that sort of thing in a class with waiting on tables. But it was important to me. I needed those people. They identified with me, with what they could see on the screen: an average fellow, from a small town, no airs, a friendly smile.

But, gradually, I came to enjoy this rather curious trade. Westerns were to movies what the sports page is to the daily newspaper: the best part of it. The toy department. But let me tell you about the line of succession.

It all started with Max Aronson, a one-time Chicago store clerk. He practically invented the whole business. In 1907, Max formed his own film company, got the idea for a cowboy hero, and looked around for the right actor. When he couldn't find one, he gave the part to himself and became Broncho Billy Anderson, the star of more than four hundred one- and two-reel Westerns. That was the ideal partnership. The star he created was himself.

William S. Hart was next. His movies were as authentic as he could make them, filled with details he had learned as a boy living with the Sioux Indians in South Dakota. He did them proudly, but adding at least a couple of show business touches. One was the ritual of the two-gun draw, shot from the hip. The other was pure genius. He invented the Horse. Soon Fritz, his pinto, was as famous as Hart himself.

Then came Tom Mix. He was discovered doing two-reel, custard-pie comedies but he copied Hart closely and came up with one trick Hart could never quite manage. A smile. The next thing anyone knew, Mix was getting fan mail.

Harry Carey, a mild and wistful man, who had the *look* of someone who had lived on the desert, came along in the wake of

Mix. So did Ed (Hoot) Gibson, who had ridden with Colonel Stanley's Rough Riders, and Buck Jones, whose family had been homesteaders in the Indian Territory. Buck died in a night club fire in Boston in 1942, died a hero, in fact, trying to rescue other trapped patrons.

The next to carve out new territory was Ken Maynard, the best horseman of all, once a trick rider with Ringling Brothers. He could get out of his saddle, pass himself under the belly of his horse, Tarzan, and come up on the other side. Ken did his own stunts, things like leaping onto the back of his horse from a cliff top.

About 1928 there began seven bleak years for Westerns. Movies had started to talk. And then it was my turn.

Let me tell you, I had more than my share of hero worship when I started out, and I lost some of it in a hurry. The first time I met Hoot Gibson he was dressed in two-tone shoes and a loud sports coat. Right then, I resolved that whatever I wore would have at least a Western touch. The kids expected that. I saw no reason to disappoint them. Besides, for me, at least, boots and suits with a Western cut were the style I liked best.

What you have to understand, about Westerns and the people who were a part of them, is that it was a great way not to grow up. It was like living in a time capsule. The American frontier and whatever role you played, the past and the present, were always entangled. Put it this way: in the costume ball of life, you never had to change clothes.

We took the work seriously, I like to think, but not ourselves. What held it together was the idea that, in even the simplest and thinnest of plots, some of it might have been that way. Once, there really were school marms and bad guys and sodbusters and nesters and cattle barons and good guys in white stetsons.

And wasn't there Tom Mix? Tom was the genuine article, an adventurer, a soldier of fortune who saw action in the Spanish-American War, in the Philippines, in the Boxer Rebellion in China, and on both sides of the Boer War. He punched cows in Texas, Oklahoma, and Kansas, and once left Mexico a few hours ahead of a firing squad. Tom deserted from the Army in 1902—according to Ripley's Believe It or Not—and never completed his military service. But no charges were ever brought against him. He was even a lawman, once a Texas Ranger and briefly a deputy U.S. marshal. Could anyone have written a character more colorful than Mix? He was no longer young when I met him, but he drove cars that were custom built and he wore lavish Western outfits. He was especially proud of a horsehair belt, fastened with a diamond-studded buckle, engraved with the legend: "Tom Mix, America's Champion Cowboy."

He took whatever movie jobs he could get, until someone learned he could ride stunts. Then he was on his way. But no part he ever played on the screen could compete with the kind of life he had lived. He lived it right up to the instant he was killed, in 1940, on a lonely stretch of road near Florence, Arizona. One more curve, taken too fast. A flood had washed out a culvert and Mix, driving a Packard with the top down, hit it going sixty. They erected a statue of a riderless horse to mark the spot.

Mix was a sentimental man, as cowboys often are. He was the kind of man who could weep at a picture on a bordello wall. He loved poetry, and read it well, with a rich, deep voice that rumbled out of his throat like a train out of a tunnel.

Old Tom was a handsome specimen even in his late fifties and quite vain about his hair. He had a full head of it, straight as a string, and he dyed it so black it was almost blue. He explained that to me once and I never forgot. You didn't forget many conversations with Tom Mix. He had been shot in the jaw in the Spanish-American War and by then his false teeth troubled him constantly. Every few sentences he would reach up and click those teeth back into place with his thumbs. His speech was what you would call deliberate.

"Wal, you know, Gene," he told me, "the La'rd was good to me. He presa'rved my ha'r. I can damned sure keep it black for Him."

Of course, hair was of some importance in Hollywood even then, two generation gaps ago, before it began to grow over the ears and necks and down the backs. When John Wayne still had a nice rack of it, he couldn't understand why his fans were writing in, deeply troubled over what they thought was an unexplained hair loss.

Wayne shoved a letter at me one day and said, "Gene, read this and tell me what the hell you make of it."

"How come," it said, *"that you appear to have plenty of hair, but in the fight scenes you're bald on top?"*

I handed the letter back to him. "Duke," I said, "have you ever taken a good look at Yak?"

I was surprised he hadn't noticed. His double, Yakima Canutt, had a nice, circular bald spot on his crown. In the fight scenes, when Yak doubled for him, that bald spot, white as a bandage, showed up clearly in the film.

On the day they started their next picture, Wayne went out and bought a bottle of brown shoe polish and made Yak stand still while he painted his head. "Now, dammit, Yak," he said, "quit squirming. That spot has to go."

Canutt also doubled for me, but it was no problem because I always kept my hat on, even in a fight scene. That was another thing people wrote letters about: why I never lost my hat in a fight scene. Used to get bags of mail about that. Amazing, the little things that worry people. The answer was simple. In the chase scenes, if you lost your hat the scene had to be reshot. So you learned to keep it pretty tight on your head. I'd jam mine down so hard that I could jump from one horse to another, bulldog a guy down, roll around on the ground with him, and still get to my feet, hat in place.

Of course, sometimes I'd need help getting it off, and for the next hour or so I'd walk around with a red line across my forehead.

Days and nights on location were the best, of course, sometimes sleeping in a van, sometimes in a bedroll under the stars. In many ways it wasn't all that different from traveling around the rodeo circuit. The stunt men and extras and others in the cast, at one point in their lives, had worked on ranches and broken horses and rounded up cattle.

Those people were a clan of their own. They'd hang around Gower and Sunset—it became known as Gower Gulch—and wait for the next casting call. The big attraction at that corner was the breakfast they served at the Columbia Drugs, scrambled eggs and bacon for forty cents. The old-timers could always be found there, dressed in costume and ready to go. And the people hurrying by on the street never blinked.

The dream of most extras was never to be the star, but to play a heavy—the villain. We divided them into two types: *smooth* and *dog*. The smooth heavy was the one they always caught at the safe, trying to get away with the money at the end of the picture. And then the hero would bend over to close the safe and his badge would fall out of his pocket and the girl would gasp, "We *knew* you were a ranger all the time. Won't you stay and be our sheriff?"

And the hero would duck his head, and say, "No, I've got to mosey on." We always had three choices of travel in a Western. We could mosey, hightail it, or skedaddle.

The dog heavy was the grubby character the smooth heavy would turn to and say, "Okay, boys, here he comes. Make it look like an accident . . . *but get him.*" The dog heavy did all the dirty work. He was a menacing figure, mean, grizzled, unshaven, unwashed, the Bob Willkie or Jack Elam type.

The earlier cowboy actors, just ahead of my time, were generally heavy drinkers and hell raisers. They used to tell a classic story about Art Acord, one of the stars of the silent era, and Hoot Gibson, and a fight they waged on the set of a movie directed by Reeves Eason, who later directed many of mine. They had been snarling at each other for days. Finally, Eason just stopped the shooting and said, "Look, you two sonsabitches been aching to fight. Well, go right ahead."

He locked them in a horse stall and they beat on each other for nearly an hour. Nobody won. They just got so tired, and arm weary, they begged Eason to open the door and let them out. When he did, Hoot dropped to one knee, wiped his mouth with the back of his hand, and said to Acord, "Let's go have a drink." They went off with their arms wrapped around each other's shoulder. No one ever did know what started the fight.

As for myself, I would rather sleep than fight. It was no choice at all. Between scenes, I'd pull up a chair, lean it against the nearest wall or tree, fold a towel behind my neck for a pillow, and drop off for ten or fifteen minutes of the purest kind of sleep. Someone would call out, *"Ready for Mr. Autry,"* and I'd jump up, comb my hair, slap the hat back on, and feel completely refreshed. That ability to cat nap helped get me through the years when I was doing three or four things at once.

It helped to have a clear head because, for one thing, I seldom followed a script. There were few writers around, at least on Westerns, who could get the dialogue down without making you sound as though your feet hurt. I just paraphrased my lines as I went along, read them in whatever way might sound natural, and tried to be Gene Autry. I often had a hellish time with names.

Once, in a movie called *Bells of Capistrano*, I had to gallop up to a border guard and, in one breath, ask a question containing three difficult Spanish names: "Did Father so-and-so from the town of such-and-such pass by here, carrying a bell to Capistrano?"

We must have reshot that scene fifteen times and with each take one, and sometimes all three, of the names came out differently. In the interest of completing the movie, we did one more take. The way it finally played, I rode up to the guard and shouted, "Did a priest go by here carrying a bell?"

Away from the set, the people involved in Westerns kept pretty much to themselves. They seldom mixed with the Robert Montgomerys or the Carole Lombards, the stars who lived in homes like monasteries in the hills behind Hollywood. Yet in the 1930s, much more so than today, there really was such a thing as a *movie colony*. It wasn't just a state of mind, invented by Louella Parsons or Hedda Hopper. You didn't often work together but your paths crossed, and everyone knew each other, and there was a community of spirit.

Sometimes when I felt a little homesick or restless during my first year or two in Hollywood, I dropped into a small saddle shop on Sunset Boulevard. I would just hang around for an hour or so, visiting with anyone who might be there and breathing that new leather smell. It was a good place to be when you had a feeling that things were moving too fast. I used to run into Clark Gable there. He loved the outdoors. We'd lean on the counter, talk about hunting gear, and run our hands over the rifle cases.

How I admired Gable! He played many a sophisticated role, and he probably wore a tux as well as any man who ever lived. But he was an earthy fellow. You could put him anywhere and he would fit, in high society or in a ditch with the other diggers. When they called Gable "The King," they were not, for once, indulging in the usual Hollywood baloney. He was.

That was an era of great box office stars. Metro was run by

Louis B. Mayer and he believed in the star system. Fan magazines were as common as blotters, and the studios used them, often paid them, to pump up their clients. It's hard to realize that one studio, at the same time, had under contract Gable, Tracy, Myrna Loy, Robert Taylor, Marie Dressler, and Wallace Beery. It was a line-up that made your head spin. It was MGM's answer to the Old Yankees, with their Murderer's Row of Lazzeri, Gehrig, Ruth, Combs, and Meusel.

Normally, I am not one of those who prefers to live in the past, and rummage in the attic of time. In fact, I have often felt that nostalgia should go back where it came from. But I have a soft spot for the Hollywood that once shed a light on our nine-to-five lives. The old stars had a mystique and they clung to it even after everything else was gone. I mean, if they went out the back door to carry out the garbage, they dressed as though they were going to a charity ball. They dressed and lived and fed on that image of glamor. It may have been a make-believe world, but at least they worked at it.

The late Errol Flynn was a symbol of that Hollywood. He was a neighbor of mine, less than a mile up the hill. Flynn collected characters. I would recognize a car in his driveway on my way into town, and I'd stop by to say hello to "Big Boy" Williams or Dick Foran or Bruce Cabot, and listen to the stories they told of whatever trouble they had recently created. Women would come strolling in as though Flynn's home was some kind of department store. In a way I guess it was.

Flynn was fifty when he died. By my reckoning he had lived a hundred years. He had lived at twice the pace of most men. He spent more time on a bar stool, or in court, or in the headlines, or in bed, than anyone I knew. He may have been the greatest swordsman Hollywood ever saw, and that covers a lot of ground. I was at Lakeside Golf Club a few months before his death, while Errol was having lunch with Beverly Aadland, his fifteen-year-old girl friend of that period. They went for a sail on his boat. The day before, he had entertained her mother.

Most men would gladly have given their right eye, in those days, to have been Clark Gable or Errol Flynn. They were great people to be, if you had the nerve or the time. But that wasn't really my Hollywood, or my lifestyle, or even a side of the acting business that attracted me. I mention it, in passing, because Gable and Flynn were a part of those years, and the orbit they moved in was out there somewhere beyond the boots and the saddles.

Guinn Williams, incidentally, was nicknamed "Big Boy" by Will Rogers. They were polo-playing buddies. "Big Boy" once owned two hundred ponies and captained a team that included Flynn and Douglas Fairbanks. That was Hollywood, too.

Rogers was at the height of his fame when I landed on the scene. I had run into him, always by chance, a few times after that night in the station in Chelsea, Oklahoma. But in the fall of 1935, we happened to be on the program together at a rodeo near Hollywood, at a place called Gilmore Stadium. My first films had been released, and *The Phantom Empire* was running as a serial, and Rogers said, "Well, Autry, I see you're doing quite well."

"Oh, we're throwin' a little meat in with the beans now," I said. "But, you know, you're kind of responsible for my being here, Mr. Rogers. If you hadn't told me I might make it as a singer, I'd probably still be punchin' a telegraph key. The railroad owes you a favor."

He laughed at that. "When I get back from a trip I'm making," he said, "I hope we can get together. Talk about Oklahoma."

I asked where he was going.

He said he was leaving on a trip around the world with Wiley Post, the aviator from Texas. "I'll look you up when I get back," he said.

Of course, he didn't get back. When the news broke that the plane carrying Will Rogers had crashed on take-off somewhere in Alaska, the entire country was plunged into mourning. He was, without question, the greatest folk humorist this country ever produced. And he came from the very soil of it, born on the Rogers ranch in what was then the Cherokee Nation. His wit struck sparks. It focused on the foibles of us all, but especially on the politicians and the rich and famous. He wrote a newspaper column every day, radio scripts and routines for the stage, and never hired other writers. Whatever material he needed came out of his own fertile mind, much of it on the spot, as he twirled a lariat, riveting the gaze of his audience in much the same way that a hypnotist uses a medallion on a chain.

He brought to the Western tradition the idea of the friendly cowboy. As much as any man, he helped establish the lore and humor of the West as part of the American heritage. And his gift for making us laugh at our own foolishness is with us still.

A little of Will Rogers must have rubbed off on anyone who met him, or was ever exposed to the land and the life he knew. Will would have enjoyed a letter I received some years later, from a fellow who said he had seen most of my movies. (I made 93 in all, consisting of maybe five basic plots and two locations—the mountains or the desert—and cowboys galloping endlessly across terrain that was always treacherous, parched, and bleak.)

"You are always fighting over that land," the man wrote. "I am wondering what the hell those cattle eat, anyway. Rocks? I wouldn't give twenty cents an acre for that land, but the railroad is always coming through or someone is about to discover oil.

"Gene, why are you always fighting over that stupid land, and never in some peaceful, beautiful valley?"

I tried to think of an answer, but I never did.

CHAPTER FOUR

The Cowboy Takes a Hike

Even a blind hog finds an acorn every now and then. That is, everybody gets lucky sometimes. But one of the hard things about success is knowing how much of it came from an effort honestly given, and how much from luck.

Listen. Never take lightly the importance of luck. Some reject it when it comes. Some don't even recognize it.

For six straight years, from 1937 until the war, I was voted the top Western star in Hollywood. No cowboy had ever before finished in the box office Top Ten. Yet I was right up there with Gable and Mickey Rooney and Shirley Temple. My friends kidded me, they still do, about going so far on such modest talent.

I always agreed with them. I had no illusions about my films, which were not always as believable as, say, the six o'clock news. Nor did I consider myself anything special as an actor or a singer. "But what is my opinion," I would add, "against that of a million other people?"

Being lucky is a kind of talent, too. It was my good fortune to come along at a moment when the industry, the Western movie industry, had reached the end of a cycle. About every ten years or so, another cowboy would arrive with a new style, or a different idea, or a better trick, and the public embraced him. The public was tolerant.

No one knew exactly what would work, but it was clear that the traditional Westerns no longer did. The Wild West of Billy the Kid's day had been done to death. So I came along, owing more to Bing Crosby than Bill Hart. My movies offered crimes of cunning, instead of crimes of violence. Dishonest salesmen and financial pirates were my villains. I ran a kind of one-man Better Business Bureau, out in the wide-open spaces.

And a funny thing about it, millions of cap pistols were sold in my name during those years. I dominated that market. Yet I was one Western star who made little use of firearms. We toned down the gunplay, as it became more obvious that women made up nearly half of my audience. At one point, Republic considered casting me in straight, romantic parts. I put a fast stop to that. "Look," I said, "a cowboy, if he doesn't let his public down, is good until he's fifty years old. A matinee idol doesn't last five years."

So I stayed with what I was doing. I stayed with it until the cows came home. My career as a movie cowboy stretched from the worst of the Depression, in the thirties, survived the war years of the forties, and lasted until the fifties, when television happened. Three decades.

Trying to single out one of my pictures is like trying to recall a particular noodle you enjoyed during a spaghetti dinner. It is easier to remember them all. There are Western movie fanatics, cultists, I suppose they are called, who will know what I mean. Many of them were children when these films were made. The fans mattered then and they do now. For them, and for the pleasure of it, I have searched through old scrapbooks and files and my own memory, indeed a dusty trail, to recover what I could of all those years, all those Saturday afternoons.

Of the actual plots, or story lines, I remember very little, in most cases. But of the ideas behind them, the people who passed through them, the oddball things they did, *we* did, I have impressions as strong today as when they happened.

It no longer surprises me to learn that what we were a part of forty years ago hadn't been done before, though no one knew it at the time. To be the first this or the first that is often an empty honor, but I still prefer it to being the second this or the second that.

Although other serials had revolved around lost and hidden cities and civilizations, ours, *The Phantom Empire*, filmed in 1935, was the first to be rated as science fiction (or, as the Star Trekkies like to put it, sci-fi.) Buster Crabbe and *Flash Gor-*

don are better remembered, but we preceded them by nearly a year.

Remember Mary Ford? She was once a member of my radio troupe. Mary and her husband, Les Paul, hit it big with their multiple-track recordings in the 1950s. I used it, for the first time, I am told, with an early version of the title song from *Tumbling Tumbleweeds*, the movie that launched the era of the singing cowboy. The multiple track allowed me to sing both the lead and the tenor; in other words, my own harmony.

At least two other trends were established in that first starring film of mine: 1) There wasn't a Reo truck or a wood-paneled station wagon on the road that my horse, Champion, couldn't outrun, and 2) Big Business and Special Interests and High-handed Villains always lost out to the pure of heart.

Until *Melody Trail*, the females in Westerns usually numbered one, only, and wore slacks. My second feature film, and most of those that followed, had pretty gals hanging all over the corral and often clad in either majorette costumes, or the forerunner of the mini. Whose idea this was I don't recall, but I'm willing to take credit for it.

In *The Sagebrush Troubador*, I tracked down the killer of a half-blind old prospector, using as clues a swayback horse and one guitar string. I then saved the life of his granddaughter and rediscovered the lost gold mine. In short, a routine day's work.

Of *The Singing Vagabond* I have no recollection at all, except that the cast included Chief Thundercloud, the original Tonto.

Red River Valley had a good mix, I thought, of action, music, comic foolery, and plot. In many ways it was the most typical of the early Autrys, pitting me against a banker conniving to grab the town water rights, a kind of TVA Goes West.

Comin' Round the Mountain was one of just two films I made for Republic actually set in the Old West. My retreat from the buckskin Western was no accident, but based on my belief that the public found me more convincing as Singin' Gene than as a Pony Express rider. This one was also notable for the fact that it produced my first screen kiss, with Ann Rutherford. The year was 1936 and it worked so well that we came right back and tried it again, four years later, with Ann Miller. And they cut the scene. But that's another story.

In case anyone still didn't know that I was a cowboy actor, and I sang, the studio decided to take the direct approach. I was asked once what *The Singing Cowboy* was about, and I replied, "Oh, about sixty-five minutes." The film marked the debut of Lon Chaney, Jr., as a Western heavy. But the action was clearly secondary to the songs, ten of them, including "Listen to the Mockingbird."

If one had to pick an example of the slice-of-life plots that tended to pop up in my films, *Guns and Guitars* would probably serve. I did not engage, for the most part, in such mundane activities as saving the old homestead or chasing bank bandits. While my solutions were a little less complex than those offered by FDR, and my methods a bit more direct, I played a kind of New Deal cowboy who never hesitated to tackle many of the same problems: the dust bowl, unemployment, or the harnessing of power. This may have contributed to my popularity with the 1930s audiences.

With *Oh, Susanna!* we began what was to become a policy for most of the movies I did at Republic: employing various country music groups, usually regional, with at least some radio fame. the Light Crust Doughboys were first, out of Fort Worth, only a few years away from seeing their leader, Pappy Lee O'Daniel, elected governor of Texas. With the exception of the Sons of the Pioneers, who appeared in *Tumbling Tumbleweeds*, the music in my previous films had been supplied by Smiley, myself, and a few, uncredited, backup musicians.

Over the years, I am told, *Ride, Ranger, Ride* has become a collector's item, in the unexplained way that those things often happen. This one is valued as the other of the two Autry scripts, at Republic, placed in the period of the American frontier. (I leave the U. S. Cavalry, rejoin the Texas Rangers, and expose the traitor who instigated an Indian uprising. I know. Why does a synopsis, even your own, always sound like a blurb for a movie ad?)

A footnote to this film was the debut of Max Terhune, who became one of the best liked, off the screen, of all Western actors. As late as 1974, a "Max Terhune Appreciation Society" still flourished. Once a ventriloquist, Max got his start, as I did, at WLS radio in Chicago. He went on to fame as one of "The Three Mesquiteers," whose ranks later included Duke Wayne.

Also in the cast was Iron Eyes Cody, who had been around Westerns since *The Covered Wagon,* in 1923. You may have seen him last in a popular TV spot, as the Indian with the big tear on his cheek, in a message about the ecology. He favored those flat-brimmed, round-crowned hats the Indians used to wear in the movies to show they had gotten religion. Sort of Amish-looking.

Tim McCoy brought Iron Eyes to Hollywood when he was twenty. Later, he toured with Ken Maynard in his circus, The Diamond K, before it went busted and Ken lost everything he had. Cody was one of the last people to visit Maynard before he died, in March of 1973. The old cowboy talked about his wife and how much he had missed her the last few years, hard ones for him. "Iron," he said, "I gotta go meet Bertha."

The men who made Western movies were a curious breed, different from other actors. Not better, or worse, or nobler, just different. In a way that surely isn't hard to understand, they all, in time, came to feel an obligation to the mythology of the West. William S. Hart could endure the fact that Thomas Ince, the head of his studio, had underpaid him, but he could never forgive Ince for his odd dislike of Hart's pony, Fritz.

No B Westerns had been produced with bigger budgets, or released with more fanfare and publicity, than mine. The Rogers films of the war years and the Hopalong Cassidys from Paramount were about the only others that had anything resembling a promotion campaign. Certain of my pictures were treated as special entries, rather than as the-next-in-an-endless series. The first to rate this handling was *The Big Show,* filmed on location, according to the lobby posters, at the Texas Centennial. That means we did the background shots and some of the specialty acts—Sally Rand (yes, *that* Sally Rand) and the SMU band—in Dallas.

The Big Show marked my only dual role. I appeared as a kind of snooty film star named Tom Ford, whose double and stunt man happened to be Gene Autry. With the exception of my part as a henchie in *Mystery Mountain*, and a later film at Fox, this was the only other time I played a character whose name was not my own.

This time we featured not one but five musical groups: Sons of the Pioneers, the Light Crust Doughboys (whose star, Bob Wills, had just quit to go out on his own), the Beverly Hillbillies, the Jones Boys, and the SMU school band. By loading up the credits, and designating the movie as an "Autry Special," Republic found that it could charge the exhibitors more than the usual flat rate. This discovery inspired a number of "Autry Specials," as well as a practice that led to my going out on strike.

Most movie buffs remember *The Old Corral*, if at all, for what must seem an ironic touch. In one scene I fought with a rude fellow, as played by an actor named Dick Weston. At gun point, I forced him to sing a song, a humiliation one and a half times worse than death. Dick Weston, of course, was the first screen name used by Roy Rogers. The plot involved a torch singer, a transcontinental bus, and some smart-apple Yankees.

In those days, Republic had a rule about titles. If it was catchy, use it. Never mind if it didn't fit the story. So you will understand when I tell you that *Round-up Time in Texas* takes place in Africa. Wild horses, a diamond mine, and a savage tribe of Zulus are the key elements. A group called the Cabin Kids provided the background music, and if you wish to know how long ago this was, all you need to be told is that a Republic press release described them as "a really swell group of pickaninnies."

How delicately the *love angle* was treated in most of my movies was vividly reflected in *Git Along Little Dogies*, the second of eight released in 1937. The rules were clear: almost no clinches, no embraces, were allowed. I could put my arm around the heroine's waist only if necessary to save her from falling over a cliff. Believe me, when your audience consisted mainly of women who craved romance, and small boys who hated it, a compromise was required to please both.

In *Git Along Little Dogies*, Judith Allen, who had once played opposite W. C. Fields, had the part of the insolent young thing.

In one scene she drove her car through a pool of oil, laughing as she splattered me from head to foot. And now I quote from a review of the film:

"Gene jumps on Champion, chases the auto, and brings it to a stop by shooting a tire. The heroine states that he is no gentleman. Gene puts a bullet through another tire. She attacks him. Gene picks her up and drops her into a brook . . . After dropping her in the water, he is allowed to be slightly contrite. He lets the girl talk him into putting on the spare tires. While he is at work, she jumps on Champion and rides away."

Now, my grade school public relished all this, while the grownups could see that the foundation was being laid for a beautiful romance. But it was essential that the love interest be disguised. One boo, or hiss, or raspberry, could cause five hundred hearts to freeze.

(A final word about *Little Dogies*. In it, we hit the ecology trail. We opposed the drilling of an oil well out of fear that it would spoil the cattle's drinking water.)

Rootin' Tootin' Rhythm was based on a story by Johnston McCulley, the creator of Zorro. But the only Spanish influence was provided by my leading lady, Armida, a Lupe Velez type. The plot was another of those mistaken-identity-through-a-clothes-swap things I got involved in, more than once.

The screen's original Peter Pan, Betty Bronson, a major star of the silent era, attempted a comeback in my next film, *Yodelin' Kid from Pine Ridge*. (The script may have convinced her it wasn't worth it. She retired soon after that.) But a supporting cast of real quality included two veterans, Charles Middleton of "Ming the Merciless" fame and Russell Simpson, a few years away from Pa Joad in *Grapes of Wrath*.

We were grinding out a picture on an average of every six weeks, one after another like link sausage. Strung together and laid bare, some of the ideas seem silly today and some were, even then. But many were fresh and inventive. In *Public Cowboy Number 1*, we used a short wave radio set to foil a cattle rustling ring that was directed from an airplane. This was 1937, remember. The movie was later re-created as a Big Little Book. That was a compliment, I guess.

By then we had practically formed our own stock company, whose cast included such semi-regulars as William Farnum, another silent screen idol, who re-established himself in the "good sheriff" roles.

The heavy in *Boots and Saddles* was Gordon Elliott, and there is a point to be made here about movie luck and people who persevere. Elliott had knocked around since 1929, playing mostly dress extras. After this film, Columbia made a serial called *The Great Adventures of Wild Bill Hickok*, and gave Elliott the starring role. The studio renamed him Wild Bill Elliott, he later became the screen's second Red Ryder, and he was still around in the early fifties when the B Western began its final spasm. By then the cowboy hero drank when he felt like it, beat up the villain while holding a gun on him, and wore his six-shooter reversed in the holster, with the butt forward. (Elliott may have been the first to wear them in that fashion.)

The credits for *Boots and Saddles* gave fourth billing—after Smiley and Judith Allen—to Ra Hould, which is not a typographical error. He was an Australian import, used on this picture because Sol Siegel, the associate producer, wanted an authentic British accent for one of the characters. Republic starred him in one or two other films, but it wasn't a good time for boomerang tossers, or something, and I lost track of him.

Republic broke new ground in *Manhattan Merry-Go-Round*, when I became the first cowboy to rate a guest star billing. The musical comedy had a powerhouse line-up with Phil Regan, Leo Carillo, Ted Lewis, Cab Calloway, and Louis Prima, but the fellow who drew the most attention was an amateur named Joe DiMaggio.

In his second season with the New York Yankees, Joe had led the league with forty-six homers, and was on his way to becoming the town's biggest hero since Babe Ruth. In the 1970s his name, and one haunting line from a Simon and Garfunkel song—

"Where have you gone, Joe DiMaggio?"—would touch off the whole blessed nostalgia boom.

In honor of Joe, the movie was premiered in San Francisco, his home grounds. During the week, we hit a few spots together, and one night we wound up in that famed tourist attraction, Finocchio's, where the female impersonators did their act. (In the late thirties, boys you could not tell from girls, and vice versa, were still a novelty.)

Between shows one of them came over to our table, sat down, placed a hand on Joe's bicep and squealed, "Jeezus, what a muscle!" With the evening gown, the wig, the make-up, the soft complexion, and what appeared to be an ample bosom, our guest confused the hell out of both of us. After a while, he/she finished a drink and left to do a routine, the eyes of DiMaggio following every step. Joe was thoughtful for a moment, then he joked, "You know, Gene, if that was a girl I could really go for her. I like 'em a little husky."

For *Springtime in the Rockies*, we used an old formula with a twist. I was the foreman of a ranch whose new owner, the spoiled heiress, arrives from the East with a carload of sheep and a degree in animal husbandry. The big story was Autry in a poker game. And this time gambling did pay. I won a worthless old spread and dumped the heiress and her sheep on it.

You would not exactly call it a case of life imitating art, but the heiress was played by Polly Rowles, a Pittsburgh socialite. At least, the studio claimed she was and the boys in the crew believed it, meaning that no matter how hard she tried to be friendly they would not accept her. We were filming in the mountains near Palm Springs, and staying at night at a motel in town. From somewhere the boys acquired a wooden Indian, the lifelike kind you used to find sitting in a chair in a cigar store. They slipped into Polly's cabin and left it there, propped up on the john.

It would not be gentlemanly to imagine the scene that evening when Polly retired to her room, undressed for bed, and walked into the bathroom. But that was one of the most piercing, blood-curdling screams I have ever heard.

Most of the hijinks on a movie location in those days were pro-

vided by the crew. It may be that way still. But I doubt it. The
money is too big, the unions too serious.

I have powerful memories of *The Old Barn Dance*, for reasons
only indirectly related to the movie. It was the last I would make
for six months. After a final, tiresome hassle with Herb Yates
over my contract, the cowboy took a walk. My absence opened
the door for Roy Rogers, who, coincidentally, had a bit part in
the picture.

On the sound track was one of my early hits, "You're the
Only Star in My Blue Heaven." Some have said, still say, that it
was the beginning of the soft-country sound. So maybe I opened
a door for Willie Nelson, granted, thirty-five years later. But I
was concerned then with doors that were closing, not opening.

I am by nature slow to anger. But once convinced I have been
wronged, and my feet planted, you cannot budge me with a trac-
tor. A man broke enough, long enough, often develops a keen
sense of his worth and does not mind fighting to get it. But my
quarrel with the studio was not entirely over dollars. I had signed
my first contract, with Nat Levine, for one hundred and fifty
dollars a week, with this understanding: If I proved myself, and
made money for Republic, I would be rewarded.

By 1937 I had moved up to first place in the box office polls
for Western stars. My pictures didn't play the luxury, four-
thousand-seat theaters. They played the rural flea pits and the little independent houses, with eight hundred seats or less. But people were standing in line and I went out to meet them. I made
personal appearances all over the country, drumming up business
for the eight films a year we were rolling out.

Herb Yates had taken over the company. Republic profits
soared. My salary had jumped to five thousand dollars a film, but
there were strings. My contract contained a clause that entitled
the studio to half of any money I received from endorsements,
radio or public appearances. No attempt had been made to
collect and I was assured that none would. But at the end of the
year I wanted the contract amended. I didn't want some lawyer
rediscovering those rights later and deciding they should be en-
forced.

I might have made none of this an issue, if not for a policy

Republic had put quietly into effect. It was called block buying. I found out about it between pictures, on the road, when I stopped by the office of a local film distributor. I put in a plug for *Boots and Saddles,* then ready for release.

"Wish I could afford it," he said.

That was a curious thing to say, I thought. "Afford it? What do you mean?"

"Can't stand the cost of the package," he said.

"Package?"

"Sure. Don't tell me you're not aware of the package deal."

"New one on me," I said. "Tell me about it."

"Just started," he said. "Now, if we want a Gene Autry film, we have to buy the entire studio line. That's a lot of loot."

I could feel my temperature rising. "Are you telling me that you can't get one of my pictures without having to take a bunch of others you may or may not want?"

He nodded. "That's about it. They're using your films to push whatever else they got going."

I hurried back to Hollywood and confronted Herb Yates. I wanted that practice stopped, those clauses removed, and, while I was about it, a fairer share of the profits my pictures were producing. That was the wrong approach to take with Yates. But if there was a better one I didn't know it then, and I don't now.

He was not unkind or ungenerous. But like a lot of studio bosses of that era, his vanity was such that he would resist doing what was right rather than yield to what he saw as pressure. Yates had a stern look about him, thin lips, a square jaw, balding, with owlish glasses. But he was unpredictable. Once he had one of the sound stages flooded and frozen so he could practice his ice skating. He was out there for hours, alone, with a little tam-o-shanter tilted to one side of his head and a scarf around his neck.

Socially, he was the best of company. He could pick up everybody's tab in a night club, lay down a thousand dollars, and think nothing of it. The next day, across a desk, if you were asking for a raise, he would throw dollars around like they were manhole covers.

I had a new movie scheduled to start in two weeks, to be called *Washington Cowboy.* When I walked out of his office, we both

1. The classic pose: Champion rearing on cue.

2. *Taking a guitar break with child star Jane Withers, later TV's Josephine the Plumber; film was* Shooting High.

3. *Two who usually got our man: with ex-heavyweight champ Jack Dempsey.*

4. Homesteaders: Ina Mae and myself, circa 1944.

5. *One of my prized possessions, a painting by the great Western artist Frederic Remington.*

6. *Champion, the horse with a high school education, and friend, on the back lot at Republic.*

7. *These boots were made for show: part of my collection of over three hundred pair.*

8. *A boot print in the sidewalk of Grauman's Chinese Theater.*

9. *Champion's turn to be immortalized in front of Grauman's Chinese Theater (1945).*

10. Sidekick Pat Buttram and Champion have an ear for good music in a scene from Texans Never Cry.

11. With Ann Miller, Jimmy Durante in Melody Ranch.

12. *Square dancing with Elena Verdugo in* The Big Sombrero; *she later answered the phone for Dr. Marcus Welby.*

knew I wouldn't be there when the cameras rolled. The trade papers made it sound like a range war.

So I had gone on strike. It wasn't the first time. Jimmy Cagney had bolted, and Olivia de Havilland, among others. It was the only weapon you had if you got into a scrap about your contract. But my idea of a strike was to keep busy and keep moving. A moving target is harder to hit. Any cowboy knew that.

Now began a chase scene that topped anything we had done on the screen. I told George Goodale to book a tour going East, as many dates and towns as he could line up. As it turned out, George had nothing better to do. He had gone out to Republic a day or so after my showdown, stiff as a board, and told off an assistant to Yates, and they barred him from the lot. That was one of the great things about George. He was the kind of fellow who, if you have been in a bar fight or something and the cops are dragging you off, will holler, *"You can't do that, he's my friend,"* and wind up in the paddy wagon with you.

Of course, when I failed to show up for the first day's shooting on *Washington Cowboy,* the studio suspended me. Yates said he would make the film without me and create a new cowboy star. That was when they gave a screen test to Leonard Slye, who had appeared in a couple of my pictures as Dick Weston, and whose name was soon to be Roy Rogers. They changed the title of the movie to *Under Western Skies,* but they kept a song called "Dust," written by Johnny Marvin and Gene Autry. In the original script, I was to go to Washington and tell the story of the dust bowl before Congress, and appeal for aid to the farmers and ranchers, whose cattle were dying. It was a Western version of *Mr. Smith Goes to Washington,* the Jimmy Stewart classic.

Yates had threatened to break me—"if you won't work here, you won't work anywhere." The studio took out an injunction to prevent me from appearing on stage until my contract had been fulfilled. We hit the road, through Arizona, New Mexico, and Texas, always one step ahead of the process server.

The darndest thing happened in Texarkana, which sits on the state line like a penny on a crack. The theater I was to play in was on the Texas side, but right across the street was Arkansas. While I was on the stage, the town marshal showed up with a warrant. My people kept talking to him, and assuring him I'd be right off, and after each act they would bring me into the wings opposite where he was waiting.

At the end of the show, instead of making my usual exit, I jumped off the stage and ran out the front of the theater, across the street and into Arkansas, where he had no authority to serve me.

Republic followed us all over the country, but they didn't catch up until the tour reached Nashville. There they served me with a subpoena, which enjoined us from appearing on the stage of the Paramount, the biggest theater in town, with two thousand seats. It was sold out, all day, for three shows.

So I took another look at the summons and I said, well, the law is very clear, and you don't mess with the law unless you have your own army, so I won't go on the stage. And I didn't. What I did was put Champion up there, and Smiley Burnette, and whatever group we had with us, and I bought a ticket and sat in the front row, in front of the orchestra pit and put Champ through his paces. So the show went on. It had been announced to the crowd, of course, that I had been served and could not perform. But people enjoy being a part of events that are out of the ordinary pattern, and they reacted warmly to everything we did.

The injunction was a temporary one and Republic took me into court, in Nashville, to make it permanent. They had a smart attorney who knew the motion picture business, and he knew the times. He didn't bother with a lot of evidence. All he said was, "Look, Republic is offering this man forty thousand dollars a year, a handsome living, a fortune. He ought to be forced to go back to work for his own good." The judge hearing the case was making, I suppose, about six thousand dollars a year. He made the injunction permanent.

I want to be honest about this. I learned long ago that whenever someone involved in a business dispute says, "It isn't the money," you can be assured that it is the money. And forty thousand dollars *was* a fortune. But I worked hard for it, seven days a week. My pictures had pulled Republic out of hock and were now bringing in millions. There was also an attitude involved, a matter of self-respect, and I was fighting for that, too.

Months had flown by. Now the rest of the tour had to be canceled. My prospects were not bright. But as Smiley often kidded me, "Whenever the wolf came to the door, Autry ended up with a fur coat."

Back in Los Angeles, I was getting help from a powerful lobby. Republic's distributors were holding their annual convention and they climbed all over Herb Yates. It was going on six months since an Autry movie had been released. They made it sound not like a business problem, but a national famine. Many of them had gone along with the block buying, to the extent that they would buy a package of twenty, my eight plus twelve others, and ship back the ones they didn't want without using them. Now they demanded some assurance I would be working for Republic next year. Otherwise, they warned Yates, their theaters would be in trouble.

At that point, Yates called. While our attorneys got together and worked out a compromise, we went off to play golf. In a curious way, there were no hard feelings. All he had done was call me disloyal and threaten to ruin me. In return, I had called him a cheap skate and a tyrant. In those years, in Hollywood, no one took anyone else seriously. So we played golf.

My salary was raised to ten thousand dollars a film (escalating to fifteen and twenty over the next seven years), and the clauses I found objectionable were removed. The package deals continued; they were by then too entrenched to undo. And I gave my permission, which they needed, for the song I had written, "*Dust*," to be sung by Roy Rogers, in a movie that had been scheduled for me.

Perhaps this is the place to say that there was never any animosity, nor jealousy, between Roy and me. He was not a factor in my dispute with the studio. A break came and he took it, just as anyone would have, myself included. I never felt we were competing. You could only film so many weeks in a year, and there were plenty of pictures and audiences for both of us, and some other fellows, too.

Of course, the studio tried desperately to create the impression of a rivalry, a feud, between us. And a few of the people around us almost got into the act. Roy was a fresh-faced kid from Ohio, but Republic skipped over that in promoting him as a cowhand from Cody, Wyoming. Goodale wanted to *expose* that, leak the story to the papers. It sounds comical now, but back then Hollywood's myths—who you were, what you came from—seemed important.

Bev Barnett, the publicity director at Republic, who had once worked for me, got wind of it. He came to me and said, "Gene, don't let George do that to us. If he does, it'll cost me my job."

I said, "Bev, no one connected with me is going to hurt you, or Roy. You have my word on that." And that was the end of it. Life was a whole lot simpler then.

CHAPTER FIVE

It Beats Working

A young film producer once had an idea for a different kind of movie. This was during a time when people were wrapping up the forties and fifties and selling them back to us as the good old days. Batman was the rage on television and Superman had made it to Broadway.

What he had in mind was a movie consisting of nothing but old trailers from coming attractions. He knew a farmer in North Carolina who had bought up thousands of them and stored them in his barn. He planned just to string them like paper clips, one after the other. Scenes of Tarzan swinging from tree to tree to tree. Five minutes of Bette Davis smoking a cigarette. Douglas Fairbanks fencing with three eunuchs. And Gene Autry kissing his horse. Things like that.

He had a great title for it: *Coming Next Week*. And he had enough footage left over, he said, for a sequel: *Coming Week After Next*.

Let me dispose right now of a malicious rumor that has haunted me all my life. I did not kiss my horse! We may have *nuzzled* a little, but we never kissed. Never. I can take a joke, but it bothered ol' Champ.

That was one way of pointing out, I guess, that Autry was about the most reluctant Romeo the screen had produced up to that time. I never kissed my leading ladies, either, except Ann Rutherford once and another time with Ann Miller that wound up on the cutting room floor. I won't go into the reason for that again, except to make one point. The leading ladies in the Autry films were not there just for decoration or to point out which way the bad guys went. As written, they gave me a lot of any-thing-you-can-do-I-can-do-better sass, smoked a lot of Kools—that era's Virginia Slims—and, in general, played a thirties' version of waiting for Gloria (Steinem). That may have been due, in no small part, to the presence of such screenwriters as Betty Burbridge, Luci Ward, and Connie Lee. We didn't exactly use them because they were experts on the West. Whatever their formula, those films were about the only ones in the B Western category, up to then, that had a mass appeal to women.

The touch of Betty Burbridge was evident again in *Gold Mine in the Sky*, my first movie after my strike against Republic had ended. For the third time in less than a year, the plot had me riding herd on a spoiled heiress. That was a favorite of Betty's, who had already milked it pretty good back in the silent film days.

After that we knocked out three quickies of no special distinction (unless you count a song by Smiley Burnette called "She Works Third Tub at the Laundry") for release in late 1938, starting with *Man from Music Mountain*. Then came *Prairie Moon* and *Rhythm of the Saddle*. The studio was trying hard to recover its losses.

Our last film that year was *Western Jamboree*, and it brought me together, for the first of three pictures, with one of the funniest humans Hollywood ever knew. The name Joe Frisco might draw a blank look today, but no one in his trade was ever more widely quoted. People collected Joe Frisco stories and held them like old coins, waiting for the value to go up.

Joe palled around with Smiley and Pat Buttram, the two sidekicks of my movie years. He had a heart as big as a blimp and whatever Joe had—clothes, booze, or debts—he shared. And Joe stuttered. That wasn't what made him funny, but it didn't detract any.

He was a racetrack junkie. Went there almost every day. One afternoon he left the set early and headed for Santa Anita. There he ran into Bing Crosby, who made the mistake of asking how he was doing.

"N-n-n-not so g-g-g-good," he said, reaching out a hand. "L-l-l-lend me a sawbuck." Bing slipped him a twenty-dollar bill.

After the next race they met near the paddock and Bing said, "How'd you do, Joe?"

"N-n-n-not so g-g-g-good," he said. "G-g-g-gimme another sawbuck."

Finally, Frisco bet a longshot and the horse came home at something like 35 to 1. Later, Bing walked into the bar and there Frisco was, a pile of money on the counter, holding court and buying drinks for his friends. When Crosby walked in Joe motioned him over, peeled off two twenties, and said, "S-s-s-say, kid, s-s-s-sing me a song."

It was important to Joe to get in the last word. Once he let a down-on-his-luck buddy sneak into his hotel room and bed down, as he waited for times to improve. A week went by before the desk clerk got wise. Then he called one night and confronted Joe with the fact that he was harboring an unpaid guest.

"You'll either have to ask him to leave," the clerk sniffed, "or we'll have to charge you the double rate."

"In th-th-that case," said Joe, with just the right touch of indignation, "s-s-s-send up another G-g-g-gideon Bible!"

Home on the Prairie marked the first appearance of June Storey, a pretty little blonde from Canada, as my favorite reinholder. June was Smiley Burnette's favorite audience. He had a conviction, it was almost a religious belief, that your feet were the key to your physical and mental health. Whenever people looked tired, Smiley would bathe and massage their feet. He carried a pail around with him on the set. June thought it was a very generous thing for Smiley to do and took frequent advantage of the service.

Still in her teens, June was one of those people who wanted to nominate you for a prize anytime you did a good deed. I found a tiny kitten once, I'm not sure where, just abandoned on the street, I guess. I brought it to the shooting that day in a sock—it was no bigger than a man's hand—and held it in my lap between scenes. June loved to tell people about that. "Have you heard," she'd ask, "about Gene and the little kitten he carried around in a sock?"

And whoever it was would wait, just wait for the rest of the story or the punch line or whatever, and that would be it. There wasn't any more.

Whenever one of my films had the same title as a current best-selling song, such as *Mexicali Rose*, the exhibitors always knew that Republic was going to hit them with a slightly higher tab. The reason being that these were usually shot on a bigger budget, and Yates liked to get back the money they spent for the rights to the song.

But I believe this one was worth the price of the ticket. The cast included Noah Beery, Sr., who could chew up as much scenery as his brother, Wallace. And we laid three big ones on them in the music department. In addition to the title song; we brought back "You're the Only Star in My Blue Heaven," and introduced "*El Rancho Grande*." That last one had more ay-yi-yi-yi's than even Desi Arnaz in his prime.

I'll only hit the high spots now. The decision had been made to tour the British Isles starting in late July 1939. We turned them out so fast in the first half of the year it was like watching a nickelodeon. One of them was *Colorado Sunset*, which had as supporting actors Elmo Lincoln, the screen's first Tarzan, and Buster Crabbe, one of his successors. This may have been the only Western ever made with two ex-Tarzans in the cast. That may not be the stuff of legend, but it should win a trivia contest. (In the movie, Buster hid behind a mustache. He was then starring as Flash Gordon. Somehow, the studio thought his fans would be less upset at his losing to Autry in a one-on-one, if he looked less like Flash.)

In Old Monterey was considered another big picture that year, mainly because you didn't find Smiley Burnette, Gabby Hayes, and myself working together very often. Gabby was wonderful, always with a yarn to spin. One was about a rodeo stunt he used to pull. He'd gallop across the arena and pick up his handkerchief with his teeth. For an encore, he said, "I'd ride back and pick up my teeth with the handkerchief."

According to some critics, the only drawback to the film was that you also got the Hoosier Hot Shots, a Western forerunner of Spike Jones and his City Slickers. This was another group out of WLS radio, identified only as Ken, Gabe, Hezzie, and Gill. They made strange noises with rub-boards, slide whistles, pig bladders, and whoopee cushions. Hezzie, the comedian of the group, could also wiggle his ears. "Are you ready, Hezzie?" was their trademark. Their biggest hit was, "I've Got Tears in My Ears from Lying on My Back in Bed While I Cry Over You."

I needed a change of pace, we all did, and Europe was certainly to be that. The tour was the brainstorm of Bill Saal, a wild man, but one of the finest PR men I ever saw. He was a Texan, from Dallas, with a thin Robert Benchley mustache and beady eyes and a jutting chin. He looked good in a trench coat.

Saal had made all the arrangements, but no one really knew what to expect when we boarded the U.S.S. *Manhattan* on July 26, from New York's Pier 58. Herb Yates and his wife were with Bill, Ina, and me. The passenger list included James A. Farley, Mr. and Mrs. John Roosevelt, and other assorted government and military people, curious about whatever was brewing in Europe.

It is hard for me, now, to separate that trip, the clamor and excitement of it, from the war that was coming sooner than any of us could have guessed. Everywhere we appeared—London, Liverpool, Dublin, Glasgow, Danzig—the theaters were filled and the streets jammed for blocks with thousands of fans, waiting to see "the American cowboy." My films, and their notions of the Old West, had made me a romantic figure.

There was no major British film industry then. Their medium was the stage; their actors were trained to Shakespeare and the Old Vic. So the *cinemas* were loaded with American movies. They knew all about Franchot Tone, Frederic March, Madeleine Carroll, Constance Bennett—and Gene Autry. It felt odd to see my name on the marquee of the Abbey Picture House. But it felt good.

The only thing that impressed me more than my reception was the British indifference to what was happening all around them. Any inconvenience was dismissed as only temporary. The phrase you kept hearing was, "when the trouble blows over." The trouble had to do with the outbreak of temper in Berlin, the daily threats by Hitler in the newspapers, the massing and movement of German troops.

It all came together for us in London after an appearance at the Paramount Theater. Outside, mounted police tried to control a crowd estimated at five thousand. Bill Saal had taken charge.

"Look, Gene," he said, backstage, "when the show is over, when you finish your act, come out the front way. I've posted some photographers there. I want to get pictures of you with that mob." I glanced out a window. It was a sea of people.

Later, I followed Bill through the front door. The instant we stepped outside, it was like getting hit by the Dallas Cowboys. I was literally thrown into the air. Arms reached out, grabbed at me. Saal was frantic, trying to run interference for me, hold off the crowd, and signal his photographers. He had hired three of them, stationed one at each side of the theater and the other in the middle of the crowd. He had instructed them to start shooting when Autry stepped into the mob.

You have to understand the leisurely British pace. At their usual gait, they remind you of a butler bringing in tea.

"SHOOT!" screamed Saal, motioning to one of his cameramen as my hat bobbed up and down in the crowd like a cork.

From his perch several yards away the cameraman pressed a thumb into his own chest and said, "Me?"

"Yes, yes," said Saal. "You."

"Now?"

The crowd was bouncing off him. Saal fought to hold his ground. He stood on his toes and at the top of his voice he yelled, "YES, NOW, YOU SONUVABITCH. That's the trouble, with you Englishmen. *Hitler has you by the nose and you don't even know it.*"

All this time—well, I suppose only a minute or two had passed —I wasn't exactly feeling terror. But it makes me very nervous when my legs are moving through no effort of my own, and I can't reach my billfold.

Finally, the photographers started snapping their pictures. And Bill began to worry about our safety. He spotted a small British car, an Austin, I think, with a canvas top. He climbed onto it and motioned for me to join him. I struggled through the crowd, took Bill's hand, and let him pull me up.

For a moment the two of us stood there, surveying the mad scene around us, kind of enjoying our triumph. And, then, as our eyes met, forming small o's of surprise, we sank slowly right through the top of that little British car, right through the center of that canvas roof.

We were looking out, from the waist up, when a British policeman, a bobby, waded over from a few feet away. He looked at Saal, touched his hat with his night stick, and shouted, "By the way, old chap, is this your car?"

Bill didn't bat an eye. "Hell, yes," he shouted back. "Now go away and don't bother me. I'm trying to watch the show."

With that the bobby pressed through the crowd and walked away, swinging his stick.

We might never have escaped from there if someone hadn't thought to back up the horse van and lower the ramp, the one we used to get Champion inside. Herb Yates had been caught in the crowd, too. Somehow the three of us met near the car, lowered our shoulders, forced our way through the people, and scrambled up the ramp. Champion didn't seem too pleased to see us, but this was no time to get picky.

With very little effort, I can close my eyes today, tug at my memory, and see that scene exactly as it happened. I have often wondered what that poor fellow thought when he returned and found a huge hole in the top of his car. We tried to locate him later but never did.

Through the entire tour, of course, Champion was treated with a courtesy and respect given few other American entertainers. They asked me to bring him to a luncheon in my honor at the Savoy Hotel, in London, and I did. I led him through the lobby of that elegant hostelry, where the princes of Europe have met, and later he walked among the tables at my reception, while the startled guests protected their plates.

A cowboy was such a novelty over there. It was almost like being from another planet. The questions. Did you ever use your gun to kill anyone? How fast is your horse? Does he understand everything you say?

I tried to give them a little of what they wanted, I suppose. The headline in the Glasgow *Bulletin*, on the morning of August 21, 1939, warned in bold, black type: "HITLER WILL ENTER DANZIG SOON."

At a luncheon that day, I raised my six guns and said, "Look, I ain't a'saying yes and I ain't a'saying no, but if those Nazis cross the border in the morning I'm a'coming in, shooting." The audience roared.

The signs of war were everywhere, unmistakable. And the people talked about it. They talked of little else. In their hearts they knew it was only a question of time. But no one seemed to be preparing for it. I couldn't understand that. I looked at the newspaper headlines years later, the ones my office saved to celebrate our trip, and they were a history lesson. "HITLER SAYS HE IS LOSING PATIENCE," read one. And underneath, in type not much smaller: "COWBOY TAKES LIVERPOOL."

I was there, in Liverpool, the day the Nazis marched into Poland. Some thought Hitler would start bombing England right away. He didn't, but the war was getting closer. The manager of the theater in Dublin was a captain in the reserve British Army. He received his orders one night before I went on stage. By the time I got off, he was gone.

We even attracted a "spy." At least, no one ever convinced me she wasn't. A beautiful black-haired Russian girl who attached herself to Bill Saal. She turned up everywhere we went. She kept asking about America, how we felt about the war, would we fight, were we prepared. She might have been nothing more than an innocent Russian tourist who loved cowboy movies, but she struck me as very worldly and very curious and she fell in love awfully fast.

But all of that, the war talk, the guns going off in our imagination, had something to do with the size of the crowds and the emotion they showered on us. It was a kind of last hurrah, I guess. People had a sense of their lives changing, of time running out on make-believe things.

In Dublin, when we paraded through town with Champion, 300,000 lined the streets to watch, what was then thought to be a world record for anyone less than the Pope. It was a record that stood, I think, until the Beatles toured New York, creating their own brand of hysteria.

The newspapers were very kind to us, but I won't bore you by repeating the details here. Once you have quoted one "MOBBED IN BELFAST" headline, it tends to get tiresome and is of interest only to the mobbee. But it was in Dublin that the tour ended and it is of Dublin that I have the strongest memory.

My dressing room was on the second floor of a large theater, with a fire escape outside my window facing an alley that led to a large parking lot. The Theater Royale was the name of it. I did five shows a day, and after each one the crowds would line up back there and shout, "We want Gene." We hooked up a microphone and loudspeakers on the fire escape, and between performances—for the people who couldn't get tickets—I'd sit there and talk to them and do two or three songs.

It was an impromptu thing, but it kept growing. My last night in Dublin there were ten thousand people out there in that alley and overflowing the parking lot. I know round numbers like that are always suspect, but the police guessed that many and the theater manager, the kind of man who would count the house at a funeral, swore to it.

So after the last show, on my last night, I went outside and sat down on the fire escape and told them how much I loved Dublin, and all of Ireland, and how great it had been, and how grateful I was. And then a curious thing happened. The crowd sang to *me*. First a few voices, then more, until it seemed all of them had joined in and you could hear it for blocks, the words of "Come Back to Erin." I tell you, no people on earth can outdrink or outsing the Irish. It was surely one of the most touching, one of the purest moments of my life. Tears welled up in my eyes. There are just not many times, once you are a grown man, or judged as one, that you feel happy enough to cry.

Heckuva way for a cowboy to talk.

We were ready to return home now. It had been a remarkable tour, in every sense a triumph, but we would get very little benefit from it. The war was going to take care of that. Whatever else America would be shipping and lend-leasing to England, Gene Autry movies would not be among them. (Yet I was amazed in 1953, when I returned to London to appear at Earl's Court, the huge indoor theater, to find I still had a following, after all those years.)

Our passage to New York was out of Plymouth harbor, on the American steamship *The Washington*. The war was getting closer. We were in our suite at the Savoy, in London, a few days before the sailing when Douglas Fairbanks, Sr., called from the lobby. I invited him up. He came right to the point. "I understand you have space on *The Washington*," he said. "My wife and

I, Lady Ashley, have been unable to get passage. This is a dreadful imposition. But we must leave England. *Now.* We'll sleep on the floor if you'll allow us. I would be much in your debt."

A bedroom and parlor had been reserved for us. I assured Doug we would make arrangements for additional beds or cots. We would be happy to share whatever space we had.

But the day before the sailing, Fairbanks called and said, in his very proper way: "Gene, I shan't forget your kind offer to share your stateroom. But I have been able to secure two seats on the *Clipper.*" At that time, Pan American had a fleet of amphibious planes called the *Clippers.* We wished each other luck and a safe journey home.

Before we left port, news had reached the ship that a German submarine had sunk a British passenger liner halfway across the Atlantic. There was no word of survivors. I noticed, as we came aboard, that a large American flag had been painted on the deck and both sides of our vessel.

The week we docked in New York, the late Bob Considine interviewed me for his syndicate. I told him what I had seen, what I felt. War was coming and England wasn't ready. Neither were we. That America would be swept up in Europe's "trouble" was obvious to many, more obvious to some.

Of course, that was one of the virtues of motion pictures. They were supposed to take your mind off the real world and, in those days, we seldom got the two confused. As luck would have it, one of the things I had brought back was the song written for me by the two British lads Michael Carr and Jimmy Kennedy—"South of the Border." There was even time for a script to be written and for the film of the same name to become our last release for 1939. Republic paid a thousand dollars for the rights to the song. Under the studio's waste-not, want-not policy, the second line of the lyrics—"down Mexico way"—was used for a title in 1941.

Indirectly, I brought home something else from that tour. P. K. Wrigley happened to be in Dublin the day Champion and I paraded through town. At the time, he had been thinking about a radio show for Doublemint gum to sponsor. He went back to his advertising agency in Chicago and told them of an unbelievable sight he had witnessed, a singing cowboy who drew 300,000 people in the streets of Dublin.

I was on the set of a movie called *Shooting High* when I answered a telephone page. The call was from Danny Danker, of the J. Walter Thompson agency, the man who made Lux toilet soap famous. When I put down the phone I turned to Carl Cotner and Frankie Marvin, who had bit parts in the film, and, said, "Hey, stick your fiddles in the car tomorrow. We're going to do an audition for CBS for a radio show for the Wrigley people." The three of us walked into the CBS studios on Sunset Boulevard the next day. Out of that came "The Melody Ranch Show." We went on the air with it in 1940. It lasted sixteen good years.

For *Shooting High,* the studio had loaned me to Twentieth Century-Fox, whose hot property then was a child actress named Jane Withers. Years later, she would appear on television commercials as Josephine the plumber. For one of the rare times in my career, I took second billing and played a character other than myself. In the movie, I "doubled" for a stuffed-shirt cowboy star played by Robert Lowery. The cast also included Jack Carson, as a high-powered press agent. A couple of scenes in the film dealt with making a film, and this gave what happened on the set a slightly madcap quality.

The film within the film had Lowery (as the cowboy star) going through the motions, until it came time for the rough stuff. The director would yell "cut!" and then I would replace Lowery. That is what you saw on the screen. What happened next, of course, was that the real stuntman replaced *me.* I never objected to doing my own stunts. But this was just good business. If a box office name got his tail bone busted during a movie and couldn't continue, someone would be out big money.

The success of our radio show led, inevitably, to a picture called *Melody Ranch.* I don't believe any Republic film in 1940 carried a bigger budget—close to $400,000—with the likely exception of *Dark Command,* starring John Wayne and Claire Trevor. *Melody Ranch* was what the studio in those days modestly referred to as a blockbuster. The cast included Jimmy

Durante, Ann Miller, Horace MacMahon, Gabby Hayes, Bob Wills and His Texas Playboys, and special music by Jule Styne.

I even had a kissing scene with Ann Miller, but when that tidbit appeared in the papers during the filming, the mail from angry and disillusioned little boys was so heavy it was cut from the movie. The mail was along the lines of the question asked by a young baseball fan of Shoeless Joe Jackson, when he was implicated in a World Series fix: "Say it ain't so, Joe."

In place of romance, the kids got Jimmy Durante. As an entertainer, Durante was in a class by himself. His comedy relied not only on what he said or how he said it, but on that cement-mixer of a voice, the roll of those eyes, the thrust of that nose. He was one of the great scene stealers of all time. And when it came to reading a script, I was Sir Laurence Olivier compared to Durante. He could not read a blessed line. When you did a scene with Jimmy you just let him go, and when he finished you tried to remember enough of what he said so that your answer made sense. Sometimes it did.

At one point in *Melody Ranch*, Horace MacMahon, who became better known for his hard-bitten cop roles, was on trial for stealing a horse. His lawyer was Cornelius J. Courtney, as played by Durante. (Yes, some of our plots did tax the imagination.) Jimmy ad-libbed the whole scene. With his client on the witness stand, he began his questioning.

"Whatcha name?"

"Jupiter," said MacMahon.

"Ahhh, Choopiter," said Durante. "Choopiter, do you swear to tell the troot, the whole troot, and nuttin' but the troot, so help ya, God?"

"I do."

Durante threw up his hands. "Aaaggh," he said, "we done lost da case, right dere."

I don't recall if we reshot the scene or not. But I thought it was funnier than the original dialogue.

Jule Styne, with his greatest hits ahead of him, had written "Melody Ranch" as a title song for the movie. At the time, we still didn't have a theme song for the radio show. Carl Cotner thought it was a natural and urged me to use it. But I had something else in mind. I had worked with Ray Whitley on a tune for an earlier film, and I planned to try it on the show.

Carl thought I was making a mistake. But I shook my head and said, "I don't think it's near the song this one is. I just have a feeling about it." I was talking about "Back in the Saddle Again." That time, at least, I think my judgment held up.

During the early forties, it must have seemed to most moviegoers that Republic couldn't make an Autry or a Rogers picture without Mary Lee cast as somebody's spoiled kid sister or resident orphan-in-trouble. *Ridin' on a Rainbow* was one of those. It was also a Western version of *Showboat*. One of the songwriters was Carson Robinson, who later made a big seller out of a small classic called, "Life Gets Teejus." Mary Lee had started out as a young singer with the Ted Weems orchestra.

Often, of course, when one of my own songs became popular we slapped it on a movie. So *Back in the Saddle* was released in March of 1941. Smiley was in it, as usual, and Mary Lee, and an interesting actress named Jacqueline Wells. She had talent, but was one of those who seemed doomed to work in nothing but B Westerns. She would change her screen name about every five years and start over; from Diane Duval to Jackie Wells to Julie Bishop. Under that name, Julie Bishop, she became a Warner's contract player and achieved semi-stardom in the war years. She is probably best remembered as the Hawaiian hooker who fell for John Wayne in *Sands of Iwo Jima*.

I always had one regret about *Back in the Saddle*. If we had known what was coming in just a few months, we could have saved it for the title of my first postwar movie.

CHAPTER SIX

The Last Good War

As they say, in every man's life there is a summer of '42. For most of my generation it actually began on a Sunday morning, the seventh of December, 1941.

You ask kids today about Pearl Harbor and some of them will think you are talking about a female country and western singer. But that is where it started, at a place called Pearl Harbor, a name strange to many of us even then. If you knew someone in the service you might have known that Pearl Harbor was the naval base at Honolulu, where the booze was cheap and every third sailor got his tattoo.

I walked into the CBS studios in Hollywood around noon that day for the rehearsal of "Melody Ranch," same as always. The actual broadcast would come hours later, live, of course—there were no tapes then—with an audience out front. Many of them had already taken their seats, for the rehearsal, buzzing with rumors. The Japanese had bombed Pearl Harbor! No one knew quite what to believe, what to do, what to expect. Backstage we wondered how much the audience had heard. And how much they thought we knew.

Ten minutes before our rehearsal the curtain was opened. The cast assembled and I strolled to the mike to start the warm-ups. I introduced the rest of the cast. We traded a few gags. And by then we knew that everyone was aware of the news.

In spite of the confusion, and all the questions that went begging, we had to put on a show as though nothing had happened. No one told us the control room had received word that "Melody Ranch" was to be delayed for a special report from the CBS newsroom in New York. At the moment our theme usually began, the report was piped into the studio. Those of us on the stage—and the hundred or so seated in the audience and the millions riveted to their radios across the land—listened numbly to the details of the attack on Pearl Harbor.

". . . at a few minutes after dawn, Hawaii time, the Japanese Imperial Air Force . . ."

I heard those words then. I hear them now. President Roosevelt had called a special session of Congress for the next morning, for the purpose of declaring a state of war. We were advised to stand by for further announcements.

For the next vacant seconds the people in the studio were like figures in a wax museum. No one stirred. Or spoke. Then the director gave a cue, my theme came up, and almost by reflex, we started the show. One of the stock questions of our time would soon become: "What were you doing when you heard the news about Pearl Harbor? And that was what I was doing a few hours after the bombs fell, what I did, a radio show. One of the most awkward of my life. We sang. Joked. Went through our lines. And when it was over the audience got up and walked out in a silence that was like leaving a tomb.

Sure, we stuck to the script. It didn't strike me as a time for making a speech. Or a pep talk. There would be plenty of those to come. People got through that day on reflex and instinct, mostly. And by following a script.

I would hate to have to count the times it has been said, or written, in reference to that day, that we knew nothing would ever be the same again. Well, that was just exactly the feeling you had. And in a way that has never happened since, and maybe never can again, there was a kind of jubilation about going to war. You were too full of the flag to feel sorry for yourself.

The bombing of Pearl Harbor had left us with over three thousand military casualties. Our fleet was at the bottom of the sea. And by nine o'clock that Sunday morning the Japanese had flown back to their ships, almost unmarked. We knew who we were fighting, and for what. Who the good guys and the bad guys were. This was cowboy and Indian stuff, a war you could understand. Korea and Viet Nam were unpopular wars. We know that. Having lived through those, it is sometimes hard to remember how united we were against the Axis powers, what an honor it seemed to wear a uniform, and yes, even to die for it. We don't send our young to kamikaze school in this country, and war no longer holds any glamor for us. But I think it is good that we felt that way once.

Almost overnight, lives were rearranged like a deck of cards you just flung into the air. For the next several weeks, all around you, that was all anyone heard: who had just gone in, who was staying out, draft cards and classifications and calls for physicals. I was thirty-five. Married. Childless. But supporting two sisters and a brother. For the first time in my career, in my life, the money had been pouring in: from movies, records, radio, rodeo appearances, and merchandising deals. In 1941, I had earned over $600,000.

I made up my mind to enlist and there was little soul-searching about it. I didn't plan on waiting for the draft board to come and get me. Nor did I intend to look for some loophole to keep me out. There was nothing noble about it. I would have much rather kept counting my money and firing blanks. But it didn't seem to me to be any choice. If you were healthy, and able, you either served or you learned how to shave in the dark.

I needed some time to get my affairs in order. Through a friend on the draft board, I learned that my number would come up in April. I asked if they could hold off until July, giving me time to fulfill the contracts I had for spring rodeos around the country. Otherwise, a lot of people were going to be stuck. An extension was granted. I intended to enlist in the Army Air Corps before the deadline. But my next move was to tell Herb Yates. My decision to join up was to bring on my final break with Republic.

We sat in his office, on the walls of which were dozens of photographs of Gene Autry, touchingly inscribed to the man who had been my boss for nearly seven years. I said, "Herb, I'm going to enlist. If you have any pictures you want me to do, you better get them scheduled now. I've talked to the draft board and I only have until July."

Herb said, "Hell, Gene, don't you worry about that. You should have come to me first. This is an essential industry. We can go to Washington and get you a deferment. You won't be touched."

Yates thought he would be doing us both a favor. But I didn't quite see it that way. "I can't do that," I said. "Jimmy Stewart has been drafted. Gable just went in. I can't justify it to myself."

He asked me to take a day or two to think it over, discuss it with friends, and I did. They saw it my way, in terms that might sound cornball now but didn't then. There were kids out there who believed that I stood for something. And what about the mothers and fathers with sons who had to leave the farm? That was essential, too.

My mind was made up when I went back to see Yates. He thought I was being a fool or, worse, that I was grandstanding. "If you do this to us," he said, "you know what will happen. By the time you get back, you'll be forgotten. You could be throwing away your whole career. And it won't hurt us. No, sir. If we have to we'll spend a million dollars to promote Rogers. A million. And we'll make him bigger than you ever were."

He was trying to get under my skin. There may have been some truth in what he was saying, but I wasn't going to lose my temper. "Herb," I said, "do what you have to do. But I'm telling you, I can't stay out. It would make me look bad and the movie business look bad. I think we better just get those pictures cranked up, if you want me to do them."

It was a strange time for the industry. There was a disposition on the part of some in motion pictures—and elsewhere—to do a little business as usual. Some marched off gladly and came home with distinction: Clark Gable. Ty Power. Henry Fonda. Robert Taylor. Red Skelton. Jimmy Stewart rose from a private to a combat pilot, flew bombers, commanded a squadron, eventually made general. A great band leader, Glenn Miller, didn't come back. Others stayed home for the reasons thousands of others in less public jobs did—health or family obligations.

Still others wrestled with their consciences and suffered for it. Lew Ayres, then at the height of his fame as "Young Dr. Kildare," had a moral objection to killing people. He refused to be inducted. He spent a year in a camp for conscientious objectors, and became a kind of national scapegoat. But Ayres established his sincerity. He was released and served, with valor, as a medical corpsman. Yet many years were to pass before he could pick up the pieces of his career.

This was the way Hollywood went to war. As for Yates, and the other, so-called movie moguls, the habits of a lifetime were hard to shake. They didn't lack patriotism. But it was in their nature to view wars, earthquakes, and other cataclysms as a personal affront. Such things were transitory. Movies were forever. The war was a kind of roulette wheel; sooner or later, the right number would turn up and everyone would be happy again.

When the planes woke up our smug, sleepy world that Sunday at Pearl Harbor, I had one movie in progress: *Heart of the Rio Grande*. Originally, it had been titled, *Deep in the Heart of Texas,* cashing in on the popularity of that hand-clapping number. But we ran into a problem. The problem was that Universal had grabbed the rights to the title. So we had to switch at the last moment. Oddly, this was the only movie of mine in which the Jimmy Wakeley Trio appeared, though they often backed me on the radio and on the road. And they wound up in Universal's picture, too, playing behind Johnny Mack Brown and Tex Ritter.

After that we did four movies in six months, including *Home in Wyomin'*, in which I sang—as a nod to the war effort—the Irving Berlin song "Any Bonds Today."

My last picture before entering the service was *Bells of Capistrano,* the one where I had such a rough time with all the long Spanish names. Republic acknowledged my departure by proclaiming Roy Rogers as "the King of the Cowboys," and increasing their B Western budgets to the kind of dollars our units saw only once in a while.

With my other obligations fulfilled, I prepared myself to enter the Air Force. I had been offered a commission by General Hap Arnold, then the head of that service, based in part on the fact that I had a private pilot's license and had flown small craft. I was to go in as first lieutenant, but I didn't, and there's a story behind that.

A few weeks earlier, a well-known actor had joined the Navy as a lieutenant commander. It then developed that he had appeared as a guest on "The Studebaker Hour," on radio, and the sponsor had provided him with a car, as they customarily did. But the actor had five or six, and he gave this one to a friend of his who happened to be a navy admiral.

This all came to the attention of a senator named Harry Truman, whose committee was investigating military malpractices. The upshot was that the actor was summoned before a court-martial board and accused of buying his commission with that car. The charge struck me as nonsense.

But soon after, a high-ranking officer called and said, "Gene, I'm sorry, but the word is out. No more commissions for Hollywood celebrities. You'll just have to go in as a GI and go through it like everyone else."

Clark Gable was caught in the same fix. Promised a captaincy, he went in as a private, worked his way through Officer's Candidate School, and took the heat.

That's what I did, and it turned out to be the best thing that could have happened to me. I played my last date in Chicago's Soldier Field on the Fourth of July, 1942, and went down to the recruiting office the next day and signed up. I was actually sworn in, at the Pentagon's request, on the air during our next broadcast of "Melody Ranch."

By the end of the year I was living it up on a tech sergeant's pay of $135 a month. Except for the fact that my salary had been cut by about $598,000, my life didn't change all that much my first year in the service. I was assigned to Special Services and appeared at many bases throughout the United States. We continued to do "Melody Ranch" on radio—sometimes on the road, most often from Phoenix, when I was stationed at Luke Field.

One of the shows I did was for General George Patton, who was then training the Eighth Army in desert warfare at a camp halfway between Palm Springs and Blythe. I had met Patton earlier, when he was a colonel in charge of a cavalry post at Fort Myer, Virginia. He invited me to perform at a horse show to benefit the March of Dimes. Patton loved horses and had organized his own elite group called "The Rough Riders," who did a series of tricks. I sang and jumped Champion through a hoop of fire. It was a social register crowd, headed by Liz Whitney.

Patton was a charmer that night. But in the desert, in his work clothes, he was another story. The Eighth Army was preparing to ship out for Tripoli, and this was the last entertainment they were going to get for a long while. The general said he would introduce me personally—I felt flattered by that—and he climbed up on the hood of his jeep. That's where I was to perform, too. On the hood of his jeep.

A PA system had been rigged and Patton gripped it by the stem and said, "Men, I know some of you bastards have been cussing me and giving me hell. I know it's hot out here. But let me tell you, it's cold compared to what you're going to run into later on."

He paused to let that sink in. I began to wonder a little about how this was going to lead into my introduction.

"Now, according to the statistics," he went on, "a lot of you aren't coming back. The ones who do are the ones who will be in condition, the ones smart enough to get themselves in shape. I ask you. Are you going to be one of the smart ones who come back, or one of the dumb sonsabitches who stay over there? It's up to you."

Then he nodded at me and said, "Here's Gene Autry."

Let me tell you, Patton was a tough act to follow. I thought about that day in the desert when I heard of his speech to the Third Army on the eve of D-Day, which included this deathless message: ". . . and when you are sitting at the fire with your grandson on your knee and he asks you what you did in the Great World War II, you won't have to say, 'I shoveled manure in Louisiana.'"

That was surely one of the reasons, a pretty good reason, I thought, for giving up whatever it was we left behind. I had mixed feelings about doing camp shows. It was soft duty. For the cut in pay I had taken, I felt I was entitled at least to get shot at. I didn't want to play show-and-tell, or beat the drums for war bonds or the Red Cross or WAC enlistment drives. I knew how to fly and, well, Patton had said it pretty good.

But I had a problem. My age was against me. I had flown only small aircraft, so just to get into flight school I needed a higher rating—so many hours flying so much horsepower. I found a private field in Phoenix and, on my own time, at my own expense, I started checking out bigger aircraft, the Stearman and Fairchild and the AT-6. They were single-engine planes, but with 400 to 450 horsepower. See, my life hadn't changed much. I had just gone from one kind of horsepower to another.

I flew two or three times a week for six months and, finally, I was accepted for flight school at Love Field, in Dallas. Believe me, when you are competing with nineteen- and twenty-year-old boys, trying to match their reflexes and their stamina, it is mighty tough. But I had no intention of washing out. And I guess I should make it clear. Being Gene Autry had nothing to do with that. Didn't help, didn't hurt. I didn't take any hazing, either. Anyone who cared to look could see I was earning my way. That's why I considered it a break, not coming in on a cushion, as an officer. Gene Autry's name and reputation meant little. But love of flying did. And I was hooked on those clouds.

I received my promotion to flight officer and was transferred to the Air Transport Command. Later, I had other chances for promotions, but I never took them. I felt comfortable as a flight officer and I wasn't rank happy. It was equivalent to a warrant officer in the Marines and you had the best of two worlds. You could drink in both the officer's club and the enlisted men's club.

Now, among fliers, the ATC wasn't where the glamor was. You were in the cargo business. The fellows who flew the fighters and the bombers sometimes compared us to truck drivers, in a friendly spirit, of course. But it was tough and important work, high risk and low profit, and it suited me fine.

I formed friendships with men who were great aviators, captains on commercial airlines, such as Hal Murray of Braniff and Clarence Childs, with Eastern, and Bill Cherry, who still flies for American.

Cherry was at the controls when the plane carrying Eddie Rickenbacker crashed in the South Pacific. Everyone knows that story, how they drifted in a raft for three weeks, killed a seagull and ate it raw. The last time I saw Bill Cherry, I was a passenger on a flight to Boston in 1974 and he was the captain. He invited me into the cockpit and we sat around, reliving the war.

I flew some beauties in the Air Corps—the Douglas dive bomber, P-51s, the C-47—but for the thrill that lasts a lifetime, nothing could beat the C-109. It had been converted into a tanker to haul fuel over the Hump and into Kunming, China. I'll never forget the first time I landed one on a metal mat, in the Azores, on a refueling stop en route to India. They just laid those mats over the sand like a giant grill. When we touched down I thought the plane was coming apart. Made the most infernal racket I had ever heard.

The C-109 did have this unfortunate characteristic. It would sometimes break in two. It was like a huge eggshell filled with gasoline. Just one great gas tank holding ten thousand gallons of fuel. Even the wings would be filled with gas, big round drums loaded and rolled in there. If you ever had to land on the belly, the plane was constructed in such a way that the wings would snap off and you would be sitting on one big torch.

Well, you take that plane and all that fuel and lift it over the roof of the world, and that was called flying the Hump. And I don't remember anyone in the Air Transport Command ever making a big deal about it. The pilots I knew *thought* about it a lot, and worried some, and kept track of the planes we were losing. This was the China-Burma-India Theater, the air zone with the highest fatality rate in the war. The thing a pilot dreaded was knowing that if he had time to bail out, his only chance was over the desert, and no one wanted to go down in a lousy desert.

The planes took off from Karachi, or Assam, always in the daytime, of course. They were in the air five hours before they reached the Himalayas, looming in front of them like a solid wall, rising 29,000 feet. They had the biggest mountain range in the world, a clumsy ship with a lot of weight, and each flight was a suspense story. They had to pick their way through the valleys. They would land in Kunming, unload the cargo, then turn around and go home. I only flew the Hump once, to see what it was like. But if you worked it right, once was enough.

The cargo included a little of everything, most of which would go bang. Fuel, ammunition, guns, supplies. Sometimes a crew would smuggle a case or two of scotch aboard for some of the boys at the other end. And, always, they had great quantities of Spud cigarettes, crates of them, the cheapest brand going. They'd buy them at the PX for a dime a pack and trade them for souvenirs. The natives sold them for a dollar.

Even in the midst of that great planetary adventure called war, I couldn't escape Hollywood. Once, we landed in Cairo and decided to take in a spot popular with American airmen called the Arizona Club. I walked in with our crew and we all sat down and ordered a round of drinks. At a table across the room a fellow kept staring at me. You couldn't miss him. He was sitting with a group that included several very pretty Egyptian girls.

He was a small man, dark, with nervous eyes. He stood up, walked to one side, tilted his head, studied me some more. The next thing I knew he was standing beside my chair. In a very heavy accent he said, "Podden me, coot you be Gene Ott-ree?"

I confessed that I was. I did quite well, I thought, not to fall off my chair.

He broke into an ear to ear grin. "Ah," he said, "I rap-prazant Par-a-mount Pic-choors in zee Mideast. Ve sell your pic-choors. Zay are very pop-u-lar vit Arabs. Zay like outdoors, horses. Ve do beeg beezness. Ve vould be honored to haf you join us"—he motioned to his table—"for a dreenk."

The crazy thing was, it was all true. Halfway across the world, I had run into a guy who worked for a company that distributed my movies. I did stop at his table for a drink, and the ladies with him turned out to be belly dancers. One of them, a little girl named Samia Gamal, was a favorite of King Farouk. She was about sixteen, a gorgeous little thing with black sparkling eyes, long hair, fine teeth.

I can't even recall the old boy's name now, I'm ashamed to say, but I honor his memory. We stayed in Cairo for three or four days, and he entertained our crew with a party in his home.

Well, time marches on. The war ended, and ten years later I was in the Stork Club in New York one night with friends. All of a sudden, I found myself enveloped in two slender arms and a holiday of kisses, and this voice kept saying, "Sheen, Sheen." It was Samia Gamal. She had married a Texas oilman named Shep King and moved to the United States. They were divorced and, years later, I read where she was working in Las Vegas.

I guess we had the usual quota of close calls and crossed paths during the war. Once, to avoid a typhoon over the Azores, a plane I was copiloting had to turn back and fly for five hours with an engine missing, low on fuel, back to Gander Bay, in Newfoundland. Then a fog bank moved in and we were stuck there for two weeks. Another night in the officer's club in Marrakesh, I looked up from a game of checkers—yes, checkers—and there was my cousin, Art Steele.

Another time, on a whim, flying over the Mideast, we radioed back to our base that we were having engine trouble and would have to put down at Haifa. We had our crew chief order some parts that we knew would take three or four days to reach us. Of course, nothing was wrong. We had been simply seized by a group urge to visit the Holy Land while we were in the neighborhood. And we did. Tel Aviv. Jerusalem. Bethlehem. And it was well worth the effort.

In Tunis, I ran into Bruce Cabot, who had been on board the U.S.S. *Manhattan* when we sailed for England in the summer of 1939. In other odd, remote places, I encountered Tyrone Power and Errol Flynn and Clark Gable, and dozens of friends from places I had lived in Texas and Oklahoma. You looked up and there they were and it never seemed strange to you. I don't know why that was.

No stories go with those meetings, nothing dramatic or funny. You met, had a reunion, shared a drink, made vague promises about getting together back home, when it was all over, and sometimes you kept them.

It was in Calcutta that I bought probably the most distinctive cowboy boots I ever owned. Well, not the boots exactly. The skin. A python skin. The natives over there would kill one, skin it, then throw the skin into a red ant bed. The red ants would eat all the flesh that was left and they'd wind up with a clean skin. Then they'd tan it. I paid five dollars for the python skin and had a bootmaker in Houston finish the job.

I was always in the market for a new pair of boots. I have never in my life felt right in shoes. They tell me, and I guess it's true, that I was the only flight officer in the Army Air Corps who had permission to wear cowboy boots while in uniform. That was just about the only privilege that being Gene Autry ever got me in the service.

Of course, as a people, Americans spend a good bit of our time gunning down the overprivileged. I was the copilot once on a flight from New York to Los Angeles, when two GI's were bumped to make room for Elliott Roosevelt's dog. It made a colossal stink when it hit the papers. The plane had a weight and balance ratio—so much cargo to so many pounds of people. They had Roosevelt's great Dane in a crate and it was equal to the weight of the two soldiers. It wasn't our decision in the cockpit—and young Roosevelt probably didn't even know there was a problem. But a flight controller on the ground figured, well, this *was* the President's son, and off went the two GI's.

That sort of incident could stir the nation's moral fury, but it was rare. If one thing impressed me most about my tour in the military, it was simply what a true melting pot it turned out to be. Oilmen, waiters, teachers, politicians, actors, merchants, mechanics, were all thrown together. No class distinction there. You couldn't tell them apart in army dungarees.

And every day, someone had a story to tell that was sadder than the one you heard yesterday. No one could wallow long in his own misery. In one of our outfits we had a private known as Perfo, a gloomy Italian who wore a glass eye. I found him one afternoon looking more depressed than usual. I asked what was the matter.

"Well, Gene, I'll tell you," he said. "First, I had the flu for a week. Then I had a reaction to my typhoid shot. Then they assigned me to the mess hall, doing pots and pans. While I was scrubbing this pot my glass eye fell into the sink and broke. When I went to the clinic to get a new one, all they had in stock was blue eyes. Now I got one brown and one blue eye."

He looked at me sadly, out of his one brown and one blue eye. Then he shrugged and gave a deep Italian sigh. "Hell, Gene," he said, "I'm ready to go over the hill."

The closest I ever came to that feeling was before my tour of overseas duty started. I was assigned to Special Services at Romulus Field in Detroit. My commanding officer in Detroit turned out to be an old friend from Abilene, Texas, a major named Joe Tompkins, later a wealthy oilman who served on the board of regents at Hardin-Simmons College.

One morning the major called me to his office. "I got orders," he said irritably, "that we have to recruit some WACs. I'm putting you in charge of this detail. You get a show together and go out and find them."

"Oh, no, Joe," I pleaded. "Don't do this to me. I don't want to do that."

"I don't want to do it, either." He spat out the words. "But those are orders and someone has to do it. You go downtown and ask for a Lieutenant Morlie. You'll do the show and someone else will handle the interviews. Get it worked out."

I had nothing against the Women's Army Auxiliary Corps. Fine ladies. And I knew there was a push on to recruit large numbers of them to free more men for combat duty. A worthy cause. But why me?

Arriving at the downtown recruiting office, I asked for the lieutenant and received my second shock of the day. The officer was a lady. A WAC. From Kentucky. About thirty, attractive, but bossy. She would remind you of Lieutenant Houlihan, the nurse in the movie *Mash*. Morlie started right in telling me how we would make our recruiting pitch. What she had in mind, she said, was a full orchestra, maybe a symphony, with a program of quality music, you know, the classics, Beethoven, Bach, Mozart.

I think I turned pale. "Lieutenant," I finally broke in, "I beg your pardon, but I can't do that kind of music. That's all foreign to me. That's longhair. The kind of show I do is nothing like that. If you want that other stuff, well, Gene Autry won't be of any use to you. Now, if you want, I can do what we've always done. Get a couple groups together that can sing country and western, add a little comedy, and put on a show."

She looked at me coldly. "No, we'll do it as I suggest."

I said, "Well, frankly, ma'am, I don't believe I can help you."

With that I went back to the field office and reported to Joe Tompkins. "Major," I said, "I don't think I can work with that gal."

"Why not?"

"Well, she's a school teacher from Kentucky. She's got a little authority over there. And she doesn't want my advice."

Tompkins rose up from behind his desk. "You just go right back down there," he said, "and tell her, dammit, this is the way it's going to be."

I said, "Look, Joe, you got the gold leaves on your shoulders. You go over there and tell her yourself."

He did. Major Tompkins went down there and she threw him right out of her office.

Finally, in the interest of time and winning the war, I convinced her to try it my way. We did put a show together and made a series of appearances around the country, and a whole bunch of recruits signed up for the women's army.

But my heart wasn't exactly in it. I was like most men about the service. In the best of times, you cussed it, resented it, gritted your teeth over the endless frustrations of it. Part of my problem was that I had gone to work for the railroad at fifteen. I had been independent so long, all that mindless obedience was distasteful to me. You would present an idea to someone and it would take three weeks to a month before anyone could tell you the answer was no.

The idea I was working on in the spring of '45 was how to get out of the service. When the air war in Europe ended I was reassigned to Special Services. If they had a job for me flying, fine. But no more garden clubs and girls' gym classes. Of all the luck, I was eligible to get out but they wouldn't release me because of my name. As one of the brass put it, if I had been Gene Smith or Gene Flushbottom I'd already be home. But they didn't want to risk more bad press, more charges of favoritism.

No old bear with a toothache ever got testier than I did about that. Look, I said, I can do a helluva lot more for the country getting back to work and paying taxes, than lying around here on my can, living off the government. It must have occurred to someone in the Pentagon that I was right. Shortly, an offer came down. I could have my discharge, I could start making movies again, on the condition that I first took a USO troupe to the South Pacific.

I jumped at it. I had flown as far as Hawaii for the Air Transport Command, but I wanted to see Australia and I was curious about what the war in the Pacific was like. We put a group together and spent the next two months hopping islands.

I am far from certain that this would qualify as a case of being in the right place at the right time. But quite by chance, we flew into Saipan on the first of August 1945. We stayed four days, while the activity and the tension grew visibly. No one really knew what was going on at Tinian, another of the Mariana Islands a few miles away. But many were curious.

There was a great deal of talk about planes and people, coming and going. It had been that way, I was told, for months. You heard about a mysterious squadron training at Tinian. And a bomb, a big one, more powerful than anything any of us had ever imagined. I pictured a bomb as big as a school bus. How would they ever get it into the air? And if they did, where would they drop it?

An old friend of mine from Texas, General Roger Ramey, was on Tinian with the Thirteenth Air Force, under the command of General Curtis LeMay. Roger got in touch with Saipan and invited us to come see him. It sounds crazy now, such a group, a bunch of minstrels, even being in the area when one of history's great events was about to take place. I can only suppose that some small attempt was being made to give an appearance that things were normal. It was like being in a bank when a holdup man ducks in, waves a gun, and tells everyone not to be nervous.

I had a highball with Ramey on the night of the fourth, two days before a plane called the *Enola Gay* took off from Tinian, carrying a bomb code-named "the Thin Man." In all, there had been fifteen planes in the squadron, going through the same training, the same exercises. No one knew until the last minute which one would have the bomb.

None of this was discussed that day. Once, I started to ask a question. I said, "General—" and that was as far as I got. Roger said, "I'll tell you about it after it all happens." He wasn't smiling. And he didn't stay long.

That is where I was when the first atomic bomb exploded over Hiroshima on August 6, 1945. Later, I talked to one of the boys on the line, in the B-29 squadron that flew cover. I asked him what it was like. All he said was, *"It was a son of a bitch."* I saw some of the early photographs they brought back and there was no way I could disagree with him.

We were back on Saipan when they dropped the second bomb, called "the Fat Man," on Nagasaki. All over the islands, the news touched off a wild celebration, the kind that ends at four in the morning with people trying to hold each other up and sing barbershop harmony. There was no question of what we felt then. Pride. Relief. In all the moral agonizing that has taken place in the years since, we sometimes seem to forget how few doubts anyone had at the time that the decision—Harry Truman's awesome decision to use atomic power—was the right one. On Saipan, I can tell you, the opinion was pretty strong that America had done what was necessary. We had been spared the invasion of Japan. We had saved maybe a half million lives, ours and theirs. Compassion is a nice quality to have, but it comes easier thirty years later. I don't remember anybody asking us, then, to apologize.

The Japanese surrender was announced August 14. Within hours my troupe was on a plane heading back to the States, back to California. I had gotten up close to a very wide screen, had felt a lot of emotions I probably would never feel again. But it was behind me now. Somewhere over the blue Pacific, a few hours outside of Honolulu, it occurred to me that I was a civilian again.

More than that, I was a free agent. The way I had it figured, my contract with Republic had run out while I was in the service. From my seat I could see the metallic blur of the plane's propellers. They were turning no faster than the thoughts turning in my mind.

CHAPTER SEVEN

The Last Roundup

It took one war to get me out of the movies, and for a time it looked as though it would take another to get me back into them.

This one was with Republic. Again. I had a notion about going into business for myself, setting up my own film company. My contract with the studio had expired while I was in the service, and I really didn't think Herb Yates would try to hold me to it.

Republic had pulled out all the stops to promote Roy Rogers in my absence, and Roy had done well for them. His movies featured big, Broadway-style musical numbers. One film historian said they were more like Romberg operettas than Westerns. They sent him out on the personal appearance circuit that I had plowed in earlier times, merchandising Roy to compete with all the countless gadgets and consumer goods that had my brand on them. Chaps and cap pistols, T-shirts and pajamas, notebook covers and lunch buckets. Roy went to NBC for Quaker Oats, as competition with my show for Wrigley's on CBS. But I had an edge there. It has never been as easy to get kids to eat oatmeal as to chew gum.

Rogers was young, fresh-looking, decent, hard-working. All the qualities you could dislike in a rival if you really needed a reason. But, again, the problem wasn't personal. I knew they had him under a contract much more favorable (to Republic) than mine. And though there was still plenty of room in the business for the two of us, it seemed clear to me that there wasn't room on the same lot, in the same corral, for two cowboy actors of the same type. At stake were scripts, casts, budgets, advertising and publicity, the full treatment.

Now, when Republic tried to claim that my contract was still in force, that it had been merely in limbo during my time in the military, I did the only thing I could. I filed a lawsuit to win my release.

The bare bones of the case were these: under California law— the Shirley Temple Law, they called it—no contract could run longer than seven years. I had signed mine in 1938, after my wildcat strike, and it had run out in 1945 while I was still in uniform. As far as I know, Olivia de Havilland had been the first to bring suit against that law, at Warner Brothers. She had won the case and so I hired her lawyer, Martin Gang.

Our position was a simple one. No contract was valid longer than seven years, and when I went into the Air Corps I could not perform through no fault of my own. I owed a higher loyalty to my country than to my employer. And, finally, the studio had not been required to pay me for those years so they had no services due them.

As it turned out, a decision I had made right after my enlistment helped our case. Yates had worked out a deal with the War Department to make me available for a limited number of pictures, with the studio donating a sum equal to my salary to Armed Forces Relief. I turned it down. The money and the exposure would have been helpful and the cause was worthy, but Stewart and Gable and Power, and dozens of others, weren't making movies on the side. I didn't want any sweetheart deals.

So we filed suit against Republic to have the contract nullified. It was to be a landmark case, with large implications for the entertainment industry. It was the first case after the war of an actor returning from military duty whose contract had expired while he was in the service.

The trial was covered by the trade papers and in the daily press. Sympathy was strong in my favor. I had been away for three and a half years, at what would have been the peak of my earning powers. The studio had gone on raking in profits, while I was knocking down a cool hundred and thirty-five dollars a month. The case was heard before Judge Louis Palmer, in Los

Angeles district court, I was on the stand for a solid week. And we won.

Republic appealed the verdict and vowed to take it to the Supreme Court. (They did, and the decision was upheld.) In the meantime, I knew the legal process would take a year or more, so I went to Yates and between us we struck a bargain. Almost a bet, actually. I agreed to make five more pictures at Republic, for a percentage of the profits. If they won the case, I would finish the contract on their terms. But if I won, then I was free to go and there would be no other attempts to hold me.

So it was done. Almost a year had passed since my Air Force discharge had come through in September of 1945. I sometimes think of that as the year everybody stopped being young. In 1944 Elizabeth Taylor was twelve years old and in love with horses. In '45 she was kissing Robert Taylor. It was the year we discovered the atom bomb, the ballpoint pen, and Kilroy. We lost FDR, Ernie Pyle, and George Patton. We won the war but at great cost. We would never feel virtuous about war again.

That was 1945. In the fall of 1946 I went back to work on my first Republic picture since the war: *Sioux City Sue*. While I was away, I had lost my sidekick. Smiley Burnette had emerged as a drawing card of his own. He became the first and only supporting actor, at least in Westerns, to receive top billing over the star (Sunset Carson), and a credit line that read: "A Smiley Burnette Production."

But gradually Republic began to have some apparent misgivings about Smiley as a headliner. A kind of cold, sad story can be detected just from reading the credits:

Code of the Prairie, starring Smiley Burnette with Sunset Carson.

Bordertown Trail, starring Smiley Burnette *and* Sunset Carson.

Pride of the Plains, starring Bob Livingston *and* Smiley Burnette.

The Laramie Trail, starring Bob Livingston *with* Smiley Burnette.

I'll tell you, old Hollywood hands could read a marquee the way a gypsy reads tea leaves.

By 1945 Smiley had left Republic and signed with Columbia to costar in the Durango Kid series with Charles Starrett. So I was in the market for a partner, though I hadn't decided if I should try to re-establish a full-time character. Tom Mix and Buck Jones and Ken Maynard, I reminded myself, never used a steady comic sideman.

For the Republic films I settled on Sterling Holloway, who had appeared in non-Westerns in the past. He had an ambling, loose-gaited look that I liked. Also, he was a veteran, and I had a notion the public would care about who served and who didn't. (I was wrong about that, of course, failing to take into account the quickness with which the public forgets.)

My leading lady in two of those pictures, including the last one, *Robin Hood of Texas*, was Adele Mara, one of Xavier Cugat's ex-singers. Cugie usually operated on the theory that the best way to keep a good band singer was to marry her. But Adele was one he missed. She played opposite Starrett and Russell Hayden in a couple of Columbia films, then moved to Republic and made a career out of second leads and femme fatales.

By the time *Robin Hood of Texas* had reached the movie houses, I had parted ways with Republic. The courts had upheld my suit and I was now free to make my own deals, and pick my own friends. We had offers from several studios. But I wanted to form my own company, frankly, because of the tax angles. If you earned over $100,000 in those days, 85 per cent of it was taxable. The only way to hang on to your money was to form a corporation. So I became the president and executive producer of Gene Autry Productions, and we signed a contract with Columbia to release our pictures. It was as good a deal as anyone in Hollywood had at that time. I had complete say over my films and I could take home half the profits.

My first picture under that alliance was *The Last Roundup*. That title wasn't exactly symbolic of a new beginning, but I wasn't looking for omens. I had returned from the war with a few very strong ideas of my own about making Westerns. I thought the day was gone when a studio could take any fellow who wasn't tone deaf, give him a few p.d.'s (songs in the public domain), slap a script together, and make money. I wanted to produce full-color Westerns. All of them. And I told Ina, songs would be more important than ever. But they had to be hit songs. Or original songs. The so-called adult Westerns really began with *High Noon*, and a title song, a sound track, that even today people can identify after hearing five notes.

But to my regret, *The Last Roundup* was shot in black and white. The demands on the new Technicolor Corporation had already plunged it a year behind schedule. There was another, more practical reason for using black and white. Columbia still had a lot of stock footage, desert chase scenes, and we could take advantage of that inventory by not using color. Anyway, the story line was so modern we showed TV sets in a couple of scenes. I was teamed again with Mandy Schaefer. *Film Daily* called his feat of procuring a script that combined an Indian uprising, a cattle stampede, and a television broadcast in a story of the 1947 West "especially notable." I reckon so.

The cast included the old character actor, Ralph Morgan, and a child actor named Bobby Blake. A graduate of the *Our Gang* comedies, in which he played the sniveling little brat Mickey, he had gone on to Westerns as Little Beaver in the *Red Ryder* series. It impressed me to rediscover him, years later, as one of the killers in the movie version of Truman Capote's book *In Cold Blood*, and as television's "Baretta."

Our first film in color, in Cinecolor, was released in August of 1948. *The Strawberry Roan* also marked the first appearance of Pat Buttram as my sidekick, and the debut of Little Champ, the son of the second screen Champion. I used three different Champions in my movies (though they all had their own understudies). Little Champ's sire had been a Tennessee Walking Horse, a dark chestnut with a flaxen tail and mane, the blazed face, and four socks to his knees. He was marked exactly like the first Champion and I paid fifteen hundred dollars, the most I ever spent for a horse.

The cast for *Loaded Pistols* included Barbara Britton, the heroine of the Hopalong Cassidy series and already a name with marquee appeal. She was the only leading lady ever to share the billing with me above the title, and *ahead* of Champion. The plot for this one provided a kind of Charlie Chan twist. I gathered all the suspects in a poker game murder around the table once again; the lights went out and someone picked up the murder weapon and fired a shot. At me. Ha. I had filled the pistol with blanks and coated it with graphite.

The killer turned out to be Robert Shayne, who later played Coach Earl Blaik in what some critics—I avoid such judgments, myself—ranked the worst sports movie ever made, *Spirit of West Point*. It starred the Academy's famed All-American backs, Doc Blanchard and Glenn Davis. But what swayed the critics, I think, was a scene near the end of the film, with Army trailing Navy, when Shayne (as Coach Blaik) glances at his wristwatch and tells an assistant that two minutes are left in the game. At his, yes, *wristwatch*.

On such fine points as these, do critics and eagle-eyed fans have a feast. As I discovered myself, a time or two.

The Big Sombrero turned out to be my only other movie photographed in color. My dream had collided with an awful thing called economic reality. The process was simply beyond our budgets. But in a sense this picture did represent the bigger and better Western I had envisioned. The plot was simple: I galloped off to Mexico and helped the small *rancheros* in their fight against the Big Enchilada. But it had the longest running time, eighty-two minutes, of any film I ever made. Twenty-five of those minutes were devoted to eight songs, including two of the year's biggest hits, "You Belong to My Heart" and "My Adobe Hacienda."

Trivia fans might enjoy knowing that my leading lady was a then slender, sexy Latin named Elena Verdugo, who in the 1970s was seen on television as Consuelo, answering the phone for Dr. Marcus Welby.

That was part of the fascination of those years. There were so many gifted actors and actresses, some whose careers were ending, some beginning, some drifting. And some who would reappear years later, bigger than ever, on a twenty-one-inch screen.

One of the bit players in *Riders of the Whistling Pines* was Jason Robards, Sr., the father of a fine and sensitive actor. In the movie, I was hired by the Forest Service to flush out a gang that *didn't* want the woods saved. After my crew would spray with DDT, they would come along by night and spray the area with poison. Of course, times have changed so, the bad guys today would be the ones using DDT.

In *Rim of the Canyon*, three escaped convicts (one of them Jock Mahoney) steal Champion and return to a ghost town to search for a missing $30,000. The swag had been taken in a robbery for which my father had jailed them twenty years before. I played both myself and my old man, Steve.

Although color was out, I tried to stick with my policy of including one or more popular songs in each picture. The plot of *The Cowboys and Indians* had me, as an Arizona ranger, helping the Navajos defend their land against the palefaces. But we still managed to work into it that year's Christmas favorite, "Here Comes Santa Claus." Please, don't ask.

Next came *Riders in the Sky*, whose title song led the "Hit Parade" and went on to sell over three million records by no fewer than thirteen artists. Stan Jones, the ex-forest ranger who wrote it, had a small part in the film, along with Hank Patterson, who was to work with Pat Buttram on many of the "Green Acres" episodes on TV.

Harking back to some of my earlier Republic plots, in *Sons of New Mexico* I again became the guardian of a snippy kid, Dick Jones. I enrolled him in military school to straighten him out. It worked. In the end I called out the cadets to help clean out the bad guys, including a crooked jockey played by Frankie Darro, my old co-star in *The Phantom Empire*.

It was Buttram who wound up with the title song in *Mule Train*, a runaway hit later for both Frankie Laine and Tennessee Ernie Ford. But that wasn't Pat's only legacy from this movie. The town sheriff turned out to be a female, Sheila Ryan, and in cahoots with a scaggy band of claim jumpers. Pat and Sheila met on the set of that picture, eventually fell in love and were married. She was pretty and independent. He was country and fun-loving. No one thought it would last, but it did, until Sheila's death from cancer in late 1975. It seems to me that more than in most fields, people who stayed in the movie business any length of time formed relationships that were like vines of ivy, so that you could hardly tell where it had begun or ended or turned into the next vine.

In *Beyond the Purple Hills*, I played the part of a sheriff who saved a judge's son from a trumped-up murder charge. One of the heavies was a young actor with high cheekbones and jet black hair named Hugh O'Brian, whose movie career would never approach his TV success as Wyatt Earp.

My films at Columbia, after the first ones, had taken on a whole new look. Gone were the fancy shirts and pants and modern trappings and settings. What emerged for the most part was Gene Autry, frontiersman. The cycle had come nearly full circle. By then we were groping, guessing, trying to find a trend. The B Westerns were slipping.

Once in a while we still found a good script with a modern viewpoint. One was *Gene Autry and the Mounties*. Buttram and I played a pair of U.S. marshals who crossed into Canada, chasing a gang of bank robbers. With right on our side, we didn't pay much attention in those days to international borders and other points of diplomatic nit-picking. This was the only other time, outside of a few Abbott and Costello films—as in *Abbott and Costello Meet the Monster*—that a star's name had been used as part of the title.

In early 1951, after a nine-year break, Smiley Burnette returned as my sidekick in a film called *Whirlwind*. There was no special emotion about it. Events and timing had caused us to split, and the same conditions brought us back. But Smiley and I had come to Hollywood together and there was always that bond between us.

It ought to be explained that in all of his Columbia films, Smiley played a character called Smiley Burnette. The reason being that Frog Millhouse, the name he made famous in my films, and a few with Roy, was the property of Republic. (Since Gene Autry happened to be my real name, there wasn't much Republic could do when I took it with me.)

I teamed up with Pat Buttram again on each of my movies through 1952, nine of them, until a near fatal accident put him on the shelf. (About that, more later.) It happened on the set of a television series, "The Gene Autry Show," which we were filming between pictures.

Time was running out on the B Western. Television had begun to seduce the whole country, and some of us saw it coming earlier than others. Around 1950, my company, now called Flying "A" Productions, began developing ideas aimed at the kids' market. In addition to my own series, the others starred Gail Davis as Annie Oakley, Jock Mahoney as the Range Rider, Dick Jones as Buffalo Bill, Jr., and Champion as himself.

I was considered the first known star to enter the new medium, a move looked on by my distributors as a betrayal. They insisted that the public would not pay to see Autry if TV brought him into their homes for free. But I saw it as the only way left, the last outlet for the cheap Western. The major studios had already sold off their inventories, either to the networks or for syndication. In a sense, we were already competing with ourselves.

It was not yet time to get sentimental, but I knew I would never grow old on a sound stage. In one of my last films, *Apache Country*, I portrayed an army scout who poses as a civilian to break up a gang using Indian raids as a cover-up. The silent movie idol Francis X. Bushman played the role of the Indian commissioner. Many a star of the silent era could be found still hanging around Central Casting, waiting for a call, but this wasn't the case with Bushman. An actor of enduring reputation, who ranked in his time with Valentino and Theda Bara, Bushman, once his peak film days had ended, earned a good living as a radio actor.

Of course, radio drama was also ending an era. Television replaced our imaginations with pictures and we may have lost something in the exchange. Creative sound effects, and our mind's eye, made radio more real than life. Every day, four million housewives listened to such soap operas as Helen Trent, in which the heroine sought to prove that "because a woman is thirty-five or more, romance in life need not be over."

But television was coming over the horizon like a great tidal wave. Soon it would turn the old Western folk hero Davy Crockett into a conglomerate of coonskin caps and T-shirts and guitars, and "The Ballad of Davy Crockett" would sell four million records. TV would make it possible to accomplish in a year, even in months, what some of us had done in a lifetime.

Roy Rogers and I had to suffer in silence as Bill Boyd got the jump on us in this new medium. All the major studios had agreed not to sell any of their new movies to television. But the Hopalong Cassidy films were owned by an independent, Harry Sherman, who wasn't bound by the agreement. Overnight, Hoppy enjoyed a national revival as TV snapped up his pictures in the late 1940s. Roy and I could only wait until our contracts expired. The waiting wasn't easy. In those days television was grabbing everything in sight. It didn't matter what they put on the air. People would watch test patterns.

With *Winning of the West*, I was rejoined by Smiley Burnette for what would be my last six motion pictures. We had gone in together and we would go out together. Fair is fair.

The year was 1953 and, for the record, those last films were: *On Top of Old Smoky, Goldtown Ghost Raiders, Pack Train, Saginaw Trail*, and—not a bad title for an exit line—*Last of the Pony Riders*. In that one, the telegraph had linked the East and West, ending the need for the Pony Express. So Express rider Autry established a stage line to carry the mail and rode off to find another challenge.

No one planned it that way, certainly not me, but that pretty well closed the pages on the series, or "B" Western chapter of Hollywood history. Allied Artists did make a few along into 1954, starring Wild Bill Elliott or Wayne Morris, but those were on a more adult scale and were sold as such. It is fair to say, I suppose, that the true Saturday afternoon matinee, the "Western pitcher," ended with *Last of the Pony Riders*. It was my ninety-third film.

There were no farewell toasts, no retirement dinner with someone handing out a pocket watch for twenty years of faithful service. Actually, nineteen years, between the release in November of 1934 of *Old Santa Fe*, when I made my first appearance with Ken Maynard, for Mascot, until Columbia released my last in November of 1953. It just kind of slipped up on us. I don't recall ever saying that I had quit, or that I would never make another motion picture.

The fact is, I never really left the business. The business left me. Hollywood started turning out a new type of Western and half of the B theaters that had carried my films, and others like them, closed down. The other half started showing porno flicks. Meanwhile, television swallowed up the rest, the old Autry and Rogers and Hopalong Cassidy movies, and swamped our homes with the made-for-TV series: "Gunsmoke," "The Virginian," "Have Gun, Will Travel," "Bonanza."

The gore and crude sex of the later Westerns, what might be called the knee-in-the-groin school of Westerns, left me cold. Had I attempted only a fraction of the Clint Eastwood dirty tricks in my films, in my day, I would have been arrested or horsewhipped. Until I quit, most movie fans thought dance hall girls actually danced. But the 1960s brought on the age of the anti-hero.

I am told that such movies reflect life, that they strive to be more honest than ours, to make a point, a social comment. They seem to be saying that life is hard and unfair and filled with traps. Maybe so. But the really wild characters of my time only hurt themselves. They didn't take so many people with them.

It may not stretch a point to say that we lost a little more of our innocence with the passing of the B Western. Sportsmanship was the cloth we peddled. The good guy always won, but how he won and by what rules counted, too. Does memory trick us into thinking our way was better, and more fun? We thought so then.

Well, it's like they say about driving a taxi. It isn't the work you remember, it's the people you run into. And don't be misled by that B rating. Those movies were made and directed and produced by men who didn't think the work was unimportant. Most were talented, and some colorful.

Mandy Schaefer was with me through most of my career. He was a fine technician who always came in on schedule and under budget, nice qualities for those times. When Mandy was producing our television series, he kept dodging Pat Buttram, who he knew wanted more money. Finally, Pat cornered him one day in the men's room at the studio.

"Mandy," he said, "I want to talk to you about a raise."

Schaefer leaned over a washbasin and said, "Okay."

Pat hesitated. He looked around him, at the stalls, at the urinals, and he said, "Do you want to talk in here?"

"Might as well," said Mandy. "You're going to end up in here anyway."

I was fortunate to work with several of the best of the B Western directors. Joe Kane, for his use of the camera, his skill at editing and cutting, was compared by some to John Ford. And B. Reeves Eason may have been the best pure action director of all. What made Breezy Eason so effective, frankly, was the fact that he had no regard for the safety of his actors, and only a little more for the animals. He made his mark as a second unit director for many of Warner's epic films, including *Charge of the Light Brigade*.

George Sherman was about the size of a popcorn kernel, but he was an artist. Like Howard Hawks, he had a taste for give-and-take dialogue and the tongue-in-cheek approach to making films. He broke in with Wayne on the *Mesquiteer* series, and the Duke went out of his way to use George again on some of his films in the seventies.

Frank McDonald and John English were among my other favorites. English was one of the people who put the "move" into moving pictures. There was just nothing static about his work. They were both fine men, straight as a flagpole.

Sol Siegel produced several of my early Republic films, until MGM hired away both Siegel and Nat Levine and gave them production units of their own. Nat didn't last, but Sol's later credits included such box office successes as *High Society*, *Les Girls*, and *Call Me Madam*.

As I recall, the he-she relationships in those films were a bit more sophisticated than the ones Sol produced for me.

June Storey was the leading lady most identified with my career, though we made less than a dozen pictures and never kissed in any of them. Later, she moved over to Fox and Columbia, appeared in several musicals and mysteries, and gave a fine performance as a nurse in *The Snake Pit*, which starred Olivia de Havilland. After the war June married and moved to Oregon, where her husband owned a ranch with Jimmy Fitler, the gossip columnist. A serious auto accident ended whatever thoughts she had of returning to pictures. She was heard on radio for a while, in Oregon, later went into private nursing, now lives in Los Angeles and still keeps in touch.

Of all the Autry ladies, Ann Rutherford became the best established. But she is more remembered now as Andy Hardy's girl friend. There were so many actresses who brightened one or more of my pictures: Ann Miller, Barbara Britton, Gail Davis, Sheila Ryan, Peggy Stewart. I am indebted to them all.

There were many others, with looks or talent or both, whose names never became known. At least, not to movie fans. One was Elaine Shepard, who had a small part in *The Singing Vagabond*, in 1935, and later was Clyde Beatty's leading lady in Republic's first serial. Elaine left films and turned to journalism. She surfaced during the early 1950s as one of the Korean War's first female war correspondents.

Thinking back over those years is like warming your hands over a low fire. The B Westerns were one fine trail ride. I have always said that stunt men belonged in a special category. No studio employed finer ones, or made better use of them, than Republic. Several actors started out as stunt men, and some went the other way. Jim Arness doubled for Wayne before he landed the lead in "Gunsmoke." Kermit Maynard, Ken's younger brother, had a starring role in sixteen films but gave it up. He enjoyed stunt work more, could do it every day, and probably earned more money at it.

Over the years, I used as doubles Dave Sharpe, an Olympic tumbling champion of the twenties, Kenny Cooper, Bob Woodward, and the best of them all, Yakima Canutt. Yak started out as a rodeo performer and entered pictures in the silent days as a star of his own series. His voice and looks shot him down when sound came in, but he hung on as a villain and stunt man and eventually was honored by the Motion Picture Academy with a special Oscar.

He performed the best single stunt I have ever seen, at least in any of my movies. The scene focused on the second-story window of a hotel room, while the bad guys were breaking in the door. The stagecoach was just below us. Yak, as Autry, had to jump through the window and onto the stagecoach and get out of town. They had three cameras on it. You only got one take and it had to be right.

To let you in on a small trade secret, the windows for such a scene were made out of rosin and candy. They were clear and would shatter like real glass, but had the advantage of not cutting your jugular. Yak went through it, tumbled in mid-air to avoid an overhang, and landed right in the driver's seat. He was the daddy of them all.

Another time, Yak drove a four-horse wagon off a cliff and into a lake, a drop of about fifty feet. Before the wagon hit the water, Yak had pulled a pin from the tongue of the wagon so the horses could swim out. Later, he directed the second unit of *Ben Hur* in Rome, and the chariot race was his scene.

For the most part, stunt men had a highly developed sense of humor. They were the last ones to bed, usually. If you had ideas about hitting the sack early, they would sometimes arrange to have a dead snake in your mattress.

Some of the pranks we played on each other were more creative than that, I am relieved to say. Once, Canutt built a home on a fine piece of property in North Hollywood. He was so proud, he kept ordering everyone to go by and see it. He insisted it was the most beautiful corner in town.

So Ken Cooper went by there one day and he came back with a gleam in his eye. "Right across from it," he told me, "there's a big vacant lot and it's for sale." Well, you remember those cartoons where a guy is thinking and a light bulb comes on over his head? This was a situation that cried for action.

Cooper climbed into my car and we drove over to that beautiful corner, parked across the street, and found the man who owned the empty lot. I slipped him a few bucks and told him we'd be back. A day or so later I had a sign painted, a huge billboard, and planted it in the middle of the property, facing Yak's new house. It said: "CHINESE LAUNDRY TO BE ERECTED ON THIS SITE."

After work that day, as Yak drove slowly down his street, taking in the view, he saw the sign. He went berserk, tore down the sign, stomped on it, called the owner, and bought the lot the same day, just to protect his corner. When Cooper and I heard about that, we laughed as hard as you can laugh without hurting yourself. But, in the end, Yak enjoyed a bigger one than we did. In a few years that property was worth a fortune.

Of course, this is the best part of any man's career, a remembrance of happy times, of experiences shared. There are odd pieces that fit somewhere into those years, vignettes I guess you would call them, about the likes of Stuart Hamblen, one of the genuine characters of my time.

Hamblen was once a first stringer at Republic as a villain, and a hillbilly singer of some note, although certain of his songs tended to raise eyebrows in the 1940s, such as the ever popular, "I Won't Go Hunting with You, Jake, but I Will Go Chasin' Women." His more enduring hits included, "This Old House" and "It Is No Secret."

At the same time, Stu had traces of religion. With a Bible in one hand and a fifth in the other, he spent a good many of his spare hours in soul-saving and like pursuits. He was a cactus version of a Damon Runyon character, and what with one thing or another saw a lot of lockups from the inside out. The son of an Abilene preacher, he eventually repented and hit the sawdust trail, full time, to hold revivals. Hamblen ran for president in the 1950s on the Prohibition ticket.

And speaking of sawdust, one young bit player at Republic, named George Letz, used to spend his off time making furniture. He was a rare bird, an extra who not only filled scenery but helped make it. He appeared in two of my movies in the late 1930s, then turned up at Twentieth-Century Fox as the star of *Riders of the Purple Sage,* under the name George Montgomery. He developed a good following, including Dinah Shore, at one time his wife. But woodcraft remained George's lifelong hobby. He could talk about mahogany the way H. L. Hunt once talked about his money.

All of that is part of what I miss about being young and in the movies; the mixture of people and colorful names and neon. There was a feeling so many of them had, the lowest extra on the lot, that they could make it if they got a break, just one. Hollywood was where you could fall off a stool in a drugstore, or fall out of bed, and wake up a star.

In 1937 I was working on a movie called *Rootin' Tootin' Rhythm,* and the musical group we used on the picture was Al Clauser and his Oklahoma Outlaws. Now there was a name. Clean and direct. Not like today's pop rock groups, with their names that are not meant to be understood, the Grand Funk Railroad, or Dow Jones and His Averages, whatever.

Al Clauser and his Oklahoma Outlaws were regulars then on WHO radio in Des Moines, Iowa. It happened that the Des Moines ball club was training down the road from us at Catalina, with all of the other Chicago Cub farm teams. One day, Clauser brought to the set a guest, the team's young play-by-play announcer. He was Ronald Reagan, known then as Dutch.

After that day's shooting, Al introduced us. We shook hands and Reagan said, "You know, just from watching, it sure looks

13. *The grand old days of radio: with Ken Murray, Harry Von Zell, and Edgar Bergen.*

14. *Talking baseball with Hall of Famer Ted Williams, then managing the Senators.*

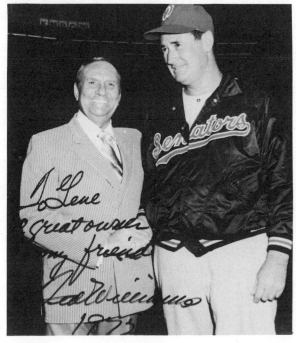

15. *Opening day at Angels' new ball park with President Richard Nixon, Casey Stengel.*

16. *With Lady Bird Johnson, whose husband the author helped in a successful campaign for Congress.*

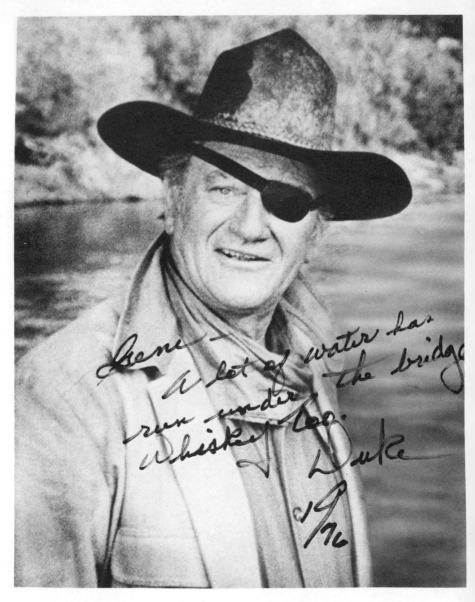

17. *True grit is having a friend named John Wayne; Duke and I started in "B" Westerns together.*

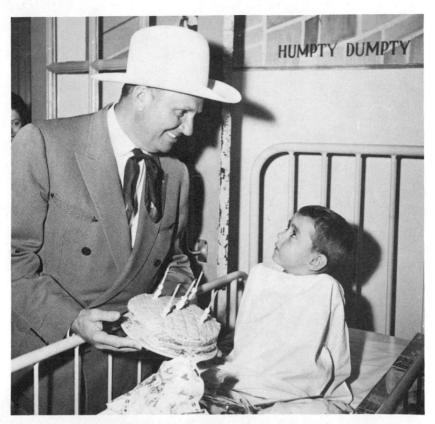

18. *A hospital is a poor place to spend a birthday, so the Singing Cowboy pays a visit.*

19. *With power vested in them, a pair of Nashville lovelies deputize me and Frank Sinatra.*

20. On "The Mike Douglas Show," chatting about the Nashville Sound, my kind of music.

21. Ex-Stanford grid stars Bob Reynolds and Bones Hamilton; Walt Disney, the author, and Bill Frawley.

22. *A diamond jubilee: ex-Giants' great Willie Mays and Cincinnati's Pete Rose.*

23. *No, it's not the mad bomber; Smiley Burnette cringes as I hoist a hot cargo.*

24. *The musical talent of the Maple City Four fails to impress.*

interesting, making pictures. I think I might like to get into that business."

I said, "Well, it seems to me you've already got one of the best jobs there is. You get into all the games free and you get to hang around with the players. And I'll tell you, this movie stuff isn't as easy as it looks."

A friendship began to form that day. Many years later, I voted for Ronald Reagan for governor of California, and I believe he made a good one. But if he had listened to me, he might still be broadcasting baseball today, probably in the big leagues, instead of traveling all over the country, as he did in 1976, looking for a job.

CHAPTER EIGHT

Sidekicks, Exalted Order of

In that part of the Southwest where I was born, on the Texas-Oklahoma line, they had a saying to describe a man who was loyal: *"He'll do to ride the river with."* I have been fortunate all of my life to be surrounded by that kind of man.

Their faces were not always known to the public. Most never appeared on a stage. They have been my friends for most of the last forty years and many are with me now. Mitch Hamilburg, my first agent, and Abe Lefton, my rodeo announcer, were with me until they died.

But the two whose names were most identified with my Western career, with the *public* Gene Autry, were Smiley Burnette and Pat Buttram. We rode a lot of trails together, on the screen and off, and most were happy. One or the other was my sidekick in all but a handful of the ninety-three movies I made, and appeared with me on stages and in rodeo arenas and radio studios beyond count.

It was through Smiley that we established the sidekick as a permanent feature of the B movie. At least, I seem to get the credit for that. I accept it with some reservation. That road—who started what—leads to argument.

Some referred to such characters as stooges, but I reject the term. Theirs were inventive roles, relying not so much on slapstick as on timing and diversion. Sure, some of it was as broad as a washtub. But it borrowed from the subtle art of the rodeo clown, drawing the angry or confused bronc away from the fallen rider. We used them in that sense to break the mood, change the pace, divert the audience.

They were meant to be seen as the well-intended, but bumbling friend in whose service all of us become trapped, at one time or another. The kind who, in trying to be helpful, lay down more obstacles than our enemies. But as I gained more control over my own films, the sidekick became more of an antic running mate than a foil.

Still, the parts were clearly defined by the times and it took a fellow with endurance and a sense of gameness to play them. In a cheerfully grousing way, Pat Buttram always fought the cause of what today would probably be called "Sidekick Liberation." He and Andy Devine organized a club they modestly called "The Exalted Order of Sidekicks." They took in such members as Bill Frawley, who did the "Lucy" show, Nigel Bruce, who was Dr. Watson, Jay Silverheels of Tonto fame, and many other traditional second bananas of the movie clan.

They printed membership cards and established a set of rules, whose acceptance they lobbied for continually but without, I regret to say, any success:

1. When a Sidekick is thrown in a water trough, the water must be heated.

2. Ice thrown in the face of a Sidekick must come from the bar of the Brown Derby.

3. The Sidekick gets the girl in every tenth picture.

4. The Sidekick must be reimbursed for money he has loaned the star.

5. The Sidekick must be reimbursed for coffee he has purchased to sober up members of the cast, including himself.

From this list you gain a reasonal insight into the trials and handicaps of being Number Two, in the era of the singing Western.

Let me clear the record on one point. I did not discover Lester (Smiley) Burnette, any more than you might discover the Atlantic Ocean. He was just there. But I did take him out of Tuscola, Illinois. He was working there in 1933 at WDZ, one of the first radio stations to be established in the United States. He was a one-man staff: announcer, newscaster, and janitor. To entertain himself, and on occasion his listeners, he also sang and played the accordion.

It happened that we were short a musician on a tour of the

Midwest. We were playing at Champaign-Urbana, in a theater near the University of Illinois, and I asked the manager if he knew where I could find an accordion player. He said, "Why, yes, there is a young feller down the road at Tuscola, about twenty-five miles south of here. Works for the radio station. Plays the piano, gittar, sings. Has lots of talent."

He gave me the name, Smiley Burnette, and the number of the station. I got him on the phone, told him who I was, and said, brightly, "I hear you play the accordion."

He said, "Yep, sure do."

I asked him how much he was making at the station.

"Eighteen dollars a week," he said.

"I'll pay you fifty," I told him, "plus your expenses on the road. You think about it and if you want to come with us let me know."

He said, "I just thought about it. You done hired yourself an accordion player."

We agreed that he would join us in Chicago at the end of the week and then we hung up. The manager looked at me curiously. "Hell, Gene," he said, "don't you think you ought to go over there and hear him? You just hired him and you don't even know if he can play."

I said, "You know, you may be right. Why don't you ride over there with me?" I called Smiley back and said I thought we ought to get together and have an understanding about a few things, and we arranged to meet in a cocktail lounge in Tuscola. An hour or so later we were settled in a booth while Smiley auditioned for me. He played the accordion, then the piano, and finally the handsaw—you hardly see those any more—and all the while he sang those eyes were bugging out of that watermelon face. I thought he was hilarious.

I wanted him with us and we were all set, except for one thing. Smiley didn't own a suit. So I just led him over to the nearest Sears, Roebuck store and we got him a wardrobe: two suits for travel and a baggy-looking outfit with a floppy, scarecrow's hat to wear in his act.

In our first movies together he played a character called Frog Millhouse, and that was his image for the next twenty-nine years. It wasn't until he took the role of Charlie Pratt on the TV series

"Petticoat Junction" that he was ever called anything else. But to at least two generations, he was Frog.

He made eighty-one features with me and seven with Roy Rogers and appeared in nearly ninety others. He thrived on work. "I'd rather wear out than rust out," he said. Smiley was like one of those old weight scales in the penny arcade. You stepped on him and out came a quaint saying. They might not strike everyone as funny or wise, but if you knew Smiley you understood exactly what he meant. "When you get to the top," he used to say, "or as far as you can go, you have to send the elevator down for somebody else."

And: "Happiness is like a butterfly. You chase 'em and never seem to catch 'em. But if you sit still long enough one will come and light on your shoulder."

He was a sweet and easygoing fellow, with a talent not everyone noticed, or appreciated, behind that zany appearance. He could play more musical instruments than I knew existed; someone once said a hundred. Yet he couldn't read a note of music. He wrote three hundred and fifty songs, some of them with me, and I never saw him take longer than an hour to compose one.

But best of all he could make children laugh. He could talk to them as few entertainers—or parents—could. He had the kind of communication with them that great animal trainers have with their . . . well, that probably isn't a good comparison. But a lot of comics would never work with kids. It could be rough. For one thing, you can't fool them. They are the best truth machines ever invented. All the publicity in the world won't help you. On that stage you *have* to be funny.

Smiley knew how to talk to them. He'd bring them into the act: "Hey, you kids know ol' Frog." And they'd send waves of love across that stage, as if some Disney character had sprung to life before their eyes.

At the end of a show, with a packed house, Smiley would say, "You kids want your pictures taken with ol' Frog?"

What they didn't know was that he had a camera on a tripod with a hood, the kind once used by vendors on the street, and they would pose with Smiley and then be handed a slip with a number on it. If they wanted the picture they had to mail a dollar to a place in Georgia and order it. Smiley must have sent them out by the tens of thousands.

He was a great one for gimmicks, coming or going. He was an incurable buyer of gadgets and novelties. I often said I was tempted to carry a trunkload of them around with me, just to sell to Smiley. If a store had an item that would peel potatoes, carve a likeness of Donald Duck, and hum a chorus of "Tie a Yellow Ribbon," he would be the first in line.

On a movie set, the relationship between the so-called star and the sidekick always reminded me of the union between a pitcher and his catcher. Not without reason, I guess, is the catcher's equipment called "the tools of ignorance."

The catcher-sidekick does at least half or more of the work, takes half or more of the risks, and settles for less than half of the glory and the money.

With both Smiley and Pat, it was a source of some kidding back and forth that I always had a fresh, rested, well-groomed horse, and they wound up with whatever old nag the studio had rented that day. I would use one horse for a chase scene and another for a close-up. Mine would be standing there like a statue, posing, his ears up. And theirs would be bumping around and neighing and shaking his head. At such times I could not resist saying, "Dammit, can't you keep that horse still?"

They would give us directions like this: "Gene, this is your scene now. You start out here, come in real fast, down that little path, the one between that big boulder and the yucca tree, and then go right on past the camera. Now watch out and don't get too close to that gully or you'll slide off."

Then the director would turn to the sidekick and say: "You just ride alongside of Gene." And, of course, alongside of me were the gopher holes and the cactus plants, and maybe a cliff.

I don't recall Smiley ever complaining. In fact, around a movie set he was a human sunbeam. In later years some people thought, mistakenly, that a slight tension developed between us when our careers took different forks. That simply wasn't so. He had one of the softest hearts I ever knew. It pleased me that he had a few good years on television, near the end, so he could relax and travel less.

We appeared together for the last time in 1965, with Rufe

Davis, as special guests on the TV version of "Melody Ranch." Although the show had gone off radio in 1956, it made a comeback of sorts in the early sixties and was on the air for seven years over local TV, on KTLA. The regular cast included Carl Cotner and Johnny Bond, the Cass County Boys and Billy Mize. By then both Smiley and Rufe had been signed for the parts of the railroad engineers on the new TV series "Petticoat Junction."

They were a pair. Rufe had a round, country face and the kind of kitchen sink talent that was once a staple of backwoods entertainment. It was in a Bob Burns movie that he made famous a song, written by Smiley, called "Mama Don't Allow No Music Played in Here." When he sang the line, "Mama don't allow no guitar, fiddle, bass, bazooka, or any *other* musical instrument played in Mama's house," he would in turn reproduce each instrument with his voice. There was no one else quite like him. Rufe could imitate birdcalls, motor boats, and all sorts of animal sounds, and do a tap dance with his teeth.

Smiley's health had already begun to decline, but we didn't know it then. He never really slowed down. When he was home, which was never often enough to suit him, he lived quietly with the last of the dozen or so kids he and his wife had adopted. She had been a small-town newspaper reporter. He was the son of two ordained ministers.

In our work habits no two people were less alike than Smiley and me. I could sit around a movie set as though it were a beach, napping or reading, not talk or move for hours at a time. Smiley was always in motion, cavorting, mugging, working to make people laugh. And he did, almost to the very end, which came too soon in February of 1967.

I didn't attend Smiley's funeral at Forest Lawn and I suppose some criticized me for it. I can understand why they would. But I quit going to them over twenty years ago. The last funeral I went to, after my mother died, was my brother Doug's and I wouldn't go near the coffin.

Death, accidents, illnesses are just difficult for me to handle. I won't attempt to explain that or defend it. Maybe it is related in a sense to why I wanted my films to entertain the spirit, not challenge it. Why the endings were always happy and the plots often implausible. I felt that people saw enough unpleasantness in the normal turn of the wheel. I saw no need to force on them more of the hard reality that each of us comes to in our own time, in our own way.

I watched my mother and brother and too many good friends suffer and leave too soon. I had fires wipe out a home and a ranch, where I had collected and stored possessions that were the irreplaceable keepsakes of a lifetime. Such thoughts bring on the gloom and I tend to avoid them.

But Pat Buttram and I touched on this once, in that quick and half embarrassed way that you sometimes treat awkward subjects. It may have been soon after Smiley's death. Without quite sorting it out, I blurted to Pat, "Now, look, let's make a promise. I'm not going to your funeral and I don't want you to come to mine."

He suppressed a smile. "Well, Gene, I'm afraid we can't work it that way," he said. "It has to go one way or t'other."

Like Smiley Burnette, Pat was the son of a minister, from Winston County, Alabama. They were so far removed from city life, said Pat, that in Winston County the "Beverly Hillbillies" show was considered a documentary. His first stage training came at church socials, where he would do a monologue, of sorts, during breaks in the fiddle contests.

But Pat always yearned for something more. Beneath his rural manner and humor, he had what not many of that generation could afford—an educated mind. He had won a scholarship to college, and studied acting at Birmingham Southern at the age of sixteen. It was a fine school and, at one time, had a reputation for producing good football teams. But when Pat went searching for the bright lights he found that most Easterners thought Birmingham Southern was a Pullman coach. He found acceptance easier if he kept quiet the fact that he was a college man.

His first break came in a fashion that sounds like the plot for a situation comedy. In 1934 Pat went to Chicago to see the World's Fair, and reporters from WLS were interviewing people to get their reactions. Pat was picked out of a crowd, and he gave them a flip answer to each question. With each answer he drew a bigger laugh. Soon he had the audience howling for him.

The manager of WLS offered him a job on the "Barn Dance," virtually on the spot. Of course, Pat knew about the show. Everyone in Alabama did. No matter what they say today about Nashville, the "Barn Dance," out of Chicago, was the granddaddy of country music. It started in 1922 and turned out a long array of new talent, including Red Foley, Rex Allen, George Gobel, and the Williams brothers. It was a great training ground and Pat grabbed at it.

That was where we first met, at the old theater on Eighth Street and Wabash. We did county fairs all week and then came back to Chicago and did the "Barn Dance" in front of a live audience of twelve hundred. We did two shows and sometimes they ran all night. The promoters charged admission and most of us never knew they were getting rich on it. Not that it mattered. Most of the kids in the cast were living on laughs and applause.

By then I had my first hit record, "Silver-haired Daddy," and had finished the Ken Maynard picture and one serial. I would stop in and appear on the "Barn Dance" for a week, then go on my tours. When I went on my strike at Republic, Pat was one of those who toured with me.

We took to each other right away. I was all business then, in a hurry to get my career and my life organized. Buttram was just starting, not yet sure of what he wanted to do or how to find out. Where Smiley loved crowds and kids and simple times, Pat had the soul of a blithe spirit and I had to keep an eye on him. Once, when he was between marriages, he made a play for a dancer who was touring with us, a real beauty. I took her aside one night and told her there was something she should know. It was all right to hold hands with Pat and maybe do a little smooching, but they had to say good night at the door because—and I lowered my voice sadly—the doctors say "he can't have any excitement." And I tapped my heart and shook my head. She understood.

For weeks after that Pat kept complaining to me that he couldn't figure the lady out. "I tell you," he said, "she literally *tears* herself away from me every night. And I know she goes for me. It's driving me up a wall."

When Pat finally wormed out of her what I had said, the story I had planted, he tried to convince her it was my idea of a joke. She refused to believe him. I mean, if you were a naïve young dancer who would you believe, Gene Autry or some comic whose intentions were less than pure?

He kept pleading with me. "Gene, for heaven's sake, tell her you were only kidding."

I said, "Pat, I got to think about it. She's mighty attractive. I'm not too sure your heart would stand it, at that." I told him he would thank me someday for looking after him, but I don't believe he ever did.

Buttram always had that precious gift of being able to laugh at himself. And us. He would break up a group of friends by quoting line after line of the corny dialogue that appeared in so many of our movie scripts:

" 'Mr. Autry, them Indians don't look too friendly.' "

" 'Pat, you stay here with six good men and I'll take the buckboard into town.' "

He used to do entire routines in his night club acts, in later years, about our days together. He would recall a scene in which he had to give Champion a kiss, an impulsive gesture to thank the horse for some heroic deed. Pat swore they had to do a dozen retakes. What really bothered him, he said, was that about the fifth take he began to like it.

Buttram was the best of company, but he honestly worried about the pace I kept and urged me to slow down and not push so hard. "Pat," I'd say, "if it was easy everybody would be doing it."

He just shook his head. "Someday," he said, "somebody will break your record for travel, for touring, for shows done and pictures made, rides and falls, rodeos and everything. But they are going to lose a helluva lot of sleep doing it."

It was several months after the war ended that Pat and I teamed up on the motion picture screen. When I returned from the service, Smiley was under contract to Columbia, where he was working with Charley Starrett. I no longer had a full-time sidekick, wasn't sure I wanted one, and tried two or three over my next few films. But the chemistry didn't seem quite right.

So I thought of Pat, and I called him in Chicago and asked him to fly out to Hollywood. He had appeared in one movie in 1941 with the great wit Robert Benchley. Benchley had a dry, languid style that mined the laughs out of everyday situations. He took a gentle approach to life and spent a good deal of it on his back. He always kept a couch in his office and referred to it as "the Track." When he decided to take a nap he would simply yawn and stretch his arms and announce, "Think I'll take a couple of laps around the Track."

Benchley gave Pat one piece of advice he never forgot. It didn't do him any good, he said, but he never forgot it. "Always describe yourself as a humorist," said Benchley. "Never let them call you a comic. That way you will always have the respect of those who never hear you perform."

Pat teamed with me on radio for fifteen years and through most of my movies at Columbia and the "Gene Autry Show" on television. And out of all those years and all those scripts, what I remember best was the goriest scene I can recall, not excluding war.

We were doing a segment of the TV series on location, in the desert near Palm Springs, and we had a scene where Pat was a professional rainmaker. He had devised a plan by which he would bring rain to a drought-stricken town by shooting off a cannon. The gods were supposed to hear the cannon, mistake it for thunder, and make it rain. Believe me, given what was to come, there is not much else you need to know about the story line.

I will say this. Pat had misgivings about it from the beginning. He is among the least mechanical of men and his contacts with machines have always been shaky. You have heard of people who talk to plants. Well, Pat always talked to machines. When he had to work with a prop he would put an arm around it and hold a brief but earnest conversation. Whenever he entered a hospital, he always made it a point to caress the X-ray machine.

This day we had one more scene to shoot and it was near six o'clock. We decided to try to get it in while we still had the sun. So we climbed to the top of a hill and hurried to set up the cameras and props.

Now this was in the early days of television in, I think, 1952, and the Screen Actors Guild did not yet cover the small screen. The fact is, some Hollywood veterans didn't think it would last. Sheila Ryan and Lyle Talbot were directors of the Guild, and they had walked out on their studios when some of their old movies were sold to TV, and no residuals were provided.

They brought it up at a Guild meeting and Walter Pidgeon rose and said, "Television! They're never going to take our pictures on television." Of course, it was already happening. But to many this new medium was a strange and unidentified species, and they didn't know whether to pet it or climb a tree. So the Guild ignored it at first, with the result that the studios paid a minimum of, say two hundred dollars a week. It was all quite loose and unregulated. In any movie you had to have a special effects man. But for television, you were not even required to have a licensed powder man for scenes that used explosives. The prop man could do it.

The cannon that was to be used in Pat's scene had been rigged with a small pan of flash powder. But instead of taping it to the lip of the cannon, the prop man put it down at the bottom and ran his wire from there, so it wouldn't show. Then he covered it with dirt, the wire leading to behind a rock, where he would set off the charge.

When Pat pulled the trigger, the prop man, out of sight, tripped his lever and the cannon literally exploded. Pat was standing less than three feet away. I was just behind him, mounted on Champion. The best we could figure later, some corrosion inside the cannon must have sealed off the opening. And flash powder, if you enclose it, can be as explosive as dynamite. Unfortunately, we learned that after the fact.

Fragments went flying in every direction. One piece hit Pat in the chest, another in the jaw, and a large chunk cut through his left boot, severing an artery. It was like shrapnel. Some of it whizzed right past my hat and Champion was nicked above the eye. Johnny Brousseau, the leathery French-Canadian who looked after my horses, had his knee broken by one scrap of flying metal. He didn't even know it until he tried to run over and help, and he just went right down. It looked like an air raid.

Pat was a mess, but the real danger was from the blood he was losing in his boot. We didn't notice that, what with his more obvious wounds, and he kept trying to tell us about it. But the rest of us insisted that he lie still and stay quiet. I guess we had seen too many movies. I know I kept saying, "Don't try to talk, Pat. It'll be all right. Don't try to talk."

Well, I knew better after that. Later, Pat lectured me, "Hell, if somebody's hurt and maybe dying let 'em talk, for crying our loud. They may need to tell you something. Like you're standing on my oxygen cord, or something."

We were camped at a place called Pioneer Town, four miles from Yucca Valley. It was getting dark. Herb Green was waiting with our plane, a twin-engine Beechcraft, at the local airstrip six or seven miles away and heard the explosion. We lifted Pat into a pickup truck and I leaped in beside him and we drove like mad down the mountain to reach the airstrip. We knew our only chance was to get Herb to fly him to the nearest hospital.

As soon as we pulled up to the plane I jumped out and said to Herb, "I think we've killed Pat. We've got to get him to a hospital." He was still conscious but just barely. There was literally a hole in his chest and you could see his lungs, and part of his chin was blown off.

Herb took one look at him and shook his head. He thought it was a miracle that Pat was still alive after the ride down the mountain. "You can't move him again," he said. "We've got to find a doctor and bring him back."

We located one and luck was with us. There was a small hospital at Twenty-nine Palms, owned by a doctor named Bill Ince. He was the son of Thomas Ince, one of the great movie pioneers, who had produced the William S. Hart movies. There was a street on the Metro-Goldwyn-Mayer lot named after Tom Ince. He had died in style, on William Randolph Hearst's yacht, at a party whose guest list included Charlie Chaplin, Marion Davies, and Louella Parsons.

The son, Bill, inherited his father's fortune, but in his will the old man stipulated that none of the money could be reinvested in movies. So young Bill decided to become a society doctor. He traveled all over the world, studied in Vienna. He loved to study. His friends suspected that he didn't really want to practice, he just loved going to school.

But he became a great doctor, settling in the Yucca Valley after his wife developed lung trouble. He built a fine hospital, equipped with the best and the latest in medical technology. That, and the techniques he learned in Europe, were to save Buttram's life.

I told Herb to take off and fly to Twenty-nine Palms and bring back Dr. Ince. In the meantime, we phoned ahead and let them know he was coming. There were no lights on the runway at the town's tiny airport, and Herb would be landing at night. So the telephone operator called all over town—they even made an announcement at a local baseball game—and people jumped into their cars and drove over to the airfield and turned on their headlights. It was one of those moonless nights you catch in the desert sometimes, but thanks to the cars lining the runway Herb was able to bring the plane down.

Dr. Ince, who didn't like to fly, scrambled aboard, carrying his medical bag. All that time I was just trying to keep Pat out of shock. I kept kidding him. "You'll be all right," I said. "All you need is a broad and a fifth of scotch."

Pat groaned and said, "Oh no, buddy, I'm gone."

I leaned over him and half shouted, "No you're not. You owe me twenty bucks and I'm not going to let you get out of it this easy."

When the doctor landed he started to work on Pat right on the spot. We had taken him off the truck and into a small office and tried to make him comfortable. We found out about the wound in his heel when someone removed his boots, and blood squirted everywhere. We had tied a tourniquet around his ankle to slow the bleeding. Now Dr. Ince put a clamp on the artery.

After that he began picking cannon fragments, dirt, and rock out of Pat's chest. He couldn't give him an anesthetic, or a pain killer, because he was just too far gone. At one point Pat said, "Don't let them put me under, Gene. I'll never come out of it."

He was so numb I guess it didn't matter much. It was just the greatest stroke of fortune that we found Dr. Bill Ince. He had learned a special stitch from an old doctor in Vienna, and he cleaned out the wounds and sewed Pat up and had the worst of it done by the time an ambulance arrived. We just could not have found a better physician, at that moment, if we had gone through the entire medical directory.

Meanwhile, Herb Green made two more quick flights, one to

bring in blood plasma, another to fly in a second doctor from Los Angeles to assist Bill Ince. When we carried Pat out to the ambulance for the ride to Twenty-nine Palms, the driver shook his head and said, "We better take those other two," pointing to Johnny Brousseau and a sound man who had been hit, "*that* guy is a goner." I stepped up then and said, through gritted teeth, "No, sir, you take *him.*"

It was a slow recovery. Pat was out of work and laid up for nine months, and Sheila Ryan moved to Twenty-nine Palms to be at his side and look after him. That clinched it. When he was on his feet again they were married.

But he can't forget the day the cannon exploded. Whenever Pat has a plane to catch and he walks through those metal detectors they go "ping, ping," from the shrapnel still in his body.

Pat went on to a career as a night club comic after our own string played out on radio and television. "Melody Ranch" went off the air in 1956, when the Wrigley people decided to pull out of radio except for a few, small daytime shows. I was sad to see it end, of course, but it had lasted for sixteen good years. I had no complaints, certainly no cause to feel bitter. "The Jack Benny Show" had been canceled earlier, with a very curt phone call from Bill Paley of CBS.

When Wrigley set the date for the last "Melody Ranch" broadcast, Buttram and the rest of the cast prepared a tribute to me as a farewell performance. They put together, on tape, some of my most popular songs and a few highlights of past shows. I wasn't there, other than in spirit.

It was a pleasant hour. Pat did a little monologue about me and, right in the middle, he got a tickle in his throat and his voice caught. Mr. Wrigley happened to be listening and he was moved by what he took to be a moment choked with emotion. Now, it was a sentimental time for all of us, but Pat was far too much of a pro to lose his composure. Whatever may have been in his throat, it wasn't emotion. But Mr. Wrigley was touched, and he reacted by signing Pat to a four-year contract to do his own daytime show.

No one deserved a break more. Anyone with an instinct for the underdog would enjoy seeing Number Two get a shot at top billing. I was pleased for Pat and he knew I was, but we both recognized a certain irony in what had happened. The sponsor had hired my sidekick because his voice broke while paying a tribute to me on a show the sponsor had just canceled. Now that, friends, is show business.

Of course, no tribute to my theatrical sidekicks would be complete without acknowledging the most enduring of them all, Champion. To be exact, I suppose the reference should be plural —*Champions*. I used three in my films, all with the distinctive blazed face and white socks. If you would like an idea of how valuable those horses were, the original Champion had four stand-ins at a time when Greta Garbo had one.

In those days the horse was virtually a co-star. The kids all knew that the Lone Ranger's mount was Silver and Roy Rogers rode Trigger. But who could tell you, years later, the name of Jim Arness' horse or Paladdin's or what the Cartwrights called theirs?

Sure, it was part of the Western myth, but often a myth is simply history with costumes. We gave our horses things to do that were important in beating the "bad guys." Remember how Champion used to nibble at the ropes that were tied around my wrists, in order to free me? How often do you remember Roy Rogers being in a tough spot, needing help, and all he had to do was slap Trigger on the flank and tell him to fetch reinforcements. Trigger would race back to the ranch and return with Roy's buddies, just in time to help Roy wipe out the heavies.

Not for nothing were they called horse operas. Champ received bag loads of his own fan mail. He practically made the gossip columns. In 1940 he created headlines by becoming the first horse ever to fly from California to New York. It wasn't exactly Lindbergh crossing the Atlantic, but he was the envy of millions of Americans who had never been higher than a barber's chair.

The flight developed into the best kind of publicity stunt, because it did not start out as one. I was lunching one day at the Roosevelt Hotel, in Hollywood, with a congressman from Oklahoma, Jack Nicholas, and with Jack Frey, then the president of TWA, an airline owned at that time by Howard Hughes. Idly I said, "Man, have I got a problem. I've signed to do a picture in

Hollywood and I don't finish until two days before we open the rodeo at the Garden. I don't know how I'm going to get my horse back here in time."

Jack Frey looked up and said, "I'll put him on one of our planes."

I thought he was kidding. "Can you do that?" I said.

"Absolutely," he said.

We started to think about the idea. Then it occurred to us that we were not even sure Champ would fit through the passenger door. The three of us caught a cab and rode out to the airport. Frey had a mechanic put a slab of cardboard against the door and cut out a silhouette the size of the opening. Then we measured the cardboard against the back of a trailer van. I shook my head. The airlines were flying DC-3's then, and if you tried to lead him straight in Champ would never make it.

But Johnny Brousseau began to tinker with the problem. One day he came to me holding a brown paper sack, on one side of which he had drawn a blueprint. "We do her like this," he said, "and she can be done." Johnny had drawn a ramp a foot lower than the door of the plane, so that Champion could walk off the van and step up, enabling his head and shoulders to clear the opening.

The airline went to great lengths to accommodate its special passenger. Five rows of seats were removed at the rear of the craft, and a private stall created, including a metal trough with hay heaped across the bottom. A harness dangled from the ceiling, so Champion could be strapped in for safety if the weather turned rough. Whenever it did I slipped the horse an apple, a small bribe to take his mind off the choppy air. By the time we landed in New York he would no longer eat oats. He had become an apple junkie.

The historic flight lasted two days. We stopped at most of the major cities along the TWA route, so the press and public could peek inside the plane and see Champion in all his high and mightiness. We stayed overnight in Chicago, made our last of six stops in Pittsburgh and flew into New York to a hero's reception. Half a dozen of us had gone along for the ride. I suppose by the end of the trip the air in the cabin had grown a little gamey, but most of us had been around stables and horses so much we thought everything smelled that way.

Of the three screen Champions, the first was probably the best-tempered. He didn't act up even when the kids at a rodeo or a parade yanked hairs out of his tail for a souvenir. In a curious way, his death led to the kind of story that gets twisted in the re-telling. (The third Champion lived until the summer of 1976. The second, my Tennessee Walker, is still alive and enjoying his retirement at Melody Ranch.)

I was in a hotel room in the East when Brousseau called to tell me the original Champ had died. Johnny was taking it hard and I tried to pick him up. "Now, Johnny, he was twenty-three years old," I said. "We'll miss him. But he lived a long time. We took good care of him."

Brousseau said he had checked with a taxidermist. For fifteen hundred dollars it would be possible, he said, to have Champion stuffed and mounted and put on display.

As gently as I could I said, "Johnny, the horse had a good life. Let's not make him work for us now. Go ahead and bury him."

By the time the story had been repeated at a banquet or two and then hit print, the punch line was, "FIFTEEN HUNDRED DOLLARS? Drag him out and plant him." I do not mind so much being made to appear thrifty, which is a staple of Hollywood humor. I do object to being made to appear insensitive.

I understood when Roy Rogers, some years later, had a taxidermist prepare Trigger for a Western museum. It is hard to let that part of your life disappear. But I could also appreciate the crack made by his wife, Dale Evans: "When Roy dies, I'm going to have him stuffed and mounted on top of Trigger."

I had a feeling close to love for Champion, for each of them. I can tell you, they were often a tough act to follow especially the first one. Once, at the Oriental Theater in Chicago, I had just put Champion through his routine. I dismounted and walked slowly to the microphone, concentrating on what I had to do.

I was unaware that behind me the horse was, shall we say, dec-orating the stage, which lent a little unwitting humor to what I said next. "Well," I told the audience cheerfully, "now that Champ has done his act, it's time for me to do mine."

The place came apart. The laughter rolled down in waves, eas-ily the loudest of my entire career. Not to mention Champion's.

CHAPTER NINE

The Road, Rodeo, and Radio

Your name up there in big letters on a marquee might qualify you as a star, but it doesn't make you a trouper. That comes from going out on the road, night after night, town after town, playing in places where the trains don't stop.

After twenty-five years I withdrew from that kind of life, I cut back on my traveling, and one of the reasons was a trip I made to Cuba in the last months of the Batista regime. Late in the fall of 1957 I was invited to bring my rodeo to Havana to open a new sports arena there in March of 1958. A minor Cuban official named Ernesto Azua called and we agreed to a deal over the phone: $25,000 up front, to be deposited in a Miami bank, and twenty-five per cent of the gross.

When December rolled around and I had heard nothing more I telephoned my man in Havana.

"Ernesto," I said, "I haven't heard from you about the rodeo. Is it still on?"

"Oh yes. The building, it will be ready on time, in March. Ees fine, everything."

I said, "Well, what about this rebellion I've been reading about. I hear there's a lot of fighting going on down there."

"Eet ees nawthing. Thees outlaw, Castro, he have a handful of *bandidos* in the mountains. But ees nawthing to worry about."

I said, "Well, what about my twenty-five thousand dollars? You were supposed to put it in the bank."

"Yes, yes. Eet weel be taken care of right away."

By January I still had not heard a word. I placed another call to Cuba.

"Ernesto, what about that rodeo?"

"Ah, Gene, ees going fine. Building ees fine. We open on time."

I said, "That's good to know. What about those rebels? I see they're still fighting."

"Poof, ees nawthing. The *federales* weel have them wiped out in a few weeks, no more."

"Yes, well, I read where you had some bombings."

"Ees nawthing."

Now we got to the serious part of the conversation. "What about my money? Where's the guarantee you were supposed to put in the bank?"

"Oh yes. We take care of that right away."

We went through one more round of this and, finally, in February, the bank in Miami notified me that the deposit had been made and the trip was set. By this time I was more concerned than ever. Two bearded revolutionaries, Fidel Castro and Che Guevara, and their followers, most of them peasants, were bleeding Batista's army like picadors weakening the wounded bull. But Ernesto kept reassuring me.

We flew to Havana—Mrs. Autry was with me—after finishing a show in San Antonio. We were welcomed at the airport by several government dignitaries, a Mariachi band, newsreel cameras, more than a dozen reporters, and three bodyguards.

I laughed and said, "Bodyguards. We don't need any bodyguards. What's this all about?"

Azua said, "We do not wish to alarm you, my friend. But we had the beeg Grand Prix auto race here two weeks ago. The rebels attempted to kidnap Juan Manuel Fangio, of Argentina, the world champion. We would not want anything like that to happen to you."

I looked at Ina. "Well, now," I said, "I sure as hell wouldn't, either."

We checked into the Nacional Hotel and two of the bodyguards instructed us to wait in the hall with the other. Meanwhile, they checked all the closets, under the beds, and on the balcony. It was not the most comfortable arrival I ever had, but they were very efficient. They were big, swarthy, unsmiling men, all with Batista's secret police. One of them, I was to remember, was named Martinez.

They said there was no reason to believe we were in any danger. But we were not to take chances. "If there is a knock at the door do not answer. If there is a call to come to the lobby, do not go down. We will be outside your door at all times." And they were, in shifts, around the clock.

We did go out to a few of the night clubs in Havana, then still renowned as one of the playgrounds of the world. But we were always under heavily armed guard. We did not go strolling, like lovers, in the moonlight.

The arena, and the rodeo, opened on schedule but to less than capacity crowds, held down by the recent bombings and the threat of more violence. Each night we would ride out to the arena with one car in front of us and another behind, each carrying two guards equipped with tommy guns.

And each night I would ride into the center of the arena on Champion, and sing my songs, while the only lights in an otherwise dark room washed over me. I felt like a clay pigeon. In each entrance I could see the shadow of a soldier with a rifle or tommy gun slung over his shoulder. Every man who entered the arena was frisked, every woman had her purse searched for bombs.

I wasn't afraid that someone would actually take a shot at me. What worried me was the prospect that a gun would go off, or for that matter a balloon, and those trigger-happy *federales* would start blazing away and I'd be caught in the crossfire under that relentless spotlight.

We were booked for ten days. After half of them I was ready to let them finish their war without me. We had opened on a Friday night. I asked Earl Lindsey, my business manager, to find Azua and settle the weekend receipts. Earl had learned all there was to know about tickets in his years with Ringling Brothers. He could riffle through a stack six inches thick and say, "There's two thousand and eighty in there."

But the problem was to find Azua. On the phone it was always *mañana*. Finally, Earl waited at the arena all day and night and caught him sneaking around at two in the morning. They went to the box office and Azua pulled out what appeared to be one of those canvas mail sacks and emptied it onto a big round table. They figured out that our share was about seventy-five hundred dollars, and Earl took as much of it as he could in American bills —the largest was probably a twenty—and stuffed it in two bags, the kind you put potatoes in. A fellow named Tommy Steiner, from Austin, was with him. He had provided the livestock.

Outside the arena they hailed a cab and Earl ducked in the door and said, "Take us to the Nacional Hotel."

The driver looked at them sideways and said, "What ees een the bag, señor?"

Earl said, "That's none of your business."

And the driver said, "Ah, but I have to know what ees een the bag."

They argued back and forth and Earl saw a policeman standing at the corner. He waved him over and explained the problem. The cop was polite but said he had to tell the driver what was in the bag. That was one of the rebel tricks, leaving a bomb in a bag outside a building and blowing it up. Earl did not look like a mad bomber. He looked like an accountant. But he explained to the officer that he worked for me, that I was appearing with the rodeo, and he was taking my money back to the hotel.

By now the cabbie was eager to take them, but Earl insisted the cop come along and they all piled in.

At the hotel, I told Tommy Steiner I was taking Ina and going home. "I got my twenty-five thousand in advance," I said, "and at least some of the percentage. To hell with the rest of it. Life's too short."

Tommy grimaced and said, "Oh, Christ, don't do that, Gene."

I asked why not.

He said, "I didn't get mine in advance. If you cancel now I'm afraid they'll say the contract was broken because you left the show, and I'll never get my money."

I groaned a little but told Tommy, sure, I couldn't do that to him. We'd stay. We finished the performances. But the night of the last one we had our bags packed, and I got them to put me on first, right after the grand entry. I had the bodyguards drive us straight to the airport and we caught a Pan Am flight and flew home. Adios, Havana.

In less than a year Castro and his band came out of the hills and overthrew the government of Fulgencio Batista. That little bunch of *bandidos*, as Ernesto described them, had not faded away, after all. I never learned what happened to Azua. But a year later I brought the rodeo back to San Antonio, and there I was sought out by one of my former bodyguards, Martinez. He had fled the country, he told me, just ahead of a firing squad. He was having a hard go. I gave him a few hundred dollars and wished him luck. Poor Cuba. Batista had been a dictator. But the liberty Castro promised them had begun with the phrase *up against the wall*.

In my time I have played shows where I wound up working for nothing, the crowds were so small. I played in a New Hampshire blizzard and a Florida hurricane and an Oklahoma dust storm. And once, just that once, in the middle of a revolution.

Of course, a rodeo was not the same as beating your way across the country in a series of one-night stands. It was bigger and in some ways easier, although not necessarily more fun. You were in one place for a week or a month, and you were part of a small traveling army. On the big tours, you worked lean.

It didn't take long to learn the tricks of the road, such as not traveling at night, when the roads were risky and the weather uncertain. Also, by staying until morning, you allowed more time to check out the box office. I learned not to leave until we got our money.

In the early days, the mid-1930s, the act often featured just three instruments: me on the guitar, Carl Cotner on the fiddle, and Frankie Marvin playing the washboard. I don't think you can say you have been in show business, really experienced it, unless you went through some of that, through the era of the one-night stand, dressing in rooms where you had to chase out the bats and spiders.

After a while we worked our way up to the old vaudeville theaters, grand and sturdy places that offered Shakespeare one night, burlesque the next, and a singing cowboy another. Every theater had its ghosts. No two performances were alike, simply because so many conditions were beyond your control.

There was a day in Wisconsin when Smiley Burnette took his bow and skipped off the stage. I stood there, leading the applause and waiting for Smiley to reappear for his encore. I waited. And waited. And waited. Finally, he staggered back out and he was just a cloud of black dust, from head to boot.

I burst out laughing and said, "What happened to *you?*"

He mumbled, "I fell into a coal bin," and the audience broke up. They thought it was part of the routine and we went on as if nothing had happened. When we came off the stage I said, "No kidding, Smiley, what the devil happened?"

He said, "Just like I told you. They got a trap door back here that opens to a coal bin, and when I ran offstage I accidentally stepped on the wrong square and just went right through the damned chute. By the time I crawled out I had soot all over me."

I suggested we keep it in the act but Smiley pretended not to hear.

Country fairs were a unique part of those years, gay and festive times, and I always learned from them. It was between shows one day, strolling around the midway, that Pat Buttram met Colonel Tom Parker in Du Quoin, Illinois.

Of course, this was many years before he became immortal as the man who discovered Elvis Presley (and Eddy Arnold, before him). He was in front of a tent with a sign that said, "COLONEL TOM PARKER AND HIS DANCING TURKEYS," and he was acting as his own barker. He was giving his spiel to a growing crowd of farmers: "They dance, they do the hoochie-coochie; come in and see these amazing creatures. Only a quarter."

It developed that he had a large table with sawdust on it and underneath was a metal plate. He would arrange about twenty live turkeys on it and then he'd throw on a switch and it would become, literally, a hot plate. At the same time the colonel would turn on the record player and the turkeys would seem to be jumping around in rhythm to the music. The farmers would turn to their wives and say, "Ma, how does he do it?" And the little kids would go home and beat their pet turkeys, trying to teach them to dance.

Pat asked the colonel just one question: When the tempo picked up, how did he get them to stay in time to the music? He

25. *The country music great, Tex Ritter, and I agree; a cowboy's best friend is his horse.*

26. *Swapping inside baseball stories with immortals Stan Musial (left), Dizzy Dean.*

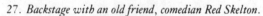

27. *Backstage with an old friend, comedian Red Skelton.*

28. *With former business partner Bob Reynolds and former baseball announcer Ronald Reagan.*

29. *With Mrs. Autry, a VIP tour of Disneyland, led by the star attraction.*

30. Baseball's opening day 1970 brought out Richard Nixon to root for the home team.

31. *High Society: with Mrs. John Hay Whitney, Franklin Roosevelt, Jr., and Dorothy Lamour, slow dancing to the music.*

32. *Our man in Havana: the Cuba trip in 1957 came amid castanets and bullets.*

33. *Frankie Marvin, Oklahoma's Singing Cotton Picker, made Tin Pan Alley rounds with author.*

34. *Comparing gavels with a politician I always admired, Sam Rayburn, of Texas.*

35. *Champion stands majestically outlined against the western hills.*

36. *There was plenty of horsepower in the Air Transport Command.*

said, "That's easy. I got a thermostat in there and when I want them to dance faster I just turn it up a little hotter."

I knew then that he was destined for greatness. It didn't surprise me when Tom Parker emerged as the genius behind Elvis. He saw the whole world as a carnival. Years later, when Buttram played a character called Mr. Haney on the television series "Green Acres," he patterned him after Colonel Parker.

Whatever contribution I did or did not make to country music, I believe I helped make it a little more respectable. It became a practice of mine to appear on the stage early, often right at the start. That was to reassure the crowd, because so many country entertainers were unreliable. They had what could best be described as a casual attitude toward the clock, and the calendar. Even the best didn't always keep their dates. Sometimes it wasn't their doing. An agent would just take five or six bookings for the same night, looking for a better deal, and forget to cancel the rest of them.

So what occasionally developed was a test of will and endurance between the local promoter and the audience. The promoter would try to wear down the crowd with warm-up acts, punctuated with frequent bulletins reporting the star's progress: "He's coming in now . . . his plane is circling the airport . . . they're cleared for landing . . . he'll be here momentarily . . ."

They would be halfway through the show before an announcement would be made that the star was not going to appear. So I don't know if I made country music more popular. I sure won't claim that I improved the quality of it. But I never missed a date, and I'm proud of that.

I remember Columbia, Tennessee—which proudly billed itself as "The Mule Capital of the World"—as the city that taught me the meaning of the phrase the show must go on. A few hours before we were to perform, George Goodale discovered that the sound system was on the fritz. No one at the theater knew how to fix it. No sound, no show.

George scouted around and learned that the only fellow in town who could repair it worked for Western Union. We needed help and we needed it fast.

The office was in our hotel, so George hustled down and asked the telegrapher if he could fix the sound system for us. "More'n likely," he said, "but can't leave the office. Nobody to run my wire."

George thought quickly. "Look," he said, "if I get you a relief operator, will you go right over to the theater and get that thing working?"

"Yup, I'll do it," he said. "But where you goin' to get another operator? I'm the only one in town."

"I'll be right back," said George.

I hadn't worked a wire in roughly ten years. But Goodale hauled me down there and when I walked in the old boy looked at me and then back at George and said, accusingly, "That's Gene Autry."

He was trying to figure out the gag but there wasn't any. I took over the wire and he went to the theater and patched the system. And the show went on. I knew that, at some point, all that honest work I once did would pay off. Offhand, I can't think of any other entertainers who were able to keep a booking because they knew the Morse Code.

Funny thing though, Goodale loved to retell that story but for three years he couldn't get it into print. It was the great frustration of his career because he knew it to be true. Press agents worked on a kind of honor system in those years. That is, they always stuck to the truth, when they could.

Finally, he was having dinner one night in Chicago with Irv Kupcinet, and he remarked that he had an anecdote about Autry that actually happened, but none of the West Coast columnists would use it. And Kup ran it a few days later in just that way: the true story Hollywood wouldn't buy.

The Colt .45 was renowned in cowboy lore as "The Gun That Won the West." On a more modest scale, I am told that the Gene Autry cap pistol once saved an entire town.

The town was Kenton, Ohio, upon which hard times had fallen in the thirties, as they had on so many places. The Kenton Hardware Company was the town's only industry. When its business fell off everyone suffered; people were thrown out of work and began to move away. The future appeared grim.

But in 1936 the Kenton Hardware Company received a contract to manufacture the Gene Autry cap pistols. Keep in mind, I had little to do with that, except indirectly. But those pistols became a spectacularly popular item among the tots of America. The company prospered. It not only rehired the people who had been laid off, but had to add extra shifts and work them around the clock. They thought highly of the Gene Autry cap pistol, in Kenton, Ohio.

So the town bounced back from the doldrums and flourished as never before. Two years later, during my strike at Republic, we were touring in Ohio and George Goodale remembered Kenton. On two days' notice he made a deal for us to play there.

That night the theater was jammed. The mayor, and half a dozen other city officials, made a speech and thanked me for saving the town. We had scheduled a second show, but after the first we couldn't get the kids out of their seats to make room for the next crowd. They just wouldn't budge. So I had to go back onstage and promise that the first twenty-five youngsters out the door would receive a *free* Gene Autry cap pistol.

Goodale was standing out in the lobby holding a box containing the toy guns when they opened the doors. Poor George. He never knew what hit him. When we helped him to his feet, the pistols were gone, half his clothes were gone, and he had footprints all over his body.

By the early 1940s, I was on the air with "Melody Ranch," and when we took to the road the show went with us. We did one broadcast from the back of a railroad flatcar in a town that, up to then, had been known as Berwyn, Oklahoma. In the fall of '41 I bought a twelve-hundred-acre ranch two miles west of there.

And an idea began to form in the mind of a man named Cecil Crosby; no relation to my announcer, Lou Crosby, who opened each show with the words: "Where the pavement ends and the West begins." Enlisting a handful of his neighbors, Cecil proposed that the name of the town be changed to Gene Autry, Oklahoma. I had brought fame to the state where I was reared, he said, as a screen cowboy and crooner. The gesture flattered me but, frankly, Berwyn didn't have a great deal to lose. With a total of 227 residents, it had for years slept quietly in the foothills of the Arbuckle Mountains.

The Santa Fe Railroad, around whose tracks the town had grown in 1886, liked the idea and the U. S. Post Office approved it. Crosby, a veteran lawman who died in 1962, got the signatures he needed on a petition approving the change. On November 4, 1941, a resolution was signed at the courthouse and Berwyn became, officially, Gene Autry, Oklahoma.

Arrangements were made for me to broadcast my weekly radio show from there on the sixteenth, a Sunday, the thirty-fourth anniversary of Oklahoma statehood. A network of Oklahoma radio stations was formed, expressly to carry one hour of the festivities just before we joined the national hookup over CBS. The Ardmore American Legion Post Drum and Bugle Corps performed. Newsreel cameras were there. *Life* magazine sent two photographers.

As far as anyone knew, I was the first motion picture star to have a town named after him. The idea had grown into perhaps the greatest one-day promotion in Oklahoma history. Berwyn had suddenly become a household word across America. The townspeople mounted a clean-up campaign that seldom had been equaled anywhere, leveling entire fields to accommodate the thousands of cars that were expected. The Jordan Bus Company offered round-trip service from Ardmore for fifty cents that day.

As an added attraction, the Santa Fe put on exhibit an old wood-burning engine and train, next to a modern streamliner. Indians were brought in from western Oklahoma and they built teepees behind the stage. Churches set up food and drink stands that featured buffalo meat sandwiches. It was unusually warm that day for November, eighty-three degrees, and a man named Pinky Crossland said he sold 7,700 pounds of ice.

At 2 P.M., the Berwyn sign at the Santa Fe Depot was replaced with a Gene Autry sign. Thereafter, all tickets and timetables would bear my name. We went on the air that day before a live audience of thirty-five thousand people.

Radio was the great medium of that day, the one best way, I found, to reach the largest audience and to meet the rich and the famous.

Mrs. Eleanor Roosevelt was a guest on one of our shows from Washington, D.C. Like her husband, she was then an inspiration to millions through her good works on behalf of the poor and the afflicted. On the same show we featured a singing preacher, a black evangelist named Elder Solomon Lightfoot Michaux. One of the reverend's flock had brought along a baby boy, with the distinguished name of Franklin Delano Gene Autry Johnston.

There were reporters and photographers on hand for the appearance of the First Lady, and they wanted pictures of us with the little boy. So Mrs. Roosevelt lifted him on her lap and I stood behind them with my hand resting lightly on her shoulder.

As the flash bulbs popped the baby tinkled all over her dress.

I have never seen such composure in all of my life. Mrs. Roosevelt was due at a formal party right after our show, and now the entire front of her dress was wet. The photographers had been snapping away and now they all looked at each other as if one of them had caused it. No one knew what to do. We were all just frozen with embarrassment.

But Mrs. Roosevelt slowly rose, handed the baby to his mother, took a handkerchief, dabbed at her dress, and reassured everyone in that familiar, high voice with the trill in it: "Don't mind that. Remember, I raised five babies."

After the war I went back to Washington with the rodeo, and a party of politicians planned to attend the opening night. Stuart Symington, then the senator from Missouri, asked a famous and crusty old congressman from Mississippi if he planned to go. "Hell, no," was the reply. "I can't stand that fellow Autry."

Symington was puzzled. "Do you know him?"

"No, I don't," said the Mississippian, "but he looks too damned much like Harry Truman."

Later I told the story to President Truman, and he looked at me with astonishment. "You mean," he demanded, "that old son of a bitch said that about you?"

Every entertainer, sooner or later, runs into a cold audience. I have seen them sit there with all the warmth of a hangman waiting for you at the scaffold. But the toughest-*looking* audience I ever encountered was at Glace Bay, Nova Scotia, in the late

1940s. They were miners and loggers, rough, unshaven men who looked as if they had just come from a raid on the nearest town.

We had toured all across Canada, sixty days of one-night stands, transporting thirty-five people by plane and bus. Often we played in the local hockey arena, with a wooden floor just laid over the ice. We hit towns with those great, colorful Canadian names, Moosejaw, Saskatchewan, Medicine Hat.

But Glace Bay was about as far east as you could go and still be in North America. It was dogsled country. You could feel it, that tough, pioneer, outback character of it. We were advised to be on our toes, those miners could get rowdy.

The balcony was packed that night but we had some empties in the higher-priced, reserved seats down in front. The first time they dimmed the house lights it sounded like a cattle stampede. Half the miners, at least, left the cheap seats and bolted to the front, and when the curtain opened there they were, these bearded, fierce-looking men in their heavy mackinaws.

We were all peeking out from the wings. I turned to Herb Green, my pilot and occasional advance man, and with a straight face, said, "Herb, get 'em out of those seats."

Green was a big, husky fellow who had won his wings dusting crops and as a barnstormer. He was no sissy. But he threw up his hands and said, "Boss, I just quit."

I gave a weak laugh and said, "Me, too." That crowd was like the old story about the four-hundred-pound gorilla. It could sit wherever it wanted to sit.

It was on that same tour, in a little town called Sault Sainte Marie, that I lost my temper about as completely as I have ever lost it. Herb had flown ahead to check out the theater, and when he got there he called and said we had a problem. The Musicians' Union was threatening to shut down our show because the contracts hadn't been signed.

That wasn't unusual, the way we moved around. Often the contracts didn't get signed until show time. Carl Cotner took the call, told Herb to let the manager know it would be taken care of the moment we arrived and to just relax.

But when Carl walked into the building the manager was waiting for him. He was frantic. He said, "You better get in my office, quick. They are going to do it. The union is going to close the whole damned show." Carl followed him into his office and a man from the union was in there, pacing.

Carl took the papers out of his coat and said, "Okay, here's the contract. I said I'd bring it with me. Now what's the problem?"

The fellow glanced at the contract and said, "You got to pay the men from our local to play."

Carl said, "Okay, how many?"

"Three."

"Fine. Let's sign the contract. What's all the talk about holding up the show?"

"Well, there's one more thing. They don't have to come down and play. You just pay 'em."

Cotner shook his head. "Nooo, sir. I can tell you right now. When Gene Autry hires somebody, they work."

The man said, "What's the difference? You got no music for them anyway."

Carl said, "Don't worry about that. I'll get the music for them. But if we have to put clown suits on 'em, they'll work."

After that was settled, they sat down and had poured the coffee, when another union official walked in, feeling pretty cocky. He was strutting around, trying to impress Cotner. "Where's that hillbilly Autry?" he asked at one point. "Which one of those hillbillies out there is Autry?"

Carl said later he could hear my spurs clinking as I came down the hall. I walked through the door just as the union man was asking for me.

I said, "So you're with the union?"

He puffed up and said, "That's right."

I rushed up to him then and, nose to nose, I said, "Let me tell you something. We're *not* hillbillies. I want you to know that, damn you. I've got a good group here. They're good sonsabitches and they're good musicians, and they're *not* hillbillies."

I was mad. And I meant every word of it.

The 1950s were the last hurrah for the kind of tour we used to do, a combination of vaudeville, barn dance, Saturday matinee, and medicine show. It was just before television blanketed the country, just before the advent of Elvis, the posh new arenas, the

Beatles, rock concerts, Aquarius, and porno movies, pretty much in that order.

It seems to me now, at least in retrospect, that those were mighty romantic times. People could still fall in love on a bus, and on at least one occasion it happened just that way.

In January of 1950 we started our tour in Pueblo, Colorado. My brother Doug was traveling with me then, and he was instantly taken with a young dancer who did rope tricks named Barbara Bardo. On the bus that night headed for Hutchinson, Kansas, Doug passed up the usual poker game in the back and sat beside the young lady.

The boys began to speculate, as they often did, on how Doug would make out. "We'll know pretty soon," one of them said.

At about three in the morning, when everyone but the card players seemed to be asleep, the silence was shattered by a girlish scream from up front. One of the poker players peeked at his watch and said, "Looks like Doug is working a little slower than usual."

The bus driver flipped on the overhead lights and asked nervously if he ought to stop.

"Hell, no," said Doug. "She's not hurt."

Later, Barbara complained to me that Doug had gotten fresh, and she had warned him she would scream if he didn't stop. He didn't, and she did. I had a big brother kind of talk with him about it, and Doug spent the next two weeks trying to make amends, as well as trying to melt some of that ice Barbara put between them.

On February 13, 1950, just five weeks later, in Bangor, Maine, they handed out wedding invitations. They made, I thought, a handsome couple.

That same year, 1950, the "Melody Ranch" broadcast passed the ten-year mark, going strong, still sponsored by Doublemint gum (with an occasional kind word for Spearmint). We enlarged the orchestra, hired more writers, singers, and actors, and put Bev Barnett, my old publicity man, to work promoting the show. All of this was intended to offset any loss of listeners to television.

Phil Wrigley had always told us never to worry about the ratings, so long as the show sold gum. I do believe we sold enough to stick to the bottom of every shoe in America.

By then new technology had changed the entire process of radio. Tape recordings were coming into wider use, which meant that shows no longer had to be live. That solved problems for both the performers and the producers. Mistakes and slips of the tongue could be edited out, and shows could be taped in advance to work around our road commitments. Oddly enough, it developed that everyone preferred the taped broadcasts except Mr. Wrigley himself.

"Some of the mistakes are the best part of the show," he insisted. "It proves you're human. Put 'em back in."

Any group that spends weeks at a time living out of suitcases needs someone like Eddie Hogan. A burly Irishman, with the square look of a Boston cop, Eddie was a combination driver, valet, and mother hen. But he had a sense of order and neatness. If I suffered some slight inconvenience, he felt that he had failed me.

It was a matter of pride with him to lay out my clothes and keep my dressing room tidy. He guarded that room as though it were a bank, always locking the door when he left. But one time we were playing in Dallas, and we had a four o'clock matinee for the kids, which left us with less time than usual to grab a break before the evening performance.

On an impulse, I picked up the key myself and locked the door as we all hurried out of the dressing room. In the rush Eddie didn't notice. But I was curious to see what would happen when Eddie discovered his key was missing.

I deliberately dawdled over dinner so we would get back to the arena at the last minute before the show. We reached the dressing room with not much time to spare, and Eddie started to fish through his pockets.

I said, "Come on, Eddie. Unlock the door."

He said, "Yessir," and started fumbling a little faster.

Eddie had one of those naturally pink Irish faces. When he was flustered he looked as though his shirt collar was choking him.

I gave him the needle again. "Come on, Hogan, where's the key? I've got to get in there."

And before I had time to anticipate what he was going to do, Eddie said, "Yessir," and backed up one step for momentum. Then he just put his shoulder into the door and went right through it.

I just stood there with my mouth open. My little practical joke had backfired. I had to pay for the door, but in a way it was worth it. I mean, what was a door compared to that kind of loyalty?

We brought the rodeo cowboy's art to old Madison Square Garden, and set attendance records almost every year. I could usually count on those trips to New York to produce at least one encounter with an old friend, with unpredictable results.

One year I ran into Glenn McCarthy, the Houston oilman, who was in town on business. He asked me to meet him after my show that night for a drink, and I said I would. Later, General John Reed Kilpatrick, who ran the Garden then, invited me to a party. When I told him I had made plans to meet Glenn, he said to bring him along.

McCarthy had already attracted national attention as a prototypical Texas wildcatter, and the builder of the spectacular Shamrock Hotel. He was said to be the inspiration for the character of Jett Rink in the Edna Ferber novel *Giant*, later a movie.

I liked Glenn. He was quick and honest and you never had to wonder where you stood. But he did everything with both fists— fight, drink, play cards.

The party was in the general's private suite at the Garden and it drew an interesting class of people. Mr. Gimbel, of the department store Gimbels, was there. And Gene Tunney, the ex-heavyweight champion. And assorted figures out of New York society. By the time we arrived McCarthy already had, as they say, a snootful. As I met some of the guests, Glenn was sitting on a couch with the general's wife, a very dignified lady with steel gray hair, a *grande dame* type. And before long Glenn had his arm around her. I thought I was going to faint. I could see the general beginning to boil and I walked over rather briskly, grabbed McCarthy, and said, "Glenn, let's go."

But it was early yet, not even midnight, so we stopped in at the Stork Club. They had the cigarette girls in the little baby doll outfits, and every time one of them went by McCarthy tried to pinch her. Finally, the owner, Sherman Billingsley, came over to me and said, "Gene, this doesn't apply to you. But that other s.o.b. has to leave."

I knew Sherman. He was an Okie, under all of that New York tailoring. And I knew he meant it. He sent over two bouncers and they practically threw Glenn out of there.

But he was undaunted. Our next stop was "21," and I could see it was going to be more of the same. After a while I said, "Glenn, let's go." That phrase seemed to account for a large part of my conversation that night. I finally got him back to the Waldorf and he wanted me to join him for a drink at the bar. I shook my head. "Glenn, I have an appointment at seven and I aim to keep it. I'm going to bed. But don't let me spoil your fun." And I don't believe anyone ever did.

It was after another rodeo night at the Garden that I saw Howard Hughes for the last time. This was in the mid-1950s, and I had stopped off at the Mocambo to meet some friends on the way back to my hotel. I had not been there long when Johnny Meyer, who worked for Hughes in mysterious ways, came over and said, "Howard is in the back room and would like you to join him." I followed Johnny and there was Howard, sitting in the darkest booth in the darkest corner of the room. No lights. Just a candle on the table.

I have no idea what we talked about, if anything. I only know that it was one of those times when Howard wanted, needed, company. He never could sleep at night, I guess. He slept all day and then sat up all night. When he kept a bungalow on the grounds of the Beverly Hills Hotel, I would see him sometimes between midnight and 1 A.M., wandering around like a ghost. He would be dressed like a hippie, except that they were not called hippies in those days. He'd have on old trousers and a T-shirt and sandals and he'd be unshaven and uncombed.

A friend of mine, Jim Granger, once ran RKO for him. The story has been told often that Howard never saw it before the purchase. And that's true. So he decided one night that he should see what he had bought, and Granger drove him out there at two in the morning. No one was around but the security guards. They walked him through every room, every stage, every office, every studio. No one ever saw him out there again, in the daylight.

I read the accounts of how he lived in his last years and how he died, friendless and neglected, one of the wealthiest men in the world dying a pauper's death. I found it hard to believe and unspeakably sad.

We never went into New York, into the Garden, without adding a few new stunts. They were often the work of Johnny Agee, a grizzled part-Indian who had trained horses for Tom Mix. Before that he was the equestrian director for Ringling Brothers Circus. He would stand in the middle of the ring, in white tie and tails, and on cue, he would rear seventy-five horses at one time. He was no longer young by the time he came to work for me, but with horses he was still magic.

Agee had broken two fingers on his right hand that didn't knit properly and would not bend. That was just part of his color. One of our tricks required him to sit at a piano, which Johnny pretended to play. He could not have, even if he knew how and his fingers were not as stiff as popsicle sticks, because the piano was a fake.

But Johnny had trained Champion to jump on top of the piano, which had been specially constructed with an extra heavy base and a thick rubber pad on top, to keep the horse from sliding. It was not a simple trick. Agee would sit at the piano as though he were Artur Rubinstein, the public address announcer would introduce Gene Autry, and I would run Champion into the arena at a full gallop and jump him smack on top of the piano.

We tried it for the first time in Madison Square Garden and it went off perfectly. The crowd actually gasped. Meanwhile, Agee sat there, pretending to play the piano, those two fingers sticking straight out. And under his breath I could hear ol' Johnny muttering to the horse, "Whoa, whoa, gawddam you, whoa." Champion looked at Agee with a look that was absolutely wild.

I no longer remember what year it was that I fell off my horse in the Garden. Possibly, the collectors of Great Moments in Show Business can tell you, but I can't and I refuse to look it up.

But it became an unforgettable night in my career and a number of creative stories have since grown up about it. So I will tell you now exactly how it happened.

I had a saddle that was made of silver and when it caught the light you needed to shade your eyes. It was so slick that if you wore regular cotton gloves you'd slide right off. I rubbed rosin on the gloves to make sure I wouldn't slip.

But this night I planned to introduce a new song, and because I was a little unsure of the lyrics I wrote them in ink in the palm of my glove, and I skipped the rosin. That night, as I rode into the center of the ring, I raised one hand to wave to the crowd and, in an instant of splendid ill timing, I lost my grip and went tumbling to the good earth.

Luckily, the microphone was only a few feet away. I stood up, dusted myself off, and said, "I've *got* to find an easier way to get off that horse."

CHAPTER TEN

Diamonds Are Forever

People invest in sports franchises for complicated reasons. An ego rub, a boyhood dream, a tax shelter. I bought one because Walter O'Malley decided in 1960 to take a summer home in the hills above Lake Arrowhead.

Otherwise, I might not be in baseball today. And there might not exist a team known as the California Angels, who have given me some of the deepest cuts and best times a grown man can have. Going into the 1978 season, I had been pursuing a pennant for seventeen years. Believe me, I rode many a chase scene during my career in films, but none compared to what I have encountered in baseball.

It has always struck me as curious that so big a hunk of a man's life can hang on something as improbable as where Walter O'Malley wanted a house. I would not pass the story on as fact, even now, except that the source of it was O'Malley himself, and only a low and suspicious mind would doubt Walter.

All of this began in 1960 when the Dodgers, wildly successful in the move from Brooklyn to Los Angeles, pulled their games off the radio station I owned, KMPC. We had a fine station, still do, with 50,000 watts. But even so the reception was sometimes weak in the mountains above Los Angeles.

O'Malley complained that he could not bring in a clear signal from his summer place on nights when the Dodgers were on the road. He would spend agonizing moments, he said, fiddling with the dial as the action faded in and out. That was the reason he gave when the broadcasts were moved to KFI, a move that left me less than elated.

We had carried the Dodgers for three years, and the minor
league games long before that. KMPC had built a reputation in
town as a sports station, a reputation I sought. As a fan, I enjoyed
the games myself. I thought they were good for business. At that
point, my interest in baseball was finding a client, not a franchise.

A rumor had been afloat that the American League wanted to
expand to the Los Angeles market. I had paid little attention,
thinking we had a deal to renew our contract with the Dodgers.
Bob Reynolds, my partner, and Stan Spero, who managed
KMPC, had personally negotiated with O'Malley and believed
they had his word.

At that point, his advertising agency called and advised us they
were switching the broadcasts to KFI. I don't know if Walter
made the final decision himself. I hoped not, because his word
meant something to me. But I reckon he was able to bring in the
signal more clearly that summer at Arrowhead. Eventually the
Dodgers, for reasons peculiar to radio, wound up on a station
whose nighttime power was only 1,000 watts. You were lucky to
pick up the games as far south as Santa Anna. Sometimes those
things even up.

I began checking into the rumors around town and learned
that Bill Veeck and Hank Greenberg expected to get the new
American League franchise. Between them they owned a piece
of the Chicago White Sox, but disposing of that interest would
be no problem. We met during one of their trips to the Coast
and agreed that if the deal went through KMPC would carry the
games.

They were the original Odd Couple: Greenberg, tall, sad-
faced, one of the game's legendary home run hitters. He had
married, and later divorced, the Gimbel department store heiress.
Veeck was the showman, a born boat-rocker, with the sly grin of
a man who is about to drop an egg in your pocket. It was Veeck
who once made the old guard cringe by sending up a midget to
pinch hit for the St. Louis Browns in another, wackier era. He
introduced the exploding scoreboard, dressed one of his teams in
short pants, on occasion opened the gates and let the crowd in
free.

Los Angeles would have loved Veeck. But the deal did not go
through. An obstacle developed named Walter Francis O'Malley.

The problem might have been money or it might have been a personality clash, or is that the same thing? O'Malley wanted to be indemnified for allowing the American League to invade his territory. Greenberg and Veeck balked at the price. Feelings hardened. The next I heard, their application had been withdrawn.

Bob Reynolds and I sat down with our staff and talked it over. How could we call KMPC a sports station and play music all summer? I said, "Listen, I think we ought to bid for the franchise ourselves, if only to protect the broadcast rights."

The next step was to telephone Joe Cronin, the president of the American League. And this was where luck and old times and a forgotten gesture played a part. I had known Cronin since his days as the shortstop, and boy manager, of the Washington Senators. He had taken over the team at twenty-seven, and won a pennant, in 1933. Cronin was managing the Boston Red Sox after the war, when I brought the Gene Autry Rodeo into Boston Gardens. The usual mob had formed outside the dressing room door before the Saturday matinee. Pat Buttram and Herb Green were outside killing time when a voice rang out, "Pat, hey, Pat."

Buttram turned around and recognized Cronin standing to one side with three small boys. Joe glanced down at them and said, "Think we could get in to see Gene?"

Pat figured it would be a tossup, whether Cronin's sons would be as excited meeting me as I would seeing Joe. So he sent them backstage with Herb, while he scurried off to find some cowboy hats. We visited in my dressing room and when Pat returned I signed the hatbands and gave one to each of the boys.

Who knows how much a memory is worth? But all these years later I called Cronin and got right to the point. "Joe," I said, "I hear Greenberg and Veeck have pulled out of the running for the expansion team here."

He said I had heard right.

"Well, I'd be interested in taking it, Joe. We have a group of radio stations out here. We've carried the Dodger games on one of them in the past. Do you think there would be any objection if we applied for the franchise?"

"Can't think of any," he said. "But it's a question of time. There is another group involved. We'd need your financial statement and a letter of credit from your bank and we need them by Monday." We were talking on a Friday afternoon.

"How big a letter?" I asked.

"A million and a half."

On that note we hung up the phone and I went to work. By Monday morning the letter of credit was on Cronin's desk in Boston.

I soon learned that the other applicant was a Chicago insurance man named Charles O. Finley, whose name meant nothing to me. A few days later we appeared before the American League owners at their annual winter meeting, in St. Louis, and won unanimous approval as the holder of the new franchise in Los Angeles. I had reason to think that Cronin had been in our corner. Although I had long since forgotten that day at the rodeo, Joe had not. He had described the scene to some of the other owners, how his kids had been taken backstage and gifted with cowboy hats. "Anybody who loves kids that much," said Cronin, "has to be good for baseball." To set the record straight, the hats had been Buttram's idea. But I paid for them.

From the moment our radio deal with O'Malley fell through, until we wrote a check for the franchise, less than three months had passed. Confusion was rampant in baseball that winter, as it frequently is. The American League had expanded into Los Angeles and Washington—the old Senators were now in Minnesota —for the 1961 season. The National League had voted to add Houston and New York but not until 1962.

And before the matter was final, we still needed the approval of O'Malley and the rest of the National League to operate a team in their territory. The vote was taken on the next to last day of the meetings, which happened to be December 7—a date, someone said, that would live in infamy.

Time had moved in a curious circle. Exactly nineteen years before, Donald Barnes, then the owner of the St. Louis Browns, had arrived at the baseball meetings in Chicago toting a briefcase filled with documents. Among them were airline schedules, railroad timetables, a sample baseball season, all intended to support his plan to move the Browns to Los Angeles. Barnes could no longer afford the financial blows he was taking in St. Louis, the last western outpost of big league baseball.

The Chicago meetings were called to order on December 8, 1941, Twenty-four hours earlier, Japanese bombers had hit Pearl Harbor. It was anybody's guess how soon they would be taking aim at our Pacific Coast. Into the ash can, unread, went the papers Barnes had so carefully prepared. California remained virgin land until 1958, when the Dodgers and the Giants crossed the continent.

The news that an American League franchise had been awarded to a group headed by Gene Autry and Bob Reynolds was greeted with some predictable whimsy. It was noted that at least some of the necessary capital had been generated by the talents of my long-time associate, Champion. For the first time in baseball history, wrote the columnist, Red Smith, a franchise "has been awarded to an entire horse."

But we were in and I was elated. We agreed to pay, as a kind of initiation fee, $2,100,000 for twenty-eight players nobody else wanted. We paid another $350,000 to O'Malley for what amounted to grazing rights. I did not consider the price unfair. Walter had to compensate the Pacific Coast League when he brought in the Dodgers, and I felt he was entitled to recover some of his cost. At the same time, he was building a new park in an area known as Chavez Ravine, and as part of the agreement we made a deal to play in the new stadium for three years after it opened. In the meantime, we would occupy Wrigley Field, the old minor League hatbox with a seating capacity of just over twenty thousand.

We had an outdated ball yard, no staff, and the right to pick twenty-eight players at a fee of seventy-five thousand dollars apiece from a list of those the other teams wanted to unload. But I could not have been more confident. Pat Buttram assured me it was the smartest move I ever made. "Hell, Gene," he said, "on the sports page a man can live forever. Look at Dempsey. They still call him 'the Champ.' Look at Joe DiMaggio. He hasn't played in years and he's bigger than ever. But if he was an actor out of work he'd be written off as a has-been. I tell you, on the sports page you never die."

Of course, I did not exactly feel like a stranger to baseball, a johnny-come-lately. I had been a frustrated player most of my life. So this was the grand old cliché, the might-have-been pro who winds up owning a team.

Baseball had been my boyhood passion. In Tioga our team was sponsored by the American Legion, as most of the teams in small towns were. I could make all the plays at shortstop and I could hit, but not with power. At nineteen, I tried out with Tulsa, a farm club of the St. Louis Cardinals. They offered me a contract for a hundred dollars a month, but I was already making a hundred and fifty as a telegrapher. If baseball had paid as well as the railroads then, who knows, I might have a line or two today in the *Encyclopedia of Baseball*.

I never tried out again, but that was a dream that didn't die easily. To play baseball, to reach the big leagues, that was the great national escape of my boyhood, especially for the poor ones looking for a way to get off the farm. Some of them made it and at least two from my neck of the woods made it all the way to the Hall of Fame: Jerome Herman (Dizzy) Dean and John Leonard (Pepper) Martin.

Dizzy was a boyhood friend. He was living near Spaulding, Oklahoma, long before his glory days with the Cardinals, when I went to work there as one of my stops on the Frisco Line. Our hangout was a grocery store across the street from the tracks, owned by an old man who sold Jamaica Ginger, a brand of white lightning whiskey widely known for giving people a condition called jake leg. He sold it in a fruit jar.

Dizzy and I played checkers by the hour with that old man and we could never beat him. He would just dig in and sit there, while his customers huddled around a potbelly stove, chewing tobacco and spitting on the floor. After about three moves he'd have me cornered. Ol' Diz would usually be finished off in two.

Dizzy was pitching for the electric company in San Antonio when the Cardinals signed him. The year he won thirty games for them he was paid seventy-five hundred dollars and for all his greatness and all his color I don't believe he ever really earned any important money until he got out of baseball.

After I broke into the movies and began to make appearances in the East, I caught a big league game whenever I could. I scheduled our World's Championship Rodeo into Madison

Square Garden every October, in the hope one of the New York teams would be in the World Series.

At one time I had stock in the old Hollywood Stars, a few thousand dollars' worth, but I sold out to Bob Cobb, who had the majority interest and owned the Brown Derby. Fred Haney had managed the team during some of those years, and went on to manage Pittsburgh, where he had to start from scratch with a bunch of raw kids like Dick Groat and Bob Skinner, and a few marginal veterans, including a catcher named Joe Garagiola. Later, Fred won pennants with the Milwaukee Braves.

Haney had been out of the game a couple years and was back in Los Angeles in 1961, working on the game of the week telecasts for NBC. We asked him to help us prepare for the expansion draft and to advise us on such items as hiring the people who would run the club. Fred handled the draft so well that on the plane coming back from New York I talked him into taking the job himself. And that was how Fred Haney became the first general manager of the new Los Angeles Angels.

We both knew the man we wanted as our manager. We offered the position to Casey Stengel, then seventy years old, fired by the Yankees in October after winning his tenth pennant in twelve years. But we believed in him and we didn't kid ourselves about needing his style and wit and legend to entertain the fans while we tried to build a respectable club. Haney told me he would follow the same plan as Branch Rickey when he took over the Pirates in the 1950s. A five-year plan. That would require a lot of patience, and suffering, and it would help to have a legend out there in front. It would be like wrapping your team in the American flag.

Casey wanted the job. But he had two problems. One, he had signed a contract for a large sum of money to serialize his story in *The Saturday Evening Post*, and as part of the agreement he had to remain out of baseball for a year. Two, he had become a director and stockholder in a bank in Glendale, and he needed to spend some time with it. He said the bank was doing well and that two sportswriters had even deposited their life savings, over two hundred dollars. That was Casey. He could never give you a plain vanilla answer.

Stengel said his situation would be different in a year, but we needed a manager then, and we hired a fine one, Bill Rigney, whose last job had been with the Giants. A year later, of course, Stengel signed to manage the New York Mets, a marriage made in heaven.

I had already figured out one of the curious truths about this game. No matter how capable or brilliant a manager was, chances were he had been fired by someone else or would be fired sometime soon.

But we didn't go into our first season thinking negative thoughts. In the beginning every day was a new thrill. In fact, after seventeen years, I am still looking for something to top the sweet excitement of opening day, 1961. The Angels were to play their first game on the road at Baltimore, against the team favored to win the American League pennant, the Orioles. They were managed by Paul Richards, a salty, angular Texan I had known for years.

At a party the night before the game, Paul clapped me on the back and said, "Well, cowboy, you're my buddy, but tomorrow the bell rings and I'm going to have to beat your ass."

I raised my glass. "More power to you, Paul," I said. "I imagine you will."

The Orioles started Milt Pappas, the ace of their staff. Our starter was Eli Grba, a former Yankee, the first pitcher we had taken in the expansion draft.

Little Albie Pearson singled to open the game. Eddie Yost walked and big Ted Kluszewski stepped up and hit one out of the park. Then Bob Cerv followed with a homer over the fence in center. After half an inning the Angels led, 4–0.

Two innings later almost the identical thing happened. Pearson singled. Yost was hit by a pitch and Big Klu homered. The Angels went on to win their first game in history by a score of 7–2. We gave away a couple of runs on errors or Grba would have finished with a shutout.

The date was April 11, 1961, and that game remains my biggest thrill in baseball. The newness, the magic of opening day, fearing the worst and getting the best, there are just not many days that golden. It was a little early for the club to peak, drat it, but I guess it will continue to be my happiest hour until the day we finally win a pennant.

Under the circumstances that first year was a fine one. The club collected seventy wins and finished eighth, ahead of our rival expansion team, Washington, and the Kansas City A's, who had a new owner that year, Charley Finley.

In 1962 we moved into Dodger Stadium (as a tenant of O'Malley's), drew over a million fans, and almost caught lightning in a bottle. We stunned just about everybody, including ourselves, by leading the league on the Fourth of July. According to one of baseball's oldest legends, a club in first place when the sun sets on Independence Day goes on to win the championship. It was a bad year for tradition but still a good one for the Angels, who stayed in contention until the middle of September and finished a strong third.

That was also the year of Robert Boris (Bo) Belinsky, left-handed pitcher, bon vivant and unreformed pool hustler. For a team known as the Angels we certainly had our share of players who were not, and I would have to say that Bo headed the list.

To begin with, he strolled into camp a week late that spring, a rookie with no reputation, except as a New Jersey truant, held a poolside press conference at the team's motel, and demanded a pay raise. Instantly, the press fell in love with him. So did the ladies. Bo just reeked of color and macho.

What happened next was not to be believed. Belinksy won six games in a row, including a no-hitter against the Orioles, the team that had originally signed him. In short order he became a favorite of Walter Winchell and the Hollywood crowd. He bought a Cadillac on the installment plan. He dated the likes of Ann-Margret and Tina Louise, was engaged briefly to Mamie Van Doren, and only our accountants know how many times he was fined for missing curfew. Once Bo was arrested for throwing a girl out of his car at five in the morning.

Belinsky's running mate was a young right-hander named Dean Chance, an Ohio farm boy who became one of the league's best pitchers. He had a fine career with us, but Bo and Dean made a devastating pair. One night during a road trip the team was rousted out of a Boston hotel at 3 A.M. when fire broke out on an upper floor and smoke filled the lobby. The players were milling around on the sidewalk outside the hotel, some of them in their pajamas and bathrobes, when a taxi slid up to the curb, almost directly in front of Bill Rigney. Without a care in the world, out stepped Belinsky and Chance.

I guess all of us connected with the club had the feeling that Bo misspent his talent and wasted his career. Bo never saw it quite that way. He always argued that he got more publicity out of less performance than anyone who ever played the game. He may have been right.

My own position with the players was as clear as I could make it. I liked them, admired their talents, enjoyed our occasional visits. But I paid their salaries, I didn't take them to raise. I was not a father figure. Around the front office, Belinsky was known as a special project. Fred Haney talked to him like a father, trying to convince Bo that he should settle down, get married, and dedicate himself to "the game." That is, baseball. At the least, Fred urged him, he should date a class of ladies not quite so exotic.

One winter Bo was trapped in New Jersey by the worst blizzard in years. He told the columnist Mel Durslag he received dozens of letters from young women in Los Angeles, offering him a place to stay if he wished to get away from the snow. Bo said he started to bundle up the mail and ship it to Haney, "so he could see what nice girls I ran around with."

Like many other night walkers, the ones who think the good times will always roll on, the ones who just can't resist the bright lights and whatever lurks around the next corner, Bo drifted out of the big leagues and out of the news. In a way it was sad. One night he took a punch at a sixty-year-old sportswriter, and that finished him with our club. He failed with the Phillies, with Houston and the White Sox, and he did a couple of turns with Hawaii in the minors.

I kept up with Bo's adventures after he left us. One spring we read that he had fallen in love with a former playmate of the year, a Miss September, and jumped the team in Houston "to be with the woman I love." Bo thought he was the Duke of Windsor. The Houston club suspended him. As they say in the song, the days grow short when you reach September. They were married, Bo and his playmate, but the marriage didn't last and his career continued to go downhill.

Then one day in the winter of 1975, five years after he had last pitched in the majors, Bo surfaced again. He had remarried, this time to an heiress, a daughter of the Weyerhaeuser family. Naturally, theirs was no ordinary story. He had saved her life on the beach at Waikiki during a surfing accident. In time he became the father of twin girls and declared himself a new man. I hoped it would work out. Bo was an appealing rogue and it is good to see the wastrels of the world win one now and then.

On the field the Angels were drifting. We finished ninth in 1963, then bounced back to fifth the next year. Dean Chance came into his own, winning twenty games, with eleven shutouts, five of them by a score of 1–0. At the age of twenty-three he became the youngest pitcher ever to win the Cy Young Award.

That year we paid a bonus of over $200,000 to a young Samson from the University of Wisconsin, an outfielder named Rick Reichardt (whose great promise would be cut short by an injury). We also signed a thirty-five-year lease to play in a new stadium to be built by the city of Anaheim. I was soon to find that you can't buy a pennant, but a new stadium can make the fans more comfortable while you try.

Anaheim was a fresh and delightful place, in the heart of the exploding Orange County. The city was famous as the home of Disneyland, and before that as part of a classic Jack Benny gag that ended with the line, "Anaheim, Azuza, and Cucamonga." I hoped we could add a new distinction, a winning baseball team.

I had long since concluded that we had no future in Dodger Stadium. The Royal Blue dominated the city, rightfully so, with its color and heritage. Our own crowds began to shrink. We had endlessly petty arguments with our landlord. At one point O'Malley was charging us for half the water and half the toilet paper, even though we had drawn only one fourth the attendance.

In 1966 we moved into our handsome new home, featuring an unusual, million-dollar, A-frame scoreboard, which gave the stadium its nickname, "The Big A." We drew nearly a million and a half fans and finished two games under .500.

By 1969 we were still struggling to finish in the first division, and I had to learn first hand about the most unpleasant side of the game—the firing of people you had come to like and admire. Fred Haney had retired and our new general manager was Dick

Walsh, one of the bright young men in O'Malley's office when the Dodgers moved West. In May the Angels had lost ten in a row. I was in New York on business when Walsh called and said he felt we had to make a managing change.

"Rig has lost control of the team," he told me. "I don't feel we can win. I don't think we can turn it around with him in there."

I swallowed hard at those words. Rigney was the only manager the Angels had ever known. "Well, Bill is a friend of mine," I said. "But if a change has to be made then let's do it now. I don't think it helps to wait on these things. Who do you have in mind?"

Dick's man was Lefty Phillips, who had joined our staff as a coach that spring and had learned his trade under Walter Alston, in the Dodger system. "Now, he's not colorful," said Walsh. "He's probably the least colorful guy we could get in here. But he knows baseball. He's strong on fundamentals and he'll build a solid team. I think he's our man."

I was in favor of promoting someone from our farm system. The fellow I had in mind was Chuck Tanner, then managing our minor league club in Hawaii. Walsh and I batted it back and forth for a few minutes. "Most of the kids on the team now came up under Chuck," I said. "He has been with us nearly ten years. He knows this pitching staff—Dean Chance, Andy Messersmith, all of 'em."

Dick said, "Gene, remember when Alston was out a couple years ago after a kidney operation? Lefty managed the club for six weeks and did a great job. I think that showed how much confidence Walter had in him."

I gave in. "Dick," I said, "I'm not going against my general manager. If you think Lefty is the right choice, go ahead."

Probably this is the place to make a point about being a club owner. There are three kinds. One type not only puts up the money, he wants to run the club himself, get involved in trades, and move the pieces around, which is where most baseball people think the fun is. This owner, in a sense, acts as his own general manager. A second type hires a professional to run the club, then stays out of his way and keeps score. Then there is the owner who keeps such a low profile, the players and the public are not sure he exists.

I like to think I belong to the second category. I have tried hard not to interfere with the men on the firing line. I am consulted on major decisions and the final approval is mine, but I don't recall ever overruling someone who felt strongly his way was right. I have made an effort to know the players. I drop by the clubhouse from time to time. I have written personal notes to each player who is traded away after long service to the Angels. But I have no urge to go on the field and shag flies with them. Nor do I call my manager at four in the morning to ask why he didn't play the infield back with two out.

Lefty Phillips was a fine man, with a record as a good coach and a shrewd scout. But as a manager he was a disaster, one of a series of mistakes that dug us a little deeper into the trench. To put it kindly, Lefty had a communications problem.

Of course, the Alex Johnson affair wasn't his fault. Alex was another of our mystery cases, an immensely talented player, a .300 hitter with great speed, which he used some of the time. Alex believed in conserving his energy. One of the ways he did this was by not running out ground balls tapped to the infield. I tell you, it was maddening. I once saw Alex thrown out at first base on a single to right field. He was a strange package. Off the field he was polite, honest, and bright. But once he put on the uniform his personality changed. He became moody and suspicious and talked only to himself. The players say he would stand behind the batting cage and just babble. He must have had some interesting conversations.

Johnson was not very popular with his teammates. He once accused Chico Ruiz, a utility infielder, of pulling a gun on him in the locker room. At the time, Ruiz may have been his best friend on the club. I am not sure that it was ever clearly established that Chico had a gun, but Alex thought he did. Possibly the boys were influenced by some of my earlier films.

The effect of a problem player on your team can be destructive. A Jim Fregosi, say, would go barreling into second base, trying to break up a double play. Then he would glance behind him and see the hitter, Johnson, jogging down the line, not even trying to get on base.

A manager must, but no owner can afford to get too involved with the players. For one thing, it undercuts the people who have to discipline them. For another, it will bring you headaches beyond relief.

I grew very fond of Jimmy Fregosi. He had talent and looks and leadership, and he was the first young one we signed to blossom into a star. He became an all-star shortstop and the symbol of the better years we knew were ahead. I also thought he had the brains and toughness to be a manager. But the day arrived when Fregosi had slowed up, lost a little range, had a personal problem, and became expendable. It was hard for me to okay the trade that sent Jimmy to the New York Mets, but in return we got Nolan Ryan and it was a great trade for us. Sentiment doesn't win many games.

Another thing I had to learn was that the owner who wants to play Dear Abby can forget about his other businesses. I had one player come to me who had gotten a girl in trouble. I sent him to a priest. Then there are always those who come around wanting advances, or loans, against their salary. The most persistent of these was Leon Wagner, known as Daddy Wags. He was another colorful fellow with the prominent cheekbones of an Indian warrior, a spectacular dresser and a big spender.

Wags went broke in the liquor business and again in the clothing business. He was very generous about giving credit to people who could not be reached by phone and left no forwarding address. I tried to give him advice about investing his money, and keeping a budget, but I don't know that it ever helped.

As a class, athletes are the only people I know who get themselves into stranger situations than people in show business. Once, when the team was in New York to play the Yankees, the police showed up an hour before game time and arrested Vic Power, our first baseman. He was hauled off to jail on a warrant signed by one of his ex-wives, who was suing for back alimony. I sent our traveling secretary down to get him out. Vic owed around fifteen hundred dollars and the club paid it off. The next day, darned if the same thing didn't happen. Another warrant was served, on behalf of another wife, and again we had to spring him from jail.

Not long after that, Fred Haney had a fit when he learned that Power had charged a set of new tires to the ball club. Fred refused to pay the bill, on the ground that Vic had no right to charge the Angels for items involving his personal automobile. Vic wouldn't pay, either. When the creditors called he refused to answer his phone, their letters were ignored, and when the bill collectors came around he ducked them. Then one night the store sent some investigators out to the ball park. They found where he parked his car and during the game they jacked it up, took off the tires, and left. When Vic got out of the clubhouse that night there was his car, sitting on the rims. For all I know, that was the way he drove it home.

Now, these stories are recalled here not to embarrass anyone, but to point up a side of the game the fans rarely see or think about. It is a big, unwieldy family and behind the box score—behind the runs and hits and errors—are all these distractions and clashes and problems, some minor and some not, that make up the long season. It looks so simple on the field, all that green geometry, and yet within even the smoothest of organizations there are enough disturbances to make an Italian opera company seem calm.

When you get down to the bottom line, the difference between a winning and losing manager is how he handles the talent he has. Sure, he has to have the players. But I agree with Billy Martin, who said that the key to managing was "keeping the five who hate you away from the five who are undecided." Most clubs work that way. And if an owner hangs around the players and listens to their complaints, he will never have confidence in his manager.

The Angels had suffered through three more losing seasons when Del Rice—the first player the team had ever signed—was hired as the club's new manager in 1972. I remembered clearly the morning Del signed with us as a player, back in 1961. We had breakfast together, with Red Schoendienst, the morning after Bob Reynolds and I had been awarded the franchise. Schoendienst had been released by the Braves and I wanted him to sign with us. But he had promised to talk with the Cardinals, with whom he had spent most of his career, before making any final decision. Bing Devine offered Red a job as a player-coach and he grabbed it. He wound up playing quite a bit at second base that year and eventually became their manager.

Del Rice also had a long history with the Cardinals, and had caught some of their great pitchers, Howie Pollet and Harry Brecheen and Murry Dickson. Rice gave us a couple of good years behind the plate, then managed for us in the minors and won a pennant for our farm club at Salt Lake City. He had earned the top job when he took over in 1972.

One of Del's first moves was to hire as a coach Bobby Winkles, who had compiled a brilliant reputation as a college coach at Arizona State, where he developed Sal Bando and Rick Monday and Reggie Jackson.

It was to be another uneven year for us. We finished next to last in our division, drew under 800,000 fans, and yet produced the most exciting pitcher in baseball in Nolan Ryan, who led the league in strikeouts. At times Ryan was just overpowering, once, against Boston, fanning the side on nine pitches. Ryan, a handsome, modest type from Alvin, Texas, was our consolation. Harry Dalton had taken over as the new general manager, landing Ryan in the deal that sent away one of my favorites, Jim Fregosi, the last of the original Angels.

At the end of the season we changed field bosses, again. It hadn't worked out with Del Rice, who would have been an ulcer case, or worse, if he had stayed on. At that point I made an effort to hire Dick Williams, who had just won the World Series for Finley in Oakland. I had Charley O.'s permission to talk with him, but Dick had a year to go on his contract. He was still enjoying the World Series glow, and didn't want to make a move.

So Bobby Winkles stepped up as manager. Harry Dalton and I both felt it was a gamble, an experiment, to give the job to a man one year removed from a college campus. But we felt his success with young players, his ability to teach, might put a new spark in the club. We were not bothered by the fact that he had no professional experience as a player. Joe McCarthy had never played in the majors and yet he became a legend with the Cubs and the Yankees. Walter Alston's big league career consisted of one time at bat. So we thought Bobby could do it.

And I still believe he might have, except that he ran into one of those no-win situations. His job was complicated by the presence of Frank Robinson, a great player in both leagues for more than fifteen years, whose ambition was to become a manager, a position no black had yet held. He realized his goal, in name as well as fact, in 1975 at Cleveland. Some thought he was running the Angels. Our younger players had a tendency to go to Frank instead of Winkles. The friction grew as the team fell into a long losing streak. Both men denied any ill feelings at the time, but I knew the tension was there.

By the middle of the 1974 season we were shopping for another manager, our fourth in five years. This time I went to Dalton and said, "I think we need the best man we can find. A proven winner. I think we ought to go after Dick Williams." His quarrels with Finley were already well documented. Dick had quit the day after leading Oakland to a second World Championship, confirming rumors that he would become the manager of the New York Yankees. But not if Finley could stop him, which he did, by taking the case to court, insisting the Yankees had never gotten his permission to negotiate with Williams. Finley wanted to be compensated, in players or cash or both, for letting his manager go. When the Yankees wouldn't or couldn't meet his price, all bets were off. New York hired Bill Virdon. Finley hired Alvin Dark. And Williams went to work for a builder in Florida, where he was sitting out the season when I placed a call to Finley in June.

I liked, even admired, Charley. I do not often agree with him but that doesn't exactly make me a rare case. Charley loves to fight—with his players, his managers, the other owners and, especially, Bowie Kuhn. I refused when Finley wanted my vote to help him dump Kuhn as commissioner.

With Finley the direct approach worked best. On that day in 1974 I told him I would like to work out a deal for Dick Williams, whose salary was still being paid by the A's. In effect, Charley was paying him not to manage the Yankees. At 6 P.M. the next day Bob Reynolds and I met Finley in a hotel in Oakland. We were with him until midnight. The hour is easy to remember because that was when the bar closed.

As we left, Finley said, "Look, when I wanted to move my team from Kansas City to Oakland you supported me. You stood up for me. What the hell. If I wanted to be difficult, I could say I had to have Nolan Ryan in return. But you couldn't afford that any more than I could afford to give up Catfish. (The reference was to Catfish Hunter, an ironic reference in view of developments soon to come.) If you want Dick, go ahead and call him."

I paid Finley $50,000 for the right to sign Williams, and he swore me to secrecy about the payment. In due time Finley told the press himself. You can't put a price on the entertainment value of doing business with Charley.

So on the first day of July, Dick Williams took over as manager of the Angels. We went on to finish last in our division, but drew nearly a million fans as Nolan Ryan helped keep the interest alive. He struck out a record 367 batters, 19 of them in one game against Boston.

As lonely as it was in the cellar, and as badly as we needed help, I hated to see Jim (Catfish) Hunter declared a free agent after the 1974 season. I won't attempt to go into the legal points, except to say that at issue was a clause in Hunter's contract with Oakland that Finley, for reasons of his own, had failed to fulfill.

The day after the ruling was announced I telephoned the owner of the A's and told him, "Charley, I disagree with the decision of the arbitration board. But since he is a free agent, and knowing that everyone is going to bid for him, I owe it to our fans to make a pitch for Hunter."

Finley said, "If you don't you'd be foolish, Gene. In fact, if we can't keep him I hope you do get him."

Here was one of the great pitchers in baseball, an established twenty-game winner, one of those rare fellows you could count on to give you a good game every time he went out. So the Angels got in line with all the other clubs and made an appointment to visit him at his home in North Carolina. We went down there —Williams, Dalton, and myself—and talked to Catfish and his attorney, a Mr. Cherry, for an hour and a half. His attorney assured us that the main thing Cat wanted was security.

"I'll tell you this," the attorney added, "it's going to take at least two and a half million dollars, tax free, to make him feel secure."

I said, "Well, to start with, the two and a half million, that scares me right there. And, secondly, I don't know of any tax-free deals. If I did I'd take 'em for myself. But somebody has to pay the tax, even if it's a gift. Hell, even if you win a bicycle on a TV show it's taxable."

By the end of the interview we had made an offer, one million dollars over five years, half of it deferred, but no tax gimmicks. I concluded by saying, "This is to take nothing away from Cat, I think he's a great pitcher, but he can't throw the ball and catch it, too. There have to be eight other guys out there who want a little security as well. He mentioned that he wanted some for himself, but what about the others who help him win his games? In the long run, it can only cause dissension if one salary is out of proportion to the others."

In a polite way, his attorney told me that was my problem, and I left there convinced our offer wasn't going to be in the running. It wasn't, and I didn't feel too badly about it, either.

Each year a little more of the fun seems to go out of baseball— out of all sports, really. If the unions and agents that represent the players don't begin to look realistically at the salaries, and at the costs of operating a team, they are going to be the ruination of a sport whose charm once was that it made us forget the bad news on Page 1. Teams can't continually lose money and stay in business. Of course, no one puts a gun to his head and forces an owner to pay the kind of salaries you might expect to be paid to the person who discovers a cure for cancer. But it doesn't take a gun. Two other factors are at work: the need to compete and human nature. It only takes one man who landscapes his yard to bring grief to every other husband in the neighborhood.

Having put myself for years on the side of sanity and common sense and no free lunch, the fact is that at the end of the 1976 season the California Angels gave contracts worth $5,000,000— according to the press—to sign three free agents, Joe Rudi, Don Baylor, and Bobby Grich. In 1960, I could not help but reflect, we had paid less than half that amount to acquire twenty-eight players.

I had long contended that winning teams had to be grown. You could not buy them. But now I felt compelled to try. My attitude had not changed since the Catfish Hunter auction, but the system had. As a result of a series of court decisions, we had moved into a nearly open marketplace. While the players are clearly elated, deliriously so, I believe the changes are not healthy for baseball and I am not happy about them. But these are the new facts of life and we have to adjust. We have a commitment to our fans, to our sponsors, and to the players who went through lean years with us. We had to improve the club.

I have never believed in washing your linen in public. But a few figures will show the trend in baseball today. The Angels had never had a player with a $100,000 contract until Frank Robinson in 1973. Now we have seven and, in 1978, our average salary, including utility men and rookies, was about $75,000.

Gone forever, I fear, is the sense of family that many teams once felt. Some critics say that attitude was paternalistic and demeaning. I never thought so.

I was infuriated once when one of our radio announcers commented on the air, after a young infielder hit his first big league homer, "That's probably the only one he'll ever hit." I let the broadcaster know that I felt the remark was disparaging and unnecessary.

I receive a lot of mail when things go wrong, as they have so often, and I try to answer as much as I can. In 1975, Dick Williams criticized an umpire named Rodriguez after a series in which several calls went against us. A number of the letters were from Latins and it was clear that they felt Williams' remarks had ethnic overtones. I wrote back that Dick's only prejudice was against bad umpiring. And for their information, our catcher thought the calls were bad, too, and his name is Rodriguez.

Arguing, comparing, second guessing, these are the joys of baseball. I can understand Charley Finley's antics, his feuds, his lawsuits and countersuits. You own the team but at heart you are a kind of superfan. I can sympathize with Ray Kroc, after he bought the San Diego Padres. They had only played a few games when Kroc took over the public address system to apologize to the crowd for his team's "stupid play." I can't picture myself on the PA mike, unless it would be to sing "That Silver-haired Daddy of Mine." But it grinds my insides to see us give a game away, to lose on a dumb play.

The vitality of the sport, and the fans, in the face of all the ways you can go wrong, is truly remarkable. The Angels observed the Bicentennial as we had so many recent seasons, by changing managers. Dick Williams bled to win, but he had been around World Series teams and he lost his patience with a roster loaded with young players. Norm Sherry, who had coached for us, finished the season as manager and was rehired for 1977. At midseason, with the club in a losing streak, Sherry was replaced by Dave Garcia.

For sure, baseball has been the most exciting and frustrating experience of my life. In the movies I never lost a fight. In baseball I have hardly ever won one. But I haven't given up. At heart I'm an optimist. No man would survive long in baseball if he wasn't.

CHAPTER ELEVEN

The Corporate Cowboy

It has always amused me when people seem surprised by my success in business. Actually, working with numbers was what I did best. What I did less well was sing, act, and play the guitar.

I can't honestly tell you what my net worth is today, although I have read stories estimating the value of companies I control at around seventy million dollars. Of course, that figure refers to property and other assets. No one has that kind of cash. The funny thing is, at no time in my life have I ever thought of myself as being rich. I sort of think of myself as independently poor.

But whatever I own, whatever I have accomplished, didn't happen by chance. Even as a boy I planned ahead. When I was a baggage smasher at fifteen for the Frisco Railroad, and later a telegrapher, I still took correspondence courses and became an accountant. This training proved useful when I started out in show business and had to check the box office myself, during the years when I had no manager.

As an actor turned businessman, I suppose my record goes against the trend. Most entertainers are thought to be about as shrewd as prize fighters. Those who became wealthy did so, usually, through high earnings or investments. Twenty years ago I put together my own company and shaped its growth. Today Golden West Broadcasters owns four radio stations, a Los Angeles television channel (KTLA), a ten-acre movie and TV production center, a national agency for selling radio time, and the California Angels baseball club.

Privately, I own a resort hotel in Palm Springs, a television and two radio stations in Arizona (in partnership with an old friend,

Tom Chauncey), and a twenty-thousand-acre cattle ranch in Winslow, Arizona. If there is a business category for fun and sentiment, I can include a collection of vintage automobiles and locomotives, recording and music publishing companies, and the one-hundred-acre Melody Ranch, on the very land where I made my first starring movies forty years ago. Until 1974 I owned ranches in Oklahoma and Colorado that raised stock for rodeos and were a source of unending pleasure to me. We sent scouts to small towns to find cattle the way you would scout baseball players. Sometimes I joined them, sitting directly over the pens, joking with the cowboys. Not many businessmen can ever beg off from an engagement, explaining they have to go scout a bull.

None of this is intended to be an inventory of my holdings. Nor do I mean to sound boastful. By design or not, there has always been a kind of linkage in my life. The money I earned from movies and records enabled me to buy my first radio stations. It was through radio that I got into baseball, and through baseball that I bought into hotels. What I found invaluable in all this is a sense of when and how to move on.

I was reminded once by Johnny Bond, who toured and worked with us on radio, of a tradition of the Old West. Whenever a lone cowboy or Indian needed to take a long journey by horseback, it was customary for him to ride one saddled horse while leading another bareback. When his mount began to tire, instead of stopping for a rest, he merely slipped the saddle onto the spare horse and rode on. In just about that way I eased out of my life as a performer and began to devote my full energy to business. I just changed horses.

I had discovered during the war how quickly your security can be threatened by conditions beyond your control. It was a jolt to the nervous system to find myself staring at an Air Force salary of less than two thousand dollars a *year*, after earning up to ten thousand dollars a *week*. I thought to myself, well, as long as I can work I know I can make money. But what if something happened to my health? Or my voice went haywire. Times change, too. If you don't part your hair right, they, the public, will find someone who does. I knew the time had come to start looking for an interest that did not depend on my being able to perform.

Over the years I probably earned five million dollars as an entertainer. The key to that success, and much of what followed, was my willingness to seek a percentage of the gross rather than a flat fee. I was among the first entertainers to do so. Wherever we appeared, I offered to work for a percentage. It was a gamble but a fair one. If my show brought in the crowds, we'd all make money. If the promoter took a loss, so did we.

I quickly established the other principles that were to guide me: Hire the best people you can find, give them trust and loyalty and pay them top money. If they do the job, that money will always come back to you. In any transaction the best deal is the one fair to both sides. You should leave a little ham on the bone.

My plunge into the world of commerce began near the end of the war, with the purchase of a radio station, KPHO, in Phoenix, while I was still on duty at Luke Field. When I was transferred to Detroit, my partner, Tom Chauncey, ran the station.

After the war ended we applied for a new radio station in Tucson and for a television franchise in Phoenix, which became KOOL. Another group applied and the FCC announced it would hold hearings to determine who would get the license. At the rate such decisions were then made, it was obvious that no one would be able to operate on that channel for years. So Tom and I went to our competitors and convinced them to join us in applying for a shared-time channel. Each group would have its own call letters and operate the station on certain hours of the day. The plan was approved. Although it had been done in radio, this was the first time the FCC had issued a shared-time license on television.

Those were the baby years of television and a lot of investors were losing their undergarments. If anything, you could lose it faster on a shared-time station, because your programs would just get rolling and then the other staff would take over. But I believed in the future of the new medium. I was considered the first of the so-called major Hollywood figures to make films especially for TV.

In Phoenix, the other owners could not stand the drain. They offered us their half of the station if we would repay the money they had lost. Tom Chauncey and I dug up the cash and bought them out. We continued to stand the losses, which were substantial, up to thirty-five thousand dollars a month. We were in hock to the bank. The profits from our radio stations didn't begin to cover the operating losses for television.

But the investment turned out to be a good one.

In the early years we financed our business growth out of bank loans and my earnings from pictures and records. I am proud of the fact that we built Golden West without public money. Even during the go-go years of the mid-1960s, when broadcasting stocks were hot, I resisted the pressure to put our shares on the market. To do so, I felt, would have meant sacrificing a certain independence and ability to make decisions. I valued that independence more than the money we might have made by going public.

Golden West was formed in 1952 with KMPC, in Los Angeles, as our flagship. In the end every business deal boils down to people and timing (if you exclude the most obvious factor, money). And KMPC was a textbook case.

George A. Richards, who owned KMPC as well as radio stations in Detroit and Cleveland, had died and his family needed to raise cash to pay the estate taxes. They decided that KMPC would have to be sold. The general manager of the station, and a minority stockholder, was Bob Reynolds, who had ideas about buying it but needed backing. As luck would have it, we were represented by the same law firm, Dow, Lohnes, and Albertson. One of the partners, Horace Lohnes, got us together.

We had known each other back in Oklahoma, where Bob's father was a driller in the oil fields. Bob had worked in the same fields in the summer, as a roughneck and tool dresser, making himself tough and mean for football. A strapping fellow, six-foot-four, with the look of cast iron, Bob went on to become an All-America tackle at Stanford. He was the only man ever to play three sixty-minute games in the Rose Bowl.

When Reynolds broke into pro football with the Detroit Lions, the owner was George A. (Dick) Richards. The years passed and Bob decided to retire. Richards persuaded him to play one more season by offering him a job as a salesman with KMPC in the off season. He worked his way up through the ranks from there. Bob had a lot going for him. He was smart, popular, modest. He liked people but was never pushy. He had a stature that made him hard to miss in a crowd.

The lawyers worked out a deal where I would own 56 per cent of the station and Bob 30 per cent, with the other shares made available to key employees. Reynolds became president of Golden West and I was chairman of the board. We were a good team. Our talents, our experiences, complemented each other. And our friendship was genuine and exists to this day, though the partnership does not.

KMPC was purchased for $800,000. We organized Golden West with paid in capital stock of $300,000, which was the down payment on the purchase price. No other cash was ever put into the corporation by the shareholders. We paid off the purchase price out of the cash flow. Quickly, we added stations in San Francisco, Seattle, and Portland. While the other two cost around a million dollars each, we paid a little less for KVI in Seattle. The station carried mostly religious music and gospel hours and was losing money. After we took over we canceled every contract and reopened with all new programming.

The stations have all been profitable and, I am proud to say, operated in the public interest.

Our efforts to increase Golden West's holdings led to my taking frequent trips to Washington. When you are involved with the public air waves you must deal with the government, and if you are not careful you may find yourself brushing history.

On one such trip, during the 1960 presidential campaign, I received a telephone call from Frank Stanton, the president of CBS-TV. He had learned that I had an appointment with Sam Rayburn, of Texas, the speaker of the House. A bill had been introduced in Congress to amend the Communications Act of 1934, in an effort to relax the equal time law and make possible a debate between the two major candidates, Richard Nixon and John Kennedy.

The bill had hit a dead end in committee hearings and there appeared to be little hope of getting it passed. Stanton asked me if I would urge Sam Rayburn to do what he could to break the legislation loose. I said I would try.

I have always found politics intruding on my life in curious ways. When I graduated from high school in Tioga, Texas, Sam

Rayburn was the principal speaker. Years later, Mr. Sam asked me to get a band and help campaign for a young protégé of his who was running for Congress. His name was Lyndon Johnson. Texas politicians had taken notice when Pappy Lee O'Daniel stumped the state with a hillbilly band and got himself elected governor in the early 1940s. So I hired a group out of Dallas, the Cass County Boys, and appeared on behalf of Lyndon Johnson during his first successful run for Congress.

Mr. Sam questioned me hard about the amendment, asking whether I really believed it was in the interest of the public, or just a gimmick for the benefit of the networks. I told him I thought it was very much in the national interest.

The speaker did break loose the bill, it was passed, the debates were held, and—many people believe—helped win the election for Kennedy. A few days after the first debate I received a letter from Sam Rayburn, dated October 4, 1960. At one point he wrote:

"I have just received from Frank Stanton a transcript of the debate between Kennedy and Nixon, and I am writing him and saying to him that there have been a lot of things said on radio and television, and in the papers, about who did what to Nixon to make him look like he did. I think he just looked like Nixon."

By 1964 I had withdrawn from show business, had made my last film and my last record. I suppose I could have dragged out my career a little longer. But as a boy growing up in the Southwest I had been taught not to stay in someone's parlor until they started to yawn.

However, the years of overlapping work had taken a toll. I was grinding out movies and records and TV shows, my own and those of other people. I was still traveling with the rodeo and making personal appearances. I had merchandising contracts to fulfill, the ranches to check on, and an expanding company to run.

A Western movie critic once wrote of me, "Autry's role as an investor has permitted him to consume alcohol at a fantastic rate and never have it negatively influence the companies he financed." I guess that is what you might call a left-handed compliment.

During the peak years of my business success, I had an on and off again battle with what is known in polite circles as a "drinking problem." Did I win? I don't think anyone ever really wins against that kind of habit. All you try to do is hold down the score. I mention this now not to be dramatic or to join the trend toward public confession. I simply want to clear the record because when you do not the rumors nearly always outdistance the truth.

I have no exotic theories to offer about why people drink or why they quit. But it has been my impression that two kinds of abnormal life often lead you down that path. People drink from boredom, not having enough to do, and they drink from having too much to do, overworking and bending under the pressure, often self-imposed.

I drank lightly, if at all, until I went into the Air Force. During a war time is the enemy, too. When you were not flying there was little to do except hang around the non-com clubs and the officers' clubs, play poker, unwind, and raise your glass. The social and military pressures were often at work.

After I left the service I had a chance to cut down, but without realizing it I had grown dependent on liquor to relax. Drinking was a way to celebrate the end of a day or a deal. My schedule was horrendous. I was always on the go, fighting another deadline, racing to a studio or a business meeting, skipping meals. The more tired one gets the easier it is to look for energy in a bottle. You just keep refueling.

It is a hard habit to resist and, after a while, you really don't want to resist. For one thing, drinking is considered a kind of American sport, red-blooded, even romantic, unlike taking drugs, which is sinister and unclean and sneaky. We have produced great and legendary drinkers in this country and tell their stories proudly: Ulysses S. Grant, Sam Houston, Barrymore, Bogart, and Joe E. Lewis. Guys have contests at bars.

Drinking was, and is, part of the Air Force mystique. Pilots cultivated that image. They would get rip-roaring drunk at night, then burn the alcohol out of their systems the next morning by sucking up pure oxygen. But I never knew anyone to hit the bottle during a flight. That was a great way to get yourself killed.

In the same spirit, there was a camaraderie among actors in the 1940s and 1950s that lent itself to long nights and wasted corks.

Drinking and fighting seemed to go together. Parties occasionally ended with people breaking up the furniture. Fellows like Bruce Cabot, Errol Flynn, Bogie, even old Hoot Gibson, were frequently barred from one club or another. I was present at a few of those brawls, usually trying to keep the peace or hoping that no one would fall down in my soup.

The best remedy for a drinking problem is a loving and understanding wife, and the loyalty and patience of those around you. Some of my friends had experienced the same problem. I once went to a meeting of Alcoholics Anonymous with Pat Buttram's wife, Sheila Ryan, to see what it was all about. I listened as the people got up and gave their testimony. I didn't join, but I admire the work the program does. I read a story once in *Reader's Digest* about a woman whose drinking reached a point where it frightened her. She piled her two kids in a car and drove two hundred miles to attend a meeting of A.A. I ordered a bunch of reprints of the story and passed them out to my friends.

One day, a few years ago, my doctor said to me, "Gene, I'll tell you flatly, you are drinking too much. And I don't have a thing in my medicine chest that will help you. This is something you're going to have to solve yourself. You are going to need will power. And a little prayer now and then won't hurt you either."

I asked the doctor what was the best way to quit. He said different people seek different cures. Some join A.A. Others check into hospitals or clinics. Still others withdraw from their friends and society. No ways are easy. He suggested that I just "sweat it out" for four or five days, and then avoid those situations where heavy drinking would take place.

And that, basically, is what I did. I reached a point where I felt I could have one drink and walk away from the bar. Some nights I didn't walk away and wished I had.

This is not an easy subject for me to confront. I respect those who have, such as Dick Van Dyke and Dana Andrews, the astronaut Buzz Aldrin, and many others in the public eye. I cannot speak for anyone else and what that person may have experienced. But I know you can be damaged by too much booze, without the problem ever reaching the proportions of Ray

Milland in *Lost Weekend*, with bottles hidden in the light fixtures.

It isn't necessary to turn mean, or unruly, or to jump in the nearest pond with a go-go dancer to show help is needed. One of the clues is when you wake up in the morning with a hangover and want a drink to get rid of it. As they say, the hair of the dog that bit you.

For a public figure there are other risks. A famous actor is observed having one drink. Within an hour someone will claim to have seen him out cold with his head in a spittoon. In my case, the stories are sometimes more cruel, and had a higher potential for harm, because of my screen image and the youthful character of my audiences.

Drinking impairs your judgment and eventually your health. I appeared on stage, a very few times, when I was less than cold sober. Socially, I said or did things that embarrassed me later. But I learned. I can't do much now about the rumors and exaggerations. I believe my success in business answers the worst of them.

I try not to offer advice or sermons or pop psychology. But no one can live in a bottle and build, or maintain, a multi-million-dollar enterprise. I hope others will be encouraged to recognize that they have a problem, deal with it, and know they still can be productive. If I had consumed the quantity of liquor some people seem to think I have, my liver would be in a jar at the Harvard Medical School.

Of course, the best way to silence a detractor anytime is to prosper. That always confounds them. There is a satisfaction that comes from success in business that is less personal, but also less selfish, than success in show business or sports. It is a special feeling to be able to look around and calculate the number of jobs you have helped create—at last count, in this case, more than twelve hundred.

Half of these are employed at Golden West, which made its biggest move in 1964, paying twelve million dollars to buy KTLA, Channel 5, from Paramount Pictures. Three years later we paid an additional six million dollars to acquire the land we had been leasing, ten acres that had served as Paramount's production facility, including the KTLA studios.

The property had once been the home of Warner Brothers, the parcel bought in 1918 from a family named Beesemyer for twenty-five thousand dollars. They bought it on the installment plan, nothing down and a thousand dollars a month. The land was ideally located, on Sunset Boulevard, between Van Ness and Bonson Avenues.

The first big movie star to emerge from the new Warner lot was Rin Tin Tin. The first sound film in history was made there, *The Jazz Singer*, starring Al Jolson. It was filmed on Stage 6, also known as the Barn, an enormous bare structure with a roof supported by fifty trusses. The main building was fifty feet wide and one hundred feet long. Attached on two sides were shops, dressing rooms, and offices.

When the Warner studios moved to Burbank, the lot at 5858 Sunset wound up as the cartoon division, featuring such actors as Porky Pig and Bugs Bunny. In 1942 Paramount purchased the property and studios for an estimated million and a half dollars.

The package was worth four times that amount when we came along twenty-five years later, including equipment, props, and costumes valued at a million dollars alone. We discovered that we owned such efforts as the golden calves used in the movie *The Ten Commandments*, as well as the tablets themselves, later stolen. (That had to be the height of lawlessness. Can you imagine anyone stealing the Ten Commandments?)

We donated most of the sets, scenery, chandeliers, and you-name-it, to the educational channel in Los Angeles, items with a history behind them, for a fund-raising telethon. The pieces brought some fantastic prices.

Paramount's merger with Gulf and Western had made the property available. Even so, we kept the purchase quiet. When our attorney, Clair Stout, and Loyd Sigman, one of our executives, needed to inspect the grounds, Paramount arranged to have them taken around at six o'clock on a Sunday morning. There were sentimental as well as business reasons for keeping it out of the news. We were aware that the sale would be upsetting to a lot of people, including the Gulf and Western stockholders. But the people who were selling were no longer the ones who had a romantic attachment to the movie business.

By June of 1968 the staffs of KMPC radio and KTLA televi-

sion were on the same lot, and Golden West Broadcasters cele-
brated its sixteenth year. What happens in the life of a company
is that circumstances change. People die, get divorced, or just
grow older and want to get their estates in order. A time comes
to cash in and your minority stockholders are entitled to that op-
portunity.

We were offered a deal by the Signal Companies, a Los Angeles conglomerate, that allowed our minority holders to sell out
and still leave control in the hands of my wife and myself. Signal
wanted as close to 50 per cent as it could get. They acquired 49.9
per cent for twenty-five million dollars, paying off the other
shareholders in cash. Mrs. Autry and I gave Signal the right to
purchase our stock—at the time of my death—for roughly the
same amount. My estate would also receive half of the company's
net profits from the time of the agreement, after deducting half
of whatever dividends had been declared.

By 1972 my shares, under those terms, would have been worth
over thirty million dollars. But a general slump had struck the
broadcasting industry and I decided that the contract wasn't fair
to Signal. Under the circumstances I felt they had overpaid. I
called in Clair Stout and asked him to contact Forrest Shumway,
the president of Signal, and advise him we wanted to lower the
sale price.

A tall, rangy, quiet-spoken man, Stout had been a partner with
the firm of Dow, Lohnes, and Albertson. When a back injury he
had suffered in the war continued to bother him, he decided to
retire and move to California, escaping the cold and damp of the
eastern winters. That was in the late 1960s and almost before
Clair knew it I had him handling all of our legal work. He had
long ago mastered one of the toughest of all tricks. He was a
lawyer who didn't talk or act like one.

As a young law clerk, he had once been given a thick bundle
of briefs to review for a senior partner. The language would
have choked a goat, and nothing was said in one page if it could
be said in ten. Clair staggered through it. The next day when the
partner asked him what he thought, Clair swallowed hard and
said, "I thought it was fine."

The older lawyer glared at him. "I'm not asking for your
praise," he said. "That isn't what we're paying you fifteen dollars

a week for." From that moment on Clair never minced words. Whenever anyone commented on his directness, he grinned and said, "That's what you're paying me fifteen dollars a week for."

My friend as well as my attorney, Clair had a fit over my proposal. He kept insisting the deal *was* fair, that such an action was unheard of, Signal had never complained, and no one in his right mind gave away ten million dollars, even on paper.

I said, "Go ahead and do it, Clair. I am just not comfortable with this contract. I feel like I've taken advantage of them."

Reluctantly, he telephoned Forrest Shumway and within a very short time he heard from the legal counsel for Signal. "Is what Forrest tells me true?"

"I'm afraid it is," said Clair.

There was a pause and then the other lawyer said, quickly, "Would you mind getting down to my office right away? If anything happens to Gene before we finalize this new agreement I'll probably get fired."

The contract was rewritten so that instead of a direct obligation to buy, Signal now had an option to acquire my 50.1 per cent—at my death—for twenty million dollars. They pay a fixed sum for that option each year, with the amount applied to the purchase price. I waived my percentage of the profits.

I never felt I was playing Santa Claus. There is a point beyond which numbers lose their meaning. What you are left with is a feeling, a weight. It's like hefting a bowling ball. You don't know how *much*, only that it seems right.

Putting across a business deal has always excited me. As with sports, the fun is in the winning, but you remember longest the ones you lose.

Our venture into the hotel business was undoubtedly a mistake. Our reasoning was right but the timing was poor. In 1960 we bought the Ocotillo Lodge in Palm Springs, figuring it would be convenient for the baseball team in spring training. Soon the Gene Autry Hotel Company was formed, with Bob Reynolds and a few other investors. We quickly bought or leased the Continental in West Hollywood, the Mark Hopkins in San Francisco, and the Sahara Inn near Chicago's O'Hare Field. By 1963 we added a second motor hotel in Palm Springs and put my name on it. I kept this one, even after the company sold all the others.

The Continental was a brand-new hotel, the only new hotel on the Sunset Strip in decades. It should have done quite well, but just about the time we opened the hippies moved onto the Sunset Strip and all but took over. They would sleep in the corridors of the hotel. Carloads of people began to cruise nightly up and down the Strip, slowly, just gawking at the characters and the weird costumes, causing massive traffic jams. West Hollywood was transformed. Instead of being a posh night club area it became a hippie ghetto. Many people were afraid to venture out there at night. Guests would make dinner reservations at the hotel and then find they couldn't park or get through the crowds. The prospects for a financial success were destroyed.

Frankly, I was tired of having the hippies and freaks walk into the lobby barefooted. We sold out to the Hyatt Corporation on January 2, 1968. The date was a practical rather than a symbolic choice. That way we kept the bar receipts for New Year's Eve.

The Mark Hopkins is one of the country's grand hotels. We signed a lease in which we were required to maintain it as a *de luxe* hotel, as the phrase is known in the industry. The Mark was making a profit, but in order to maintain that rating—it had become a little dowdy—every nickel we made had to be poured right back. No matter how well we did the money went right back into maintaining the quality.

You do get a sense of the life, of the small universe a good hotel becomes. It is quite an experience to buy or sell one. You discover that you are really involved in about ten different businesses. You don't have a beginning or ending of a day where a sale can be cut off. You might not sell the bar until two o'clock in the morning because that is when the bar closes. You can't take inventory of the whiskey and money at midnight because that hour is when you are the busiest. You have a laundry and a newstand and perhaps several restaurants that close at different times. You even operate a small bank on the premises, having provided your guests with safety deposit boxes.

The Sahara in Chicago completed our education. The hotel had been built by what is known in police circles as a shady element, with financing by the Lincoln Savings and Loan Association. The Chicago *Tribune* learned of the connection and ran a series of explosive stories. There was a run on the Savings and Loan, whose officers decided they needed an operator with a clean image to counteract the terrible publicity. The hotel had not even opened when our company was contacted and offered a thirty-year lease, with nothing down. The deal included uniforms and linen and dishes, the works. They just wanted whatever respectability my name could give them. They were like the mouse who decided he didn't want the cheese. He just wanted to get his tail out of the trap.

We entered into a lease and took over the hotel's management. The Sahara had a Las Vegas flavor, with a vast night club area on the second floor that might have been designed for eventual use as a casino.

We had not been open long when the hotel was bombed. An explosive was placed against an outside wall, knocking out a window or two. The damage was slight, but the blast frightened our guests and some employees quit. By the time we got rolling again another bomb went off. Again the damage was slight, but this time we received a subpoena from the Illinois Crime Commission, wanting our books and records. I asked Clair Stout to call the chairman of the commission and learn what they were looking for.

The chairman said, "We're trying to find out why you were bombed."

"We'd sure like to know that, too," said Clair. "We haven't any idea. What theory do you have?"

He said, "We don't think you were buying from the right suppliers."

Clair said, "No one ever told us who the right ones were."

But we quickly figured it out. You had to buy products and services—meat, cutlery, whatever—from businesses that were mob-related. At that point all I wanted was to get out of the lease. We opened negotiations with the Savings and Loan people, who were nervous that the news of my pulling out would start another run on their deposits.

In the meantime, we discovered that some of the furniture, fixtures, and equipment had been stolen. It was crazy. One day a

37. *With Ina Mae in snow country, waiting for Rudolph.*

38. *Kids get a close-up of Champ in Madison Square Garden.*

39. *Greeting a couple of guests: baseball's Yogi Berra (left), home run hero Roger Maris (1963).*

40. *Out of the saddle, but I still have a place for my ten-gallon hat.*

41. A Hollywood sports night turns out Bob Reynolds (left), Pat Boone (center), and author.

42. *What the well-dressed singing cowboy wore in his heyday—some outfits cost up to one thousand dollars.*

43. *Putting Champ through his paces (1948).*

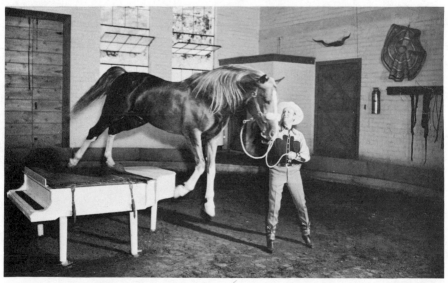

44. The corporate cowboy at work, handling business interests that include radio, TV stations, a baseball club, hotel, and ranch.

45. *In* Indian Territory, *Pat Buttram and I come to the rescue of the cavalry.*

46. *Riding the sagebrush trail with Judith Allen and Weldon Heyburn.*

47. *A quiet night with Ina Mae in the old bunkhouse, in Hollywood Hills.*

truck had pulled up to the entrance and the driver said, "We've come for the sofa in the lobby." The bellboys helped them load it onto the truck and that was the last we ever saw of it.

We were liable for such losses. Stout notified the Savings and Loan that a number of items were missing. But he pointed out, "If you want a full inventory taken everyone will know that Gene Autry is moving out of this hotel and you're going to be in deep trouble." They settled with us and we paid seventy-five hundred dollars for the wear and tear and missing equipment. As part of the settlement, we gave them the rights to my name for three more months while they looked for a purchaser. After three months my name had to be taken off the bath mats and swizzle sticks and matchbook covers.

Not long after we concluded the deal the Savings and Loan went into receivership and the state of Illinois took it over. Four months later, Clair Stout happened to be in Chicago and he stopped by the Sahara and saw my name still plastered all over it. He called the attorney general and suggested strongly that he read the contract. The result was that the state of Illinois paid us fifteen thousand dollars for the unauthorized use of my name and then removed it from the marquee and all the hotel accessories.

We had paid seventy-five hundred dollars to settle the lease and got back twice as much for compensation. We still took a loss on the Sahara, but under the circumstances that negotiation was one of our better ones.

No charges were ever brought in the two bombing incidents. The original owner of the hotel, the one who had been the subject of the *Tribune* stories, called to assure me he had nothing to do with them. I believed him. A year or two later he was murdered.

CHAPTER 12: EPILOGUE

Riding into the Sunset

Fans are wonderful. They write you long and personal letters. They hang your photograph on a wall, collect your clippings, make you rich and famous, and ask almost nothing in return. Except, possibly, that you stop aging at twenty-six.

Well into my sixties, slower of foot and no longer clear of eye, I still find myself asked if I plan to make another movie. As flattering as the question is, the answer is no. Thank you, but no. Part of that interest, I realize, is the result of Roy Rogers' appearance in 1976 in *Mackintosh and T.J.*, his first picture in twenty-two years.

I am pleased for Roy, who has earned every good thing that has happened to him. He remains as trim and fit as the first day I saw him, and he still has the squinty-eyed look of the real ranch hand. In typical Hollywood fashion, the studio once tried putting drops in Roy's eyes to eliminate the squint, until they found out the public liked it.

I know Roy and it wasn't vanity that brought him back. Nor is it vanity that keeps me away. I am like an old ball player who understands his time has passed. But an old ball player who was fortunate enough to wind up owning the team.

I am secure about who I am and what my place has been. I was the first of the full-time singing cowboys. I am not sure I was the best but when you are first it really doesn't matter. Even if everybody else is better, no one can ever be first again.

My friend Pat Buttram once said, "Autry used to ride off into the sunset; now he owns it." Pat exaggerates. But it always has been my favorite time of day and now, these sunset years, a pleasant time of life. I was fortunate to have kept my name and played myself on the screen. When the time came to turn down the lights, I just went back to being me. Meanwhile, my pictures have been in places not even on the maps.

Of all the locations in which my movies have appeared, the strangest had to be in an African village in 1963. Stanley Baker, the Welsh-born actor and producer, was filming his jungle classic *Zulu,* starring the late Jack Hawkins and backed by Joe Levine.

The movie had a budget of four million dollars. But it was beset by problems, one of which was to convince the Zulu tribesmen that the camera was not an "instrument of death," as many of them believed. To help educate them, Baker sent to Hollywood for a movie, and what he got back was one of mine. I never knew which one, but he said later, "They all wanted to act like cowboys afterward. They even tried to make guitars."

All of which tends to prove, if anything, that no entertainer picks his audience. It picks you. One of my oldest friends, the singer Gene Austen, used to recall how the mobsters in Chicago would flock to whatever club he was playing, just to request a song called, "When They Changed My Name to a Number They Broke My Mother's Heart." Those tough, beefy hoods would sit there and listen, with tears rolling down their cheeks. Gene said they sometimes tipped him as much as a thousand dollars.

Well, we reach people in curious ways. Language and culture are not natural barriers after all. When I came along the country was on the edge of a sweeping change. Great inventions would reshape our comforts and our habits and shrink the globe. Yet the lines were long outside the soup kitchens and violent crime was in its romantic heyday.

I have no exact social theories to offer, but I believe that motion pictures helped us through the Depression. You have to understand how the youngsters, especially those in the hard scrabble country towns, worked and scratched to earn their ninety minutes of escape on Saturday. They would sell eggs door to door and maybe save up a quarter. A movie cost fifteen cents and that left a dime for popcorn and a drink. The kids would stay all day, watching the feature over and over, then go home and relive it in the back yard. "I'll be Gene and you be Frog." "I'll be Roy and you be Gabby." The ones who were too small or too timid to speak up first had to portray the Indians or the bad guys. The play-acting would last them until the next Saturday. There was no teen-age drug problem that anyone knew or heard about. The kids got high on the fumes from a cap pistol.

I make no claims for improving their intellects. But the boys of that time—and a few of the girls—would try to imitate what they saw in an Autry movie, or a Roy Rogers movie, and they were not influenced in a harmful way. A ghetto kid in Detroit or Philadelphia, of course, had no horses or much of anything else, so he rode around on a broomstick. Today the young people go to a movie and they see the hero doing dangerous stunts in cars and motorcycles and they attempt to copy them. And the doctors get richer.

No, this isn't meant to be another wail of regret across the generation gap. The old days were not necessarily better. I only know they were slower and less cynical. You could talk about setting an example for young people without blushing.

Over the years I have taken some ribbing about my Cowboys' Code, the set of rules I evolved to govern the role of the B Western hero. They must sound naïve to today's do-your-own-thing disciples. But we took such matters seriously then and the code tapped a spirit that was alive in the land. It went like this:

1. The cowboy must never shoot first, hit a smaller man, or take unfair advantage.

2. He must never go back on his word, or a trust confided in him.

3. He must always tell the truth.

4. He must be gentle with children, the elderly, and animals.

5. He must not advocate or possess racially or religiously intolerant ideas.

6. He must help people in distress.

7. He must be a good worker.

8. He must keep himself clean in thought, speech, action, and personal habits.

9. He must respect women, parents, and his nation's laws.

10. The cowboy is a patriot.

Under this code, some have said, the cowboy became a sort of adult boy scout. Maybe so. I am aware that sophisticated people might snicker at such sentiments. They would not be classified as very modern, certainly not *macho*—a word that became popular in the seventies when men needed an image to counter women's lib. But I didn't exactly move in sophisticated circles. I never felt there was anything wrong with striving to be better than you are.

Of course, not all of this morality was of my own design. The censors of that period would not permit me to do many of the things that are now routine in the so-called adult Westerns—in violation of rules one through ten. Yet I always thought the pictures we made starting in 1934 were the hardest of all, because they mixed such an unlikely stew—songs, comedy, a little romance, lots of action, and scenic background. I miss the great action stunts today, the chases, the running mounts. Barroom fights are now often played for laughs, if they are played at all. We have not replaced a generation of great stars, such as John Wayne, Jimmy Stewart, Gary Cooper, Henry Fonda, Randolph Scott, and Joel McCrea.

Wayne, of course, threatens to go on forever. He started out in the days of the two-reeler, then broke into the B Westerns about the time I did, and moved on to the big-budget, technicolor features that established him as the most enduring actor Hollywood has ever known. To many movie-goers, no Western or war picture is acceptable without John Wayne.

Although the Duke and I were the first two players under contract when Republic was formed, only once did we ever appear on the same set. We came together late in my career, in June 1958, on a television special called simply, "The Western," for the NBC series "Wide, Wide World." Directed by John Ford and filmed at my own Melody Ranch, the ninety-minute show was essentially a history of the Western movie, with a cast that included Walter Brennan, Ward Bond, James Arness, Gabby Hayes, James Garner, and dozens of familiar cowboy and Indian faces.

The novelty of working for the first time with Wayne, after some thirty years, would have been reason enough to remember that show. But what has stayed with me in the years since then was the unique relationship between Wayne and John Ford.

Wayne is a man without pretense. He could be tough and rowdy, but in the presence of Ford, whom he revered, he could be as obedient and innocent as an altar boy.

The night before the telecast Duke lost track of the time, did some serious partying, and arrived on the set two or three hours late with a head quite sensitive to loud noises. Ford's voice must have sounded like a hammer beating against the lid of a garbage can. He was furious. He berated Wayne for holding up rehearsal and inconveniencing the rest of the cast. Duke just kept ducking his head and scuffing his toe in the sand and repeating, "I'm sorry, boss."

Wayne's part required him to walk down the Western street where *High Noon*'s immortal face-down occurred, as he recited his lines from the script. Ford punished him by demanding endless run-throughs over that quarter mile stretch of red dust, under a blistering desert sun. "And you'll not get so much as a drop of water," roared Ford. "Do you HEAR me?"

"Yes, boss," Wayne replied.

While the Duke was suffering his penance, Ford sidled up to me and said, "Gene, about twenty minutes before we go on the air I want you to give Duke a good healthy slug of Bourbon. And halfway through the show give him another. But don't let him know that I know."

I understood. I walked over to the ranch house, took a Coke out of the refrigerator, emptied half of it into the sink, and filled up the bottle with Bourbon. As I recall, we rehearsed until four-thirty and were to hit the air live half an hour later, catching the East at prime time.

Wayne was standing off-camera with his tongue hanging out when I sauntered up to him, holding out the bottle of Coke. "Here, Duke," I said, "have a swallow of this. I think it will help you."

His face puckered up and he waved the offer aside with a short chop of his hand. "Get that mouthwash away from me," he growled. "You want to get me sick?"

As sternly as I could, I said, "Duke, I'm telling you, this is just what you need. Try it. Take a sip."

He looked at me a little suspiciously, took the bottle, and tilted it to his lips. His eyes got as round as saucers. When he handed me the empty he said, "Autry, you may have saved a man's life."

Halfway through the show I performed the same errand. The second time Wayne didn't have to be persuaded. Years later, after his success in the movie *True Grit,* I received a package in the mail one day from Wayne. It contained a glossy photograph of himself as Rooster Cogburn, with the patch over one eye. The inscription said: "To Gene Autry. A lot of water has gone under the bridge. And whiskey, too."

Among the people I have enjoyed most on this wrinkled prune of a planet, Duke Wayne ranks near the top. I believe he has been good for motion pictures and good for America. Our politics are not very far apart. My roots are in the Democratic Party, but I consider myself an independent. At that, I may be the only living sometimes Democrat who ever said no twice to Lyndon Johnson.

After campaigning for LBJ when he ran for Congress, I had to decline when he asked for my help in his Senate race against Coke Stevenson in 1948. I knew Coke, the former Texas governor, and I had been in his home in Junction. I told Lyndon I'd have to sit that one out. This was the Democratic primary election that Johnson won by eighty-seven votes, gaining him the nickname of Landslide Lyndon.

In 1964 he called me again and wanted me to endorse him against Barry Goldwater during the campaign for the presidency. It so happened that I had served in the war with Barry, in the same squadron, and had learned a lot about flying from him. I liked and admired them both. So I told Lyndon, "I'll give you both money but this is another of those times when I just don't want to take sides."

I have learned that it isn't easy to be neutral in this country. We tend to be wary of people who have no passions. But I have never been one for displays of emotion. The loss of something near has always seemed a private matter to me. Where I came from, if someone kept harping on his grief or his troubles after a time people would just walk around him as though he were a swamp.

When a fire all but devastated Melody Ranch in August 1962, what I lost could not be replaced or even measured. The ranch was in the path of the terrible fire storm that raged through the San Gabriel Mountains. Covering one hundred acres, the ranch had once been the Monogram Studio, one of the finest in the business. I had purchased the ranch ten years before the fire, leasing it for the filming of such shows as "Gunsmoke" and "Wyatt Earp," as well as those produced by my own company.

I had always planned to erect a Western museum there, but priceless Indian relics and a collection of rare guns, including a set used by Billy the Kid, went up in smoke. Thank God, the ranch hands and all fourteen of our horses were uninjured. The fire left the terrain so convincingly battle-scarred that it was used two months later for an episode of television's war series "Combat."

The network special with Wayne and John Ford was the last time I went before the cameras at Melody Ranch. I have been back only a very few times.

Given a chance, I prefer to dwell on the brighter side. I am not troubled by the question of how I want to spend the rest of my life. I am doing it. My days are divided between our ten-room, colonial-style home in the Hollywood Hills, and the Gene Autry Hotel in Palm Springs, which still serves as spring headquarters for the California Angels.

I have formed certain habits that regulate my time. When I am in Los Angeles, my day nearly always begins with an early morning round at the Lakeside Golf Club with Clair Stout. I usually reach the office at eleven, leave at five. When I'm in Palm Springs I stay in touch by phone, daily, with our key people—John Reynolds, a former president of CBS-TV, who runs the television side; Bert West in radio; Buzzie Bavasi and Red Patterson at the ball park.

All of my years I have been a compulsive gatherer of information, reading three or four newspapers every day, right down to the classified ads. At night I often fall asleep with a radio earplug in my ear, tuned into an all-news station. When I wake up the next morning, I can tell Ina most of what was said while I slept.

Every now and again in the papers I read, I find my name in places other than the sports page, where I am usually reminded how fast the price of baseball talent keeps rising. In one of the last columns Bob Considine wrote before his death, he praised

America's swift and forceful response to the pirating of the freighter, the *Mayaguez*. He summed up the incident with the line: "Don't mess around with Gene Autry, see."

I take that as a salute to the kind of Westerns Hollywood once made, where the bad guys were always brought to justice. It is a nice way to be remembered, if you feel a need to be remembered.

It is pleasant to look back, though not nearly so much as to be able to look ahead. A reporter for the Los Angeles *Times* once asked me if a story was true: that when I came back from my salary strike Republic was ready to sweep Roy Rogers aside, but I refused to let them, insisting they continue the build-up for the young cowboy who would later become my chief competitor.

As nice as it would be to take credit for such a gesture, I'm not certain I can. I only told Herb Yates that there was no need to push anyone out. There was room for all of us.

Later, when Republic decided to sell our films to television—mine and Roy's—we teamed up in a legal battle to prevent the sale. We lost. But years later I bought my old movies outright and began to dole them out as reruns every few years. When they reappear, they remind a new generation of what the Western vision once was: rearing horses and blazing six guns, guitars by an open campfire, comic sidekicks, and as one writer put it, silver saddles at the old corral.

A generous nature is easily bruised in show business, but not always. Once we brought our road show into Milwaukee during a polio epidemic, and played all week to a nearly empty house. The theater owner was frantic. It is a sad thing, watching a man who believes he is going broke. At the end of the week I went to him and tore up the contract and took the loss out of my own pocket. I am not telling this story now to pat myself on the head, but only to put in perspective a point Herb Green once made to an interviewer: "Gene is a giver. But try to cheat him out of a dollar and he'll fight you like a grizzly . . ."

On the whole my life has been favored by friendly winds. I watched, and was a part of, the development of talking pictures, the heyday of radio, the birth and incredible growth of television. I saw country music leap out of the haylofts and honky tonks and become a new national religion. I had the best of two eras—mine and the one I re-created on the movie screen.

I have never felt that what I did for a living made me a big shot. I don't feel that way now and I hope I never will. You don't give up the values of a lifetime simply because you discover that people will pay to look at and listen to you. They will do the same to watch trained seals catch fish.

Anyway, my wife would never allow my head to get too big for my stetson. One night over dinner with friends in Palm Springs, in a mellow and teasing mood, I looked across the table at the former Ina Mae Spivey, who is as slender and radiant today as the college girl I met forty odd years ago. I tapped the table with a spoon and said, "Yep, it's about time for me to think about trading Ina for a new one . . . get me a younger model."

Very coolly, very sweetly—she had heard it all before—Ina smiled and said, "You know, I have always said you could do that, dear, any time you wanted. Of course, you'd wind up right where you started, with a guitar and a saddle."

We both laughed. That really was how it all started, with a guitar and a saddle.

Discography*

Listed is the year in which the songs were first recorded by Gene Autry. The asterisk * before a title indicates a gold record. Many of the songs were reissued under several labels. Name of the composer appears in parentheses.

1929 – "My Dreaming of You" (Johnny Marvin); "My Alabama Home" (Jimmy Long).

"Blue Yodel Number 5" (Jimmie Rodgers); "Left My Gal in the Mountains" (Carson Robinson).

"Why Don't You Come Back to Me" (Gene Autry); "Hobo Yodel" (Autry); "Dust Pan Blues" (Frankie Marvin); "No One to Call Me Darling" (Autry); "Frankie and Johnnie" (Public Domain).

"The Railroad Boomer" (Robinson); "Slue Foot Sue" (F. Marvin); "Stay Away from My Chicken House" (F. Marvin); "Waiting for a Train" (Arranged by J. Rodgers); "Lullaby Yodel" (J. Rodgers).

"Blue Yodel Number 4" (J. Rodgers); "Daddy and Home" (J. Rodgers).

* Gold Records

1930– "My Oklahoma Home" (F. Marvin); "I'll be Thinking of You, Little Girl" (Autry); "Living in the Mountains" (F. Marvin); "Cowboy Yodel" (Autry).

"That's Why I Left the Mountains" (F. Marvin); "My Rough and Rowdy Ways" (J. Rodgers).

"Whisper Your Mother's Name" (Braisted-Rodgers); "The Girl I left Behind" (J. Marvin); "In the Shadow of the Old Pine Tree" (Raskin-Brown-Eliscu).

"Texas Blues" (J. Rodgers); "Hobo Bill's Last Ride" (Waldo Lafayette O'Neal); "My Carolina Sunshine Girl" (J. Rodgers); "Train Whistle Blues" (J. Rodgers); "Anniversary Blue Yodel" (J. Rodgers); "In the Jailhouse Now Number 2" (J. Rodgers); "That's Why I'm Blue" (J. Rodgers-Elsie MacWilliams).

"Yodeling Hobo" (Autry); "Pictures of My Mother" (Autry); "Blue Days" (Autry).

"Dad in the Hills" (Autry); "High Powered Mama" (J. Rodgers).

1931 – "Mean Mama Blues" (J. Rodgers); "Blue Yodel Number 8" (J. Rodgers); "Pistol Packin' Papa" (J. Rodgers-O'Neal).

"Any Old Time" (J. Rodgers); "Money Ain't No Use Anyway" (Autry).

"A Gangster's Warning" (Autry); "That's How I Got My Start" (Autry); "True Blue Bill" (F. Marvin).

"Do Right Daddy Blues" (F. Marvin); "Bear Cat Papa Blues" (F. Marvin).

"I'll Always Be a Rambler" (F. Marvin); "Death of Mother Jones" (Public Domain).

"High Steppin' Mama Blues" (F. Marvin); "She Wouldn't Do It" (F. Marvin); "Don't Do Me That Way" (F. Marvin); "TB Blues" (J. Rodgers); "Jimmie the Kid" (J. Rodgers); "Travelin' Blues" (J. Rodgers-Shelly Lee Alley).

"There's a Good Gal in the Mountains" (Autry); "She's a Lowdown Mama" (F. Marvin); "The Old Woman and the Cow" (F. Marvin); "Bearcat Mama from Horner's Corner" (Jimmie Davis); "She's a Hum-Dum Dinger" (Davis); "Old Man Duff" (Public Domain); "I'm a Truthful Fellow" (F. Marvin); "Valley in the Hills" (Public Domain); "She's Just That Kind" (Fleming-Townsend); "She's Always on My Mind" (Fleming-Townsend); "I'm Blue and Lonesome" (Fleming-Townsend).

"Jailhouse Blues" (Autry); "Methodist Pie" (Public Domain).

"Dallas County Jail Blues" (F. Marvin); "She Wouldn't Do It" (Autry).

"Rheumatism Blues" (Autry); "I'm Atlanta Bound" (Autry); *"That Silver-haired Daddy of Mine" (Autry-Long); "Missouri is Calling" (Autry).

"Mississippi Valley Blues" (Autry-Long); "My Old Pal of Yesterday" (Long-Autry); "My Cross-eyed Gal" (Long-Autry).

"I'm Always Dreaming of You" (Long-Autry); "Why Don't You Come Back to Me?" (Autry); "Wild Cat Mama" (F. Marvin).

"Birmingham Daddy" (Autry); "I'm a Railroad Man (Without a Railroad Fare)" (Autry); "Under the Old Apple Tree" (Autry).

1932 – "That Ramshackle Shack" (Autry-Hugh Cross); "Back to Old Smokey Mountain" (Autry).

"Back Home in the Blue Ridge Mountains" (Autry); "The Crime I Didn't Do" (Autry-Long); "Kentucky Lullaby" (Autry); "Alone with My Sorrows" (Autry-Long).

"Moonlight and Skies" (Rodgers); "Returning to My Cabin Home" (Autry-Burton); "In the Cradle of My Dreams" (Long).

"My Carolina Mountain Rose" (Long); "Have You Found Someone Else" (Long); "In the Hills of Caroline" (Autry-Burton); "Black Bottom Blues" (Autry).

1933 – "Cowboy's Heaven" (F. Marvin-Autry); "Little Ranch House on the Old Circle B" (Autry-Blanchard); "The Yellow Rose of Texas" (Public Domain); "Your Voice is Ringing" (Percy Wenrich); "Louisiana Moon" (Autry).

"If I Could Bring Back My Buddy" (Long); "Gosh I Miss You All the Time" (Long); "The Answer to Twenty-one Years" (Bob Miller); "Lamplighting Time in the Valley" (Joe Lyons-Sam Hart); "Watching the Clouds Roll By" (Long); "Don't Take Me Back to the Chain Gang" (Autry).

"Roll Along Kentucky Moon" (Bill Halley); "That Mother and Daddy of Mine" (Autry).

"Way Out West in Texas" (Autry); "The Dying Cowgirl" (F. Marvin-Autry); "When the Hummingbirds are Humming" (Autry); "The Death of Jimmie Rodgers" (Miller); "In the Valley of the Moon" (Burke-Tobias); "If You'll Let Me Be Your Little Sweetheart" (Autry-Slim Bryant).

"That Old Featherbed on the Farm" (Autry-Louis O'Connell); "There's an Empty Cot in the Bunkhouse Tonight"

(F. Marvin-Autry); "A Hillbilly Wedding in June" (Freddie Owen-Frankie More); "Moonlight Down in Lovers' Lane" (Pitman-Kortlander); "The Last Round-Up" (Billy Hill).

"When Jimmie Rodgers Said Good-by" (Dwight Butcher-Lou Herscher); "Good Luck Old Pal (In Memory of Jimmie Rodgers)" (Autry).

1934 – "The Round-Up in Cheyenne" (Smiley Burnette); "Memories of That Silver-haired Daddy of Mine" (Autry); "Eleven Months in Leavenworth" (Autry).

"Little Farm Home" (Burnette-Long-Autry); "Dear Old Western Skies" (Burnette); "Beautiful Texas" (W. Lee O'Daniel); "Little Old Lady Waiting" (Burnette-Autry-Long).

"When the Moon Shines on the Mississippi Valley" (Burnette); "My Shy Little Blue Bonnet Girl" (Long); "Shine on Pale Moon" (Long).

1935 – "Angel Boy" (Long-Paul Dennis); "Red River Lullaby" (Long-Autry); "Someday in Wyoming" (Burnette-Autry); "The Old Covered Wagon" (Burnette-Autry); "Hold on Little Dogies, Hold On" (Burnette); "Answer to Red River Valley" (Burnette-Autry); "That Silver-haired Mother of Mine" (Long); "Ridin' Down the Canyon" (Burnette-Autry).

"Wagon Train" (Burnette); "Old Missouri Moon" (Long-Dennis); "Ole Faithful" (Michael Carr-Jimmy Kennedy).

"Vine-covered Cabin in the Valley" (Burnette); "Rainbow Valley" (Burnette-Autry); "I'd Love a Home in the Mountains" (Burnette-Autry); "Nobody's Darling But Mine" (Davis); *"Tumbling Tumbleweeds" (Bob Nolan); "Texas Plains" (Stuart Hamblen); "Uncle Noah's Ark" (Burnette).

"My Old Saddle Pal" (Autry-Odie Thompson); "Riding the Range" (Fleming Allan-Autry-Nelson Shawn); "End of the Trail" (Burnette); "Don't Waste Your Tears on Me" (Autry); "You're the Only Star in My Blue Heaven" (Autry).

"Mexicali Rose" (H. Stone-J. B. Tenney); "Answer to Nobody's Darling but Mine" (Davis); "Riding All Day" (Burnette).

1936 – "The Old Gray Mare" (F. Marvin); "Guns and Guitars" (Oliver Drake-Autry); "I'll Go Ridin' Down That Texas Trail" (Burnette).

1937 – "The Convict's Dream" (Autry-Hadley Hooper); "That's Why I'm Nobody's Darlin'" (Davis).

"The One Rose" (Lani McIntire-Del Lyon); "Sing Me a Song of the Saddle" (Autry-Frank Hartford); "With a Song in My Heart" (Richard Rodgers-Larry Hart); "I Hate to Say Good-by to the Prairie" (Autry-Thompson); "When Golden Leaves are Falling" (C. A. Havens).

"Blue Hawaii" (Robin-Rainger); "Rhythm of the Range" (J. Marvin-Autry); "Eyes to the Sky" (J. Marvin-Autry).

"Old Buckaroo Good-by" (J. Marvin-Autry); "Down in the Land of the Zulu" (J. Marvin-Autry); "It's Round-Up Time in Reno" (Owens-Lawrence-Autry); "Were You Sincere?" (Autry-Mark Halliday); "End of My Round-Up Days" (Pee Wee King-J. L. Frank-Estes).

"My Star of the Sky" (Autry); "When the Tumbleweeds Come Tumbling Down Again" (Autry); "When It's Springtime in the Rockies" (Woolsey-Taggart-Sauer); "I Want a Pardon for Daddy" (Charles Roat); "Take Me Back to My Boots and Saddle" (Powell-Whitcup-Samuels).

"There's a Gold Mine in the Sky" (Charles and Nick Kenny); "Sail Along Silv'ry Moon" (Tobias-Wenrich); "At The Old Barn Dance" (Tinturin-Lawrence).

1938 – "Ride Tenderfoot Ride" (Johnny Mercer-Richard Whiting); "Good-by Pinto" (J. Marvin-Freddie Rose-Autry); "As Long as I've Got My Horse" (J. Marvin-Rose-Autry); "If Today Were the End of the World" (Autry); "The Dude Ranch Cowhands" (Autry-Rose-J. Marvin); "The Old Trail" (Autry-Rose-J. Marvin).

1939 – "Paradise in the Moonlight" (Autry-Rose); "Old November Moon" (J. Marvin-Autry); "I Just Want You" (Autry-Rose-J. Marvin); "I Don't Belong in Your World" (Autry-Rose); "Blue Montana Skies" (Autry-Rose-J. Marvin).

"When I First Laid Eyes on You" (Autry-Marshall); "If It Wasn't for the Rain" (Autry-Rose); "Little Old Band of Gold" (Autry-Charles Newman-F. Glickman); "Rhythm of the Hoofbeats" (Autry-Rose-J. Marvin); "Little Sir Echo" (Smith-Fearis).

"I Wonder If You Feel the Way I Do" (Bob Wills); *"Back in the Saddle Again" (Autry-Ray Whitley); "I'm Gonna Round Up My Blues" (Autry-J. Marvin); "We've Come a Long Way Together" (Sam Stept-Koehler).

*"South of the Border" (Carr-Kennedy); "Little Pardner" (Autry-Rose-Marvin); "The Merry-Go-Roundup" (Autry-Rose-J. Marvin).

"Gold Mine in Your Heart" (Autry-Rose-J. Marvin); "I'm Beginning to Care" (Autry-Rose-J. Marvin); "Darling, How Can You Forget So Soon?" (Autry-King-Frank).

1940 – "The Singing Hills" (Mack David-Dick Sanford-Sammy Mysels); "Good-by, Little Darling, Good-by" (Autry-J.

Marvin); *"El Rancho Grande"* (Uranga-Costello); "Mary Dear" (Public Domain, arranged by Gene Autry and Cactus Mac); "There's Only One Love in a Lifetime" (Autry-Marvin-Tobias); "When I'm Gone You'll Soon Forget" (Keith).

"Blueberry Hill" (A. Lewis-L. Stock-V. Rose); "Be Honest with Me" (Autry-Rose); "The Call of the Canyon" (Hill).

"There'll Never Be Another Pal Like You" (Autry-Marvin-Tobias); "Broomstick Buckaroo" (Autry-Hartford-J. Marvin); "Sycamore Lane" (Autry-Rose); "There Ain't No Use in Crying Now" (Autry-Marvin).

"You Waited Too Long" (Autry-Whitley-Rose); "That Little Kid Sister of Mine" (Autry-Rose); "What's Gonna Happen to Me" (Autry-Rose); "Tears on My Pillow" (Autry-Rose); "Sierra Sue" (Joseph Carey).

"Good Old-fashioned Hoedown" (Autry-Lee Penney); "When the Swallows Come Back to Capistrano" (L. Rene); "We Never Dream the Same Dream Twice" (Autry-Rose); "Cowboy's Trademarks" (Arranged by Autry); "The Last Letter" (Rex Griffin); "I'll Never Smile Again" (Lowe).

1941 – *"You Are My Sunshine" (Davis-Charles Mitchell); "It Makes No Difference Now" (Davis-Floyd Tillman); "A Year Ago Tonight" (Autry-Rose).

"I'll Never Let You Go Little Darlin'" (Jimmy Wakely); "I'll Be True While You're Gone" (Autry-Rose); "Under Fiesta Stars" (Autry-Rose); "Spend a Night in Argentina" (Autry-Rose).

"I'll Wait for You" (Autry-Rose); "Too Late" (Wakely); "Don't Bite the Hand That's Feeding You" (Hoier-Morgan); "After Tomorrow" (Autry-Rose).

"God Must Have Loved America" (Autry-Rose); "You Are the Light of My Life" (Autry-Rose); "Lonely River" (Autry-Rose-Whitley); "Dear Little Girl of Mine" (Autry-Rose).

"Purple Sage in Twilight" (Autry-Jules Styne-Meyer); "Dear Old Dad of Mine" (Autry-J. Marvin); "I'm Comin' Home Darling (Autry-Eddie Dean-Hoefle).

"If You Only Believed in Me" (Autry-Rose); "Keep Rollin' Lazy Longhorns" (Autry-J. Marvin); "Blue-eyed Elaine" (Ernest Tubb).

"I Wish All My Children Were Babies Again" (Jack Baxley); "Amapola" (Gamse-Lacalle); "Maria Elena" (Russell-Barcelata); "I Don't Want to Set the World on Fire" (Seiler-Marcus-Benjamin-E. Durham).

"Take Me Back into Your Heart" (Autry-Rose); "Sweethearts or Strangers" (Davis); "I Hang My Head and Cry" (Autry-Rose-Whitley).

1942 – "Tweedle-o-Twill" (Autry-Rose); "Deep in the Heart of Texas" (Hershey-Swander); "I'm thinkin' Tonight of My Blue Eyes" (A. P. Carter); "Rainbow on the Rio Colorado" (Autry-Rose).

"Private Buckaroo" (Wrubel-Bob Newman); "Call for Me and I'll Be There" (Autry-Rose); "Yesterday's Roses" (Autry-Rose).

"Jingle Jangle Jingle" (Loesser-Lilley); "I'm a Cowpoke Pokin' Along" (Autry-Rose).

(During 1943, Gene Autry made no commercial recordings. However, he recorded a number of sides for the War Department, including "There's a Star Spangled Banner Waving Somewhere," "Home on the Range," and "When the Lights Go On Again.")

1944 – "Don't Fence Me In" (Cole Porter); "I'll Be Back" (Autry-Dean-Rex Preis-Bill Bryan); "Gonna Build a Big Fence Around Texas" (Friend-Phillips-Olsen); "Darlin' What More Can I Do?" (Autry-Jenny Lou Carson).

"I Guess I've Been Asleep for All These Years" (Autry-Rose); "At Mail Call Today" (Autry-Rose).

1945 – "Don't Hang Around Me Any More" (Autry-Denver Darling-Vaughn Horton); "Address Unknown" (Autry-Darling-Horton); "I Want to be Sure" (Autry-Merle Travis); "Don't Live a Lie" (Autry-Johnny Bond).

"Don't Take Your Spite Out on Me" (Autry-Rose); "Silver Spurs" (Autry-Cindy Walker); "I'm Learning to Live Without You" (Autry-Bond-Billy Folger); "Have I Told You Lately that I Love You?" (Scott Wiseman).

1946 – "I Wish I Had Never Met Sunshine" (Autry-Dale Evans-Oakley Haldeman); "You Only Want Me When You're Lonely" (Autry-Steve Nelson); "You're Not My Darlin' Any More" (Rosalie Allen-Rose-Sam Martin); "Ages and Ages Ago" (Autry-Rose-Whitley).

"You Laughed and I Cried" (Whitley-Milton Leeds-Billy Hayes); "Over and Over Again" (Autry-Walker); "Sioux City Sue" (Dick Thomas-R. Freedman); "Wave to Me My Lady" (Loesser-Stein); "Rounded Up in Glory" (Public Domain); "When It's Roundup Time in Heaven" (Davis).

"Ole Faithful" (Carr-Kennedy); "Home on the Range" (Public Domain).

"Cowboy Blues" (Autry-Walker); "Gallivantin' Galveston Gal" (Nelson-Leeds-Wise); "Someday" (Jimmy Hodges).

"Can't Shake the Sands of Texas from My Shoes" (Autry-Pitts-Johnson); "Twilight on the Trail" (Mitchell-Alter);

"Here's to the Ladies" (Autry-Walker); "The Last Mile" (Autry-Haldeman-Rose); "Dixie Cannonball" (Autry-Red Foley-Horton).

1947 – "When the Snowbirds Cross the Rockies" (Autry-Joy-Howard); "A Broken Promise Means a Broken Heart" (Autry-Rex Allen-Dave Bohm); "The Leaf of Love" (Tex Williams-Bob Newman); "The Angel Song" (Curt Massey-Millard-Autry).

"An Old-fashioned Tree" (Becker-Williams); "Here Comes Santa Claus" (Autry-Haldeman-Melka); "Pretty Mary" (Autry-Haldeman-Mitchell-MacDonald).

"I'm a Fool to Care" (Ted Daffan); "I've Lived a Lifetime for You" (Whitley-B. Newman); "They Warned Me About You" (Autry-Bond).

"Kentucky Babe" (Buck-Geibel); "Missouri Waltz" (Shannon-Eppel-Logan); "Rolling Along" (Kotel-Cooper); "Play Fair" (Whitley-Leeds-Hayes).

"Serenade of the Bells" (Twomey-Goodhart-Urbano); "Lone Star Moon" (Friend-Franklin); "Loaded Pistols and Loaded Dice" (Johnny Lange-Hy Heath); "Buttons and Bows" (Livingston-Evans).

1948 – "A Boy from Texas, a Girl from Tennessee" (McCarthy, Jr.-Segal-Brooks); "Blue Shadows on the Trail" (Lange-Daniel).

"The Bible on the Table" (Cunningham-Whitcup-Bennett); "I Lost My Little Darlin'" (Oakley Haldeman-Kraus-Coburn).

1949 – "My Empty Heart" (Autry-Porter-Mitchell); "Sunflower" (Mack David); "Ellie Mae" (Autry-Favilla).

*"Rudolph the Red-nosed Reindeer" (Johnny Marks); "He's a Chubby Little Fellow" (Autry-Haldeman).

"Santa, Santa, Santa" (Autry-Haldeman); "If It Doesn't Snow on Christmas" (Pascal-Marks); "Story Book of Love" (Eaton).

"Whirlwind" (Stan Jones); "Riders in the Sky" (Jones); "When the Silver Colorado Turns to Gold" (Paul Herrick-Mitchell); "Texans Never Cry" (Haldeman-Autry-Hank Fort).

"Mule Train" (Lange-Heath-Glickman); "A Cowboy's Serenade" (N. Kenny-C. Kenny-Fina).

"Poison Ivy" (George Wyle-Eddie Pola); "The Roses I Picked for Our Wedding" (Peter Tinturin-Autry); "Love is So Misleadin'" (Autry-A. Simms); "A New Star is Shining in Heaven" (Tinturin).

1950 – *"Peter Cottontail" (Nelson-Jack Rollins); "The Funny Little Bunny" (Autry-Bond).

"Don't Send Your Love" (Haldeman-R. Wright); "Roses" (Tim Spencer-Glen Spencer); "Mississippi Valley Blues" (Autry-Long).

(Duets with Dinah Shore) "The Old Rugged Cross" (Reverend George Bennard); "In the Garden" (Miles).

"Blue Canadian Rockies" (Walker); "I Love You Because" (Leon Payne); "The Last Straw" (Tillman).

"When Santa Claus Gets Your Letter" (Marks); "Frosty the Snowman" (Nelson-Rollins); "Onteora: Great Land in the Sky" (Anderson-Andrea).

"Bucky the Bucking Bronco" (Gerald Marks-Milton Pascal); "Rusty the Rocking Horse" (John Jacob Loeb); "Little Johnny Pilgrim" (Kane-Fidler); "Guffy the Goofy Gobbler" (G. Marks-Pascal); "Goodnight Irene" (Huddy Ledbetter-John Lomax).

"The Statue in the Bay" (Monte Hale-Wagner-Carlyle); "Let Me Cry on Your Shoulder" (Hershey-Swander); "Rose-colored Memories" (Autry-Haldeman-Wright).

"Teardrops from My Eyes" (Rudolph Toombs); "My Heart Cries for You" (Percy Faith-Carl Sigman); "The Place Where I Worship" (Tarr-Foster-Goodhart).

1951 – "Bunny Round-Up Time" (Stephen Gale-Leo Israel); "Sonny the Bunny" (Tommy Johnston).

"Mister and Mississippi" (Irving Gordon); "Stop Your Gambling" (Robison-Pepper).

"How Long Is Forever" (Marks); "Gold Can Buy Anything But Love" (B. Sherman-D. Sherman); "Crime Will Never Pay" (Robinson-Pepper).

"Old Soldiers Never Die" (arranged by Autry); "God Bless America" (Irving Berlin).

"He'll Be Coming Down the Chimney" (J. Fred Coots-Al Neilburg); "Thirty-two Feet, Eight Little Tails" (John Redmond-James Cavanaugh-Frank Weldon); "The Three Little Dwarfs" (Hamblen); "Poppy the Puppy" (Johnston).

"Buffalo Bill" (Jay Glass-Nelson-Fred Wise); "Kit Carson" (Glass-Nelson-Wise).

"On Top of Old Smoky" (Public Domain); "The Old Chisholm Trail" (Public Domain); "Clementine" (Public Domain); "The Big Corral" (Public Domain); "I Was Just Walking Out the Door" (Walker); "A Heartsick Soldier on Heartbreak Ridge" (Fidler-Kane); "Am I Just a Pastime" (Bond-Autry).

1952 – "Smokey the Bear" (Nelson-Rollins); "God's Little Candles" (Kennedy).

"The Night Before Christmas Song" (Marks); "Look Out the Window" (Lew Porter-TeePee Mitchell).

"Johnny Appleseed" (Henry Harvey Walsh-Gale); "The Night Before Christmas in Texas" (Leon A. Harris, Jr.-B. Miller); "Merry Texas Christmas You All" (Harris, Jr.-Miller).

1953 – "Where Did My Snowman Go?" (Venis-S. Mann-Poser); "Freddie, the Little Fir Tree" (Travis-Fairchild).

"Santa Claus Is Comin' to Town" (Haven Gillespie-Coots); "Candy Round-Up" (Autry-Haldeman).

"Up on the Housetop" (Jane Whitman); "Happy Little Island" (Gale-Hector Marchese).

"I Wish My Mom Would Marry Santa Claus" (Autry-Carr); "Sleigh Bells" (Autry-Carr); "A Voice in the Choir" (Autry-Carr).

"Bimbo" (Rodney Morris); "Angels in the Sky" (Glasser); "Holy Poly" (Rose-Autry).

1954 – "Easter Mornin'" (June Winters-Mary Alice Ruffin); "The Horse with the Easter Bonnet" (Al Hoffman-Dick Manning); "Closing the Book" (Burnette); "It's My Lazy Day" (Burnette).

"When He Grows Tired of You" (Aldrich); "You're the Only Good Thing That Happened to Me" (J. Toombs); "It Just Don't Seem Like Home When You're Gone" (Tex Atchison); "I'm Innocent" (King-Redd Stewart); "You're an Angel" (Byrum); "20/20 Vision and Walking Around Blind" (Allison-Estes).

"God's in the Saddle" (J. Hope-Moraine); "Barney the Bashful Bullfrog" (Gene Evans); "Little Peter Punkin' Eater" (Langeston-Hampton-Moore-Underwood).

1955 – "Round, Round the Christmas" (Fred Stryker); "Merry Christmas Waltz" (Inez Loewer-Bot Batson); "You've Got to Take the Bitter with the Sweet" (Fotine-Miles).

"Two Cheaters in Love" (J. Toombs); "If Today Were the End of the World" (Autry).

1956 – "You Are My Sunshine" (Davis); "I Hang My Head and Cry" (Autry-Rose-Whitley).

"Everyone's a Child at Christmas" (Marks); "You Can See Old Santa Claus" (J. Johnson-L. Frizzell-B. Adams).

1957 – "Johnny Reb and Billy Yank" (Charles Tobias); "Darlin', What More Can I Do" (Carson-Autry); "Half Your Heart" (Blair-Duhig).

"No Back Door to Heaven" (Dave Burgess).

Album: "Jingle Bells" (arranged by Carl Cotner); "Silver Bells" (Livingston-Evans); "Here Comes Santa Claus"; "Up on the Housetop" (arranged by Carl Cotner); "Rudolph the Red-nosed Reindeer"; "Santa Claus is Coming to Town"; "Sleigh Bells" (Autry-Carr); "O Little Town of Bethlehem"; "Silent Night"; "Joy to the World."

1958 – No releases.

1959 – "*Buon Natale*" (Bob Saffer-Frank Linale); "Nine Little Reindeer" (Autry-Marks-Travis); "Santa's Comin' in a Whirlybird" (Ashley Dees).

1961 – Album: "You're the Only Star in My Blue Heaven";
—62 "Tweedle-o-Twill," "You Are My Sunshine"; "Lonely River" (Autry-Whitley-Rose); "San Antonio Rose" (Wills); "Trouble in Mind" (Richard M. Jones); "Hang Your Head in Shame" (Rose-Ed Nelson-S. Nelson); "Be Honest with Me"; "Blues Stay Away from Me" (Delmore-Raney-Glover); "Tears on My Pillow" (Autry-

Rose); "I Hang My Head and Cry"; "Ages and Ages Ago" (Autry-Rose-Whitley); "Darlin' What More Can I Do"; "Good-by, Little Darlin', Good-by."

1963 – No releases.

1964 – One Solitary Life (Public Domain); A Cowboy's Prayer (Public Domain).

Filmography*

1. IN OLD SANTA FE (Mascot, 11-15-34)
   Cast: Ken Maynard, Evalyn Knapp, George Hayes, H. B.
   Warner, Kenneth Thompson, George Chesebro, George Burton,
   Wheeler Oakman, Jack Rockwell, Lester (Smiley) Burnette . . .
   and Introducing Gene Autry
   Director: David Howard
   Producer: Nat Levine

2. MYSTERY MOUNTAIN (Mascot, 12-1-34)
   Cast: Ken Maynard, Verna Hillie, Edward Earle, Edmund Cobb,
   Lynton Brent, Syd Saylor, Carmencita Johnson, Lafe McKee, Al
   Bridge, Edward Hearn, Bob Kortman, Wally Wales, Tom Lon-
   don, George Chesebro, Philo McCullough, Frank Ellis, Steve
   Clark, Gene Autry, Smiley Burnette, James Mason, Lew Meehan,
   Jack Rockwell, Art Mix, William Gould
   Directors: Otto Brower, B. Reeves Eason
   Producer: Nat Levine
   Story: Sherman Lowe, Barney Sarecky, B. Reeves Eason
   Screenplay: Ben Cohen, Armand Schaefer
   Camera: Ernest Miller, William Nobles
   Editors: Wyndham Gittens, Earl Turner
   Musical Score: Lee Zahler
   A twelve-chapter serial.

3. THE PHANTOM EMPIRE (Mascot, 2-23-35)
   Cast: Gene Autry, Frankie Darro, Betsy King Ross, Dorothy
   Christie, Wheeler Oakman, Charles K. French, Warner Rich-
   mond, Lester Burnette, William Moore, Ed Piel, Sr., Jack Carlyle,

* All Republic films, unless otherwise noted.

Wally Wales, Jay Wilsey (aka Buffalo Bill, Jr.), Fred Burns,
Stanley Blystone, Dick Talmadge, Frank Ellis
Directors: Otto Brower, B. Reeves Eason
Producer: Nat Levine
Supervisor: Armand Schaefer
Story: Wallace MacDonald, Gerald Geraghty, Hy Freedman,
    Maurice Geraghty
Screenplay: Armand Schaefer, John Rathmell
Camera: Ernest Miller, William Nobles
Music: Lee Zahler
Editor: Wyndham Gittens
Song: "That Silver-haired Daddy of Mine," by Gene Autry
A thirteen-chapter serial.

4. TUMBLING TUMBLEWEEDS (9-5-35)
Cast: Gene Autry, Smiley Burnette, Lucille Browne, George
Hayes, Norma Taylor, Edward Hearn, Jack Rockwell, Frankie
Marvin, George Chesebro, Tom London, Slim Whitaker, Corne-
lius Keefe, Cliff Lyons, Tracy Layne, Charles King
Director: Joe Kane
Supervisor: Armand Schaefer
Producer: Nat Levine
Story: Alan Ludwig
Screenplay: Ford Beebe
Songs: "Tumbling Tumbleweeds," by Bob Nolan; "Corn-fed and
        Rusty," "The Old Covered Wagon," and "Ridin' Down
        the Canyon," by Gene Autry and Smiley Burnette

5. MELODY TRAIL (9-24-35)
Cast: Gene Autry, Smiley Burnette, Ann Rutherford, Wade
Boteler, Willy Costello, Al Bridge, Fern Emmett, Marie Quillan,
Gertrude Messinger, Tracy Layne, Abe Lefton, George DeNor-
mand, Jane Barnes, Ione Reed, Marion Downing, Champion
Director: Joe Kane
Supervisor: Armand Schaefer
Producer: Nat Levine
Story: Sherman Lowe, Betty Burbridge
Screenplay: Sherman Lowe
Editor: Joseph H. Lewis
Camera: Ernest Miller
Songs: "Hold On, Little Dogies, Hold On," "Melody Trail," and
        "A Lone Cowboy on the Lone Prairie," by Gene Autry
        and Smiley Burnette; "Way Down on the Bottom," and
        "My Neighbor Hates Music," by Smiley Burnette

6. THE SAGEBRUSH TROUBADOR (11-19-35)
   Cast: Gene Autry, Smiley Burnette, Barbara Pepper, Frank
   Glendon, Dennis Meadows (aka Dennis Moore), Hooper Atch-
   ley, Fred Kelsey, Julian Rivero, Tom London, Wes Warner,
   Frankie Marvin, Bud Pope, Tommy Gene Fairey, Champion
   Director: Joe Kane
   Supervisor: Armand Schaefer
   Producer: Nat Levine
   Story: Oliver Drake
   Screenplay: Oliver Drake, Joseph Poland
   Editors: Joseph H. Lewis, Les Orlebeck
   Camera: Ernest Miller
   Songs: "Way out West in Texas," "End of the Trail," "On the
      Prairie," "My Prayer for Tonight," "I'd Love a Home in
      the Mountains," "Mississippi Valley," and "Someday in
      Wyoming," by Gene Autry and Smiley Burnette

7. THE SINGING VAGABOND (12-11-35)
   Cast: Gene Autry, Smiley Burnette, Ann Rutherford, Barbara
   Pepper, Warner Richmond, Bob Burns, June Thompson, Elaine
   Shepard, Grace Goodall, Tom Brower, Ray Benard (aka Ray
   Corrigan), Allan Sears, Charles King, Marion O'Connell, Frank
   LaRue, Niles Welch, Robinson Neeman, Chief Thundercloud,
   Chief Big Tree, Marie Quillan, Edmund Cobb, Champion
   Director: Carl Pierson
   Supervisor: Armand Schaefer
   Producer: Nat Levine
   Story: Bill Witney
   Screenplay: Oliver Drake, Betty Burbridge
   Editor: Les Orlebeck
   Songs: "Wagon Train" and "Farewell Friends of the Prairie," by
      Gene Autry and Smiley Burnette

8. RED RIVER VALLEY (3-2-36)
   Cast: Gene Autry, Smiley Burnette, Frances Grant, Boothe
   Howard, Jack Kennedy, Sam Flint, George Chesebro, Charles
   King, Eugene Jackson, Edward Hearn, Frank LaRue, Ken
   Cooper, Frankie Marvin, Cap Anderson, Monty Cass, John Wil-
   son, Lloyd Ingraham, Hank Bell, Earl Dwire, George Morrell,
   Champion
   Director: B. Reeves Eason
   Supervisor: Armand Schaefer
   Producer: Nat Levine
   Story/Screenplay: Dorrell and Stuart McGowan

Editors: Joseph H. Lewis, Carl Pierson
Camera: William Nobles
Music Director: Harry Grey
Songs: "Red River Valley" and "Where a Waterwheel Keeps
       Turning On," sung by Gene Autry; "Hand Me Down
       My Trusty Forty-five," sung and written by Smiley Bur-
       nette

9. COMIN' ROUND THE MOUNTAIN (3-31-36)
Cast: Gene Autry, Ann Rutherford, Smiley Burnette, LeRoy
Mason, Raymond Brown, Ken Cooper, Tracy Layne, Bob
McKenzie, Laurita Puente, John Ince, Frank Lackteen, Frankie
Marvin, Jim Corey, Al Taylor, Steve Clark, Frank Ellis, Hank
Bell, Dick Botiller, Champion
Director: Mack Wright
Supervisor: Armand Schaefer
Producer: Nat Levine
Story: Oliver Drake
Screenplay: Oliver Drake, Dorrell and Stuart McGowan
Editors: Joseph H. Lewis, Les Orlebeck
Camera: William Nobles
Music Director: Harry Grey
Songs: "Chiquita," "When the Campfire is Low on the Prairie,"
       and "Don Juan of Sevillo," by Sam Stept, sung by Gene
       Autry

10. THE SINGING COWBOY (5-13-36)
Cast: Gene Autry, Smiley Burnette, Lois Wilde, Creighton
Chaney (aka Lon Chaney, Jr.), John Van Pelt, Earle Hodgins,
Ken Cooper, Harrison Greene, Wes Warner, Jack Rockwell,
Tracy Layne, Fred (Snowflake) Toones, Oscar Gahan, Frankie
Marvin, Jack Kirk, Audrey Davis, George Pierce, Charles
McAvoy, Ann Gillis, Earl Erby, Harvy Clark, Alf James, Pat
Caron, Champion
Director: Mack Wright
Supervisor: Armand Schaefer
Producer: Nat Levine
Story: Tom Gibson
Screenplay: Dorrell and Stuart McGowan
Editor: Les Orlebeck
Camera: William Nobles

Music Director: Harry Grey
Songs: "Empty Cot in the Bunkhouse," "Yahoo," "We're on the Air," "True Blue Bill," "Rainbow Trail," "Slumberland," "Listen to the Mockingbird," "Washboard and Room," "Saddle Pal," "I'll Be Thinking of You, Little Gal"

11. GUNS AND GUITARS (6-22-36)
Cast: Gene Autry, Smiley Burnette, Dorothy Dix, Tom London, Charles King, J. P. McGowan, Earle Hodgins, Frankie Marvin, Eugene Jackson, Jack Rockwell, Ken Cooper, Harrison Greene, Pascale Perry, Bob Burns, Jack Don, Tracy Layne, Wes Warner, Jim Corey, Frank Stravenger, Jack Kirk, Audrey Davis, Al Taylor, George Morrell, Sherry Tansey, Jack Evans, George Plues, Denver Dixon, Champion
Director: Joe Kane
Supervisor: Robert Beche
Producer: Nat Levine
Story/Screenplay: Dorrell and Stuart McGowan
Editors: Murray Seldeen, Les Orlebeck
Camera: Ernest Miller
Music Director: Harry Grey
Songs: "Ridin' All Day" by Smiley Burnette; "The Cowboy Medicine Show" by Gene Autry and Smiley Burnette; "Guns and Guitars" by Oliver Drake; "Dreamy Valley" by Oliver Drake and Harry Grey

12. OH, SUSANNA! (9-19-36)
Cast: Gene Autry, Smiley Burnette, Frances Grant, Earle Hodgins, Donald Kirke, Booth Howard, Clara Kimball Young, Ed Piel, Sr., Frankie Marvin, Carl Stockdale, Gerall Roscoe, Roger Gray, Fred Burns, Walter James, Lew Meehan, Fred Toones, Earl Dwire, Bruce Mitchell, Jack Kirk, George Morrell, the Light Crust Doughboys, Champion
Director: Joe Kane
Supervisor: Armand Schaefer
Producer: Nat Levine
Screenplay: Oliver Drake
Camera: William Nobles
Music Director: Harry Grey
Songs: "Dear Old Western Skies," "By a Waterwheel," "Ti Yi Yippi I O," "Old Susanna," "Hold That Tiger," "Don't Trust a Bicycle Racer," and "Ride On Vaquero"

13. RIDE, RANGER, RIDE (9-30-36)
    Cast: Gene Autry, Smiley Burnette, Kay Hughes, Monte Blue,
    Max Terhune, George J. Lewis, Robert Homans, Chief Thun-
    dercloud, Frankie Marvin, Iron Eyes Cody, Sunny Chorre, Bud
    Pope, Nelson McDowell, Shooting Star, Arthur Singley, Greg
    Whitespear, Robert Thomas, the Tennessee Ramblers, Champion
    Director: Joe Kane
    Producer: Nat Levine
    Story: Bernard McConville, Karen DeWolf
    Screenplay: Dorrell and Stuart McGowan
    Camera: William Nobles
    Music Director: Harry Grey
    Songs: "Ride, Ranger, Ride," "On a Sunset Trail," "Going Down
        the Road," "Bugle Song," "Yellow Rose of Texas," "Song
        of the Pioneers"

14. THE BIG SHOW (11-16-36)
    Cast: Gene Autry, Smiley Burnette, Kay Hughes, Max Terhune,
    Sally Payne, William Newill, Charles Judels, Rex King, Harry
    Worth, Mary Russell, Christine Maple, Jerry Larkin, Jack
    O'Shea, Wedgewood Norrell, Antrim Short, June Johnson,
    Grace Durkin, Slim Whitaker, George Chesebro, Edward Hearn,
    Cliff Lyons, Tracy Layne, Jack Rockwell, Frankie Marvin,
    Cornelius Keefe, Martin Stevenson, Horace B. Carpenter, Helen
    Servis, Frances Morris, Richard Beach, Jeanne Lafayette, Art
    Mix, I. Stanford Jolley, Vic Lacardo, Sally Rand, the SMU 50,
    the Sons of the Pioneers, the Light Crust Doughboys, the Beverly
    Hillbillies, the Jones Boys
    Director: Mack Wright
    Story: Dorrell and Stuart McGowan
    Producer: Nat Levine
    Camera: William Nobles, Edgar Lyons
    Music Director: Harry Grey
    Songs: Included "Lady Known As Lulu" by Washington and
        Stept and "Mad About You" by Koehler and Stept

15. THE OLD CORRAL (12-21-36)
    Cast: Gene Autry, Smiley Burnette, Hope Manning, Lon
    Chaney, Jr., Cornelius Keefe, Marc Kramer, Milburn Moranti,
    Frankie Marvin, Abe Lefton, Buddy Roosevelt, Lynton Brent,
    Charles Sullivan, John Bradford, Dick Weston (Roy Rogers),
    Merrill McCormack, Lew Kelly, Oscar and Elmer (Ed Platt and
    Lou Fulton), Jack Ingram, the Sons of the Pioneers, Champion

Director: Joe Kane
Producer: Nat Levine
Story: Bernard McConville
Screenplay: Sherman Lowe, Joseph Poland
Music Director: Harry Grey
Songs: "The Old Corral" and "Old Pinto"

16. ROUND-UP TIME IN TEXAS (2-28-37)
Cast: Gene Autry, Smiley Burnette, Maxine Doyle, LeRoy Mason, Earle Hodgins, Buddy Williams, Dick Wessell, Cornie Anderson, Frankie Marvin, Ken Cooper, Elmer Fain, Al Ferguson, Slim Whitaker, Al Knight, Carlton Young, Jim Corey, Jack C. Smith, Jack Kirk, George Morrell, the Cabin Kids, Champion
Director: Joe Kane
Producer: Nat Levine
Associate Producer: Armand Schaefer
Screenplay: Oliver Drake
Editors: Murray Seldeen, Les Orlebeck
Camera: William Nobles
Music Director: Harry Grey
Songs: Included "Old Chisholm Trail," "Dry, Dry, Dry," and "Noah's Ark"

17. GIT ALONG LITTLE DOGIES (3-27-37)
Cast: Gene Autry, Smiley Burnette, Judith Allen, Weldon Heyburn, William Farnum, Willie Fung, Carleton Young, Raymond Nye, Frankie Marvin, George Morrell, Horace Carpenter, Rose Plummer, Earl Dwire, Lynton Brent, Jack Kirk, Al Taylor, Frank Ellis, Jack C. Smith, Murdock McQuarrie, Oscar Gahan, Monte Montague, Sam McDaniel, Eddie Parker, Bob Burns, the Maple City Four, Will and Gladys Ahern, the Cabin Kids, Champion
Director: Joe Kane
Associate Producer: Armand Schaefer
Screenplay: Dorrell and Stuart McGowan
Camera: Gus Peterson
Music Director: Harry Grey
Songs: "Git Along Little Dogies," "Honey, Bringing Honey to You," "Chinatown," "If You Want to Be a Cowboy," "Stock Selling Song," "Wait for the Wagon," "Red River Valley," "Comin' 'Round the Mountain," "Long, Long

Ago," "In the Valley Where the Sun Goes Down," "Oh, Suzanna," "Goodnight, Ladies," "After You've Gone," "Happy Days Are Here Again"

18. ROOTIN' TOOTIN' RHYTHM (5-12-37)
Cast: Gene Autry, Smiley Burnette, Armida, Monte Blue, Ann Pendleton, Hal Taliaferro, Charles King, Max Hoffman, Jr., Frankie Marvin, Nina Campana, Charles Mayer, Karl Hackett, Henry Hall, Curley Dresden, Art Davis, Al Clauser and His Oklahoma Outlaws, Champion
Director: Mack Wright
Associate Producer: Armand Schaefer
Screenplay: Jack Natteford
Story: Johnston McCulley
Camera: William Nobles
Editor: Tony Martinelli
Music Supervisor: Raoul Kraushaar
Songs: Included "The Old Home Place" by Sol Meyer and Jule Styne; "Mexicali Rose" by H. Stone and J. B. Tenney; "Rootin' Tootin' Rhythm" by Raoul Kraushaar

19. YODELIN' KID FROM PINE RIDGE (6-14-37)
Cast: Gene Autry, Smiley Burnette, Betty Bronson, LeRoy Mason, Charles Middleton, Russell Simpson, Jack Dougherty, Guy Wilkerson, Frankie Marvin, Henry Hall, Fred Toones, Jack Kirk, Bob Burns, Al Taylor, George Morrell, Lew Meehan, Jim Corey, Jack Ingram, Art Dillard, Art Mix, Bud Osborne, Oscar Gahan, the Tennessee Ramblers (Dick Hartman, W. J. Blair, Elmer Warren, Happy Morris, and Pappy Wolf), Champion
Director: Joe Kane
Associate Producer: Armand Schaefer
Story: Jack Natteford
Screenplay: Jack Natteford, Stuart and Dorrell McGowan
Camera: William Nobles
Editors: Murray Seldeen, Les Orlebeck
Music Director: Raoul Kraushaar
Songs by: Gene Autry, Frank Hartford, Smiley Burnette, William Lava, Jack Stanley

20. PUBLIC COWBOY NUMBER 1 (8-23-37)
Cast: Gene Autry, Smiley Burnette, Ann Rutherford, William Farnum, James C. Morton, Maston Williams, Arthur Loft,

Frankie Marvin, House Peters, Jr., Frank LaRue, Milburn Moranti, King Mojave, Hal Price, Jack Ingram, Ray Bennett, George Plues, Frank Ellis, James Mason, Doug Evans, Bob Burns
Director: Joe Kane
Associate Producer: Sol C. Siegel
Story: Bernard McConville
Screenplay: Oliver Drake
Camera: Jack Marta
Editor: Murray Seldeen, Les Orlebeck, George Reid
Music Director: Raoul Kraushaar
Songs: "Wanderers of the Wasteland," "The West Ain't What It Used to Be," "Old Buckaroo," "I Picked Out a Trail to Your Heart" and "Defective Detective From Brooklyn"

21. BOOTS AND SADDLES (10-4-37)
Cast: Gene Autry, Smiley Burnette, Judith Allen, Ra Hould, Gordon Elliott (aka Bill Elliott), Guy Usher, John Ward, Frankie Marvin, Chris-Pin Martin, Stanley Blystone, Bud Osborne, Champion
Director: Joe Kane
Associate Producer: Sol C. Siegel
Story: Jack Natteford
Screenplay: Oliver Drake
Camera: William Nobles
Editor: Les Orlebeck
Music Director: Raoul Kraushaar
Songs: "Take Me Back to My Boots and Saddles" by Teddy Powell, Leonard Whitecup and Walter Samuels; "Riding the Range" by Fleming Allan, Gene Autry and Nelson Shawn; "The One Rose" by Lani McIntyre and Del Lyon; "Cielito Lindo" (P.D.)

22. MANHATTAN MERRY-GO-ROUND (11-13-37)
Cast: Phil Regan, Leo Carrillo, Ann Dvorak, Tamara Geva, Ted Lewis, Cab Calloway, Joe DiMaggio, Louis Prima, Henry Armetta, Max Terhune, Smiley Burnette . . . and Guest Star Gene Autry
Director: Charles Riesner

23. SPRINGTIME IN THE ROCKIES (11-15-37)
Cast: Gene Autry, Smiley Burnette, Polly Rowles, Ula Love, Ruth Bacon, Jane Hunt, George Chesebro, Alan Bridge, Tom

London, Edward Hearn, Frankie Marvin, William Hale, Edmund Cobb, Fred Burns, Art Davis, Lew Meehan, Jack Kirk, Frank Ellis, George Letz (George Montgomery), Robert Dudley, Jack Rockwell, Jimmy's (Wakely) Saddle Pals, Victor Cox, Jim Corey, Champion
Director: Joe Kane
Associate Producer: Sol C. Siegel
Story/Screenplay: Betty Burbridge, Gilbert Wright
Camera: Ernest Miller
Editor: Les Orlebeck
Music Director: Raoul Kraushaar
Songs: "Give Me My Pony and an Open Prairie" by Gene Autry and Frank Hartford; "Down in the Land of the Zulu" and "Hayride Wedding in June" by Gene Autry and Johnny Marvin; "When It's Springtime in the Rockies" by Woolsey, Taggart and Sauer.

24. The Old Barn Dance (1-29-38)
Cast: Gene Autry, Smiley Burnette, Helen Valkis, Sammy McKim, Ivan Miller, Earl Dwire, Hooper Atchley, Ray Bennett, Carleton Young, Frankie Marvin, Earle Hodgins, Gloria Rich, Dick Weston (Roy Rogers), Denver Dixon, the Stafford Sisters, the Maple City Four, Walt Shrum and his Colorado Hillbillies, Champion
Director: Joe Kane
Associate Producer: Sol C. Siegel
Screenplay: Bernard McConville, Charles Francis Royal
Camera: Ernest Miller
Editor: Les Orlebeck
Music Director: Alberto Columbo
Songs: "You're the Only Star in My Blue Heaven" by Gene Autry; "The Old Mill" by Johnny Marvin; "Ten Little Miles" and "At the Old Barn Dance" by Lawrence and Tinturin

25. Gold Mine in the Sky (7-4-38)
Cast: Gene Autry, Smiley Burnette, Carol Hughes, Craig Reynolds, Cupid Ainsworth, LeRoy Mason, Frankie Marvin, Robert Homans, Eddie Cherkose, Ben Corbett, Milburn Moranti, Jim Corey, George Guhl, Jack Kirk, Fred Toones, George Letz, (George Montgomery), Charles King, Lew Kelly, Joe Whitehead, Matty Roubert, Anita Bolster, Earl Dwire, Maude Prickett,

Al Taylor, Art Dillard, Stafford Sisters, J. L. Frank's Golden
West Cowboys of WSM Nashville
Director: Joe Kane
Associate Producer: Charles E. Ford
Story: Betty Burbridge
Screenplay: Betty Burbridge, Jack Natteford
Camera: William Nobles
Editor: Les Orlebeck
Musical Score and Direction: Alberto Columbo
Songs: "There's a Gold Mine in the Sky" by Charles and Nick
    Kenney, "As Long As I Have My Horse" and "Dude
    Ranch Cowhands" by Gene Autry, Fred Rose, and
    Johnny Marvin; "Hummin' When We're Coming 'Round
    the Bend" by Eddie Cherkose and Alberto Columbo;
    "That's How Donkeys Were Born" by Eddie Cherkose
    and Smiley Burnette

26. MAN FROM MUSIC MOUNTAIN (8-15-38)
Cast: Gene Autry, Smiley Burnette, Carol Hughes, Sally Payne,
Ivan Miller, Al Terry, Dick Elliott, Hal Price, Cactus Mack, Ed
Cassidy, Howard Chase, Lew Kelly, Frankie Marvin, Earl Dwire,
Lloyd Ingraham, Lillian Drew, Al Taylor, Joe Yrigoyen, Gordon
Hart, Rudy Sooter, Harry Harvey, Meredith McCormack, Chris
Allen, Polly Jenkins and her Plowboys, Champion
Director: Joe Kane
Associate Producer: Charles E. Ford
Story: Bernard McConville
Screenplay: Betty Burbridge, Luci Ward
Camera: Jack Marta
Editor: Les Orlebeck
Music Director: Raoul Kraushaar
Songs: "Love, Burning Love," "There's a Little Deserted Town,"
    "I'm Beginning to Care," and "Good-by Pinto" by Gene
    Autry, Fred Rose, and Johnny Marvin; "All Nice People"
    and "She Works Third Tub at the Laundry" by Smiley
    Burnette

27. PRAIRIE MOON (9-25-38)
Cast: Gene Autry, Smiley Burnette, Shirley Deane, Tommy
Ryan, Tom London, William Pawley, Warner Richmond,
Walter Tetley, David Gorcey, Stanley Andrews, Peter Potter,

Bud Osborne, Ray Bennett, Jack Rockwell, Hal Price, Merrill
McCormack, Lew Meehan, Jack Kirk, Champion
Director: Ralph Staub
Associate Producer: Harry Grey
Screenplay: Betty Burbridge, Stanley Roberts
Camera: William Nobles
Editor: Les Orlebeck
Music Director: Raoul Kraushaar
Songs: "Girl in the Middle of the Night," "Welcome Strangers,"
and "Story of Grigger Joe" by Eddie Cherkose and W.
Kent; "Rhythm of the Hoofbeats" by Johnny Marvin; "In
the Jailhouse Now" by Jimmie Rodgers; "The West, a
Nest, and You" by Yoell and Hill

28. RHYTHM OF THE SADDLE (11-5-38)
Cast: Gene Autry, Smiley Burnette, Peggy Moran, Pert Kelton,
LeRoy Mason, Arthur Loft, Ethan Laidlaw, Walter De Palma,
Archie Hall, Eddie Hart, Eddie Acuff, Douglas Wright, Kelsey
Sheldon, Lola Monte, Alan Gregg, Rudy Sooter, James Mason,
Jack Kirk, Emmett Vogan, Tom London, William Norton
Bailey, Roger Williams, Curley Dresden, Champion
Director: George Sherman
Associate Producer: Harry Grey
Screenplay: Paul Franklin
Camera: Jack Marta
Editor: Les Orlebeck
Music Director: Raoul Kraushaar
Songs: "The Old Trail," "Oh, Ladies!" and "The Merry-Go-
Roundup" by Gene Autry, Fred Rose, and Johnny Marvin

29. WESTERN JAMBOREE (12-2-38)
Cast: Gene Autry, Smiley Burnette, Jean Rouveral, Joe Frisco,
Esther Muir, Kermit Maynard, Jack Perrin, Jack Ingram, Frank
Darien, Margaret Armstrong, Harry Holman, Edward Raquello,
Bentley Hewitt, George Walcott, Ray Teal, Frank Ellis, Eddie
Dean, Davidson Clark, Champion
Director: Ralph Staub
Associate Producer: Harry Grey
Story: Patricia Harper
Screenplay: Gerald Geraghty
Camera: William Nobles
Editor: Les Orlebeck

Music Director: Raoul Kraushaar
Songs: "Roll On, Little Dogies, Roll On," "Old November Moon," "I Love the Morning," "Balloon Song," and "Round-up Time in Texas"

30. HOME ON THE PRAIRIE (2-3-39)
Cast: Gene Autry, Smiley Burnette, June Storey, George Cleveland, Jack Mulhall, Walter Miller, Gordon Hart, Hal Price, Earle Hodgins, Ethan Laidlaw, John Beach, Jack Ingram, Bob Woodward, Sherven Brothers Rodeoliers, Champion
Director: Jack Townley
Associate Producer: Harry Grey
Screenplay: Arthur Powell, Paul Franklin
Camera: Reggie Lanning
Editor: Les Orlebeck
Music Director: Raoul Kraushaar
Songs: "I'm Gonna Roundup My Blues" by Johnny Marvin; "Big Bullfrog" and "Moonlight on the Ranch House" by Walter Samuels

31. MEXICALI ROSE (3-27-39)
Cast: Gene Autry, Smiley Burnette, Noah Beery, Sr., Luana Walters, William Farnum, William Royle, LeRoy Mason, Wally Albright, Kathryn Frye, Roy Barcroft, Dick Botiller, Vic Demourelle, John Beach, Henry Otho, Joe Dominguez, Al Haskell, Merrill McCormack, Fred Toones, Sherry Hall, Al Taylor, Josef Swickward, Tom London, Jack Ingram, Eddie Parker, Champion
Director: George Sherman
Associate Producer: Harry Grey
Story: Luci Ward, Connie Lee
Screenplay: Gerald Geraghty
Camera: William Nobles
Editor: Tony Martinelli
Music Director: Raoul Kraushaar
Songs: "Mexicali Rose" by Tenney and Stone; "You're the Only Star in My Blue Heaven" by Gene Autry; "My Orchestra's Driving Me Crazy" by Smiley Burnette and "El Rancho Grande" by Costello, Morales, and Uranga

32. BLUE MONTANA SKIES (5-4-39)
Cast: Gene Autry, Smiley Burnette, June Storey, Harry Woods, Tully Marshall, Al Bridge, Glenn Strange, Dorothy Granger, Ed-

mund Cobb, Robert Winkler, Jack Ingram, John Beach, Elmo
Lincoln, Jay Wilsey, Allan Cavan, Augie Gomez, Walt Shrum
and his Colorado Hillbillies, Champion
Director: B. Reeves Eason
Associate Producer: Harry Grey
Story: Norman S. Hall, Paul Franklin
Screenplay: Gerald Geraghty
Camera: Jack Marta
Editor: Les Orlebeck
Music Director: Raoul Kraushaar
Songs: "Rocking in the Saddle," "Old Geezer," " 'Neath the
  Blue Montana Sky," "I Just Want You," and "Away
  Out Yonder" by Fred Rose

33. MOUNTAIN RHYTHM (6-9-39)
Cast: Gene Autry, Smiley Burnette, June Storey, Maude Eburne,
Ferris Taylor, Walter Fenner, Jack Pennick, Hooper Atchley,
Bernard Suss, Ed Cassidy, Jack Ingram, Tom London, Roger
Williams, Frankie Marvin, Champion
Director: B. Reeves Eason
Associate Producer: Harry Grey
Story: Connie Lee
Screenplay: Gerald Geraghty
Camera: Ernest Miller
Editor: Les Orlebeck
Music Director: Raoul Kraushaar
Songs: "Knights of the Open Road," "Only a Hobo's Dream,"
  and "A Gold Mine in Your Heart" by Fred Rose

34. COLORADO SUNSET (7-31-39)
Cast: Gene Autry, Smiley Burnette, June Storey, Barbara Pepper,
Larry "Buster" Crabbe, Robert Barratt, Patsy Montana, Purnell
Pratt, William Farnum, Kermit Maynard, Jack Ingram, Elmo
Lincoln, Frankie Marvin, Ethan Laidlaw, Fred Burns, Jack Kirk,
Budd Buster, Ed Cassidy, Slim Whitaker, Murdock McQuarrie,
Ralph Peters, the CBS-KMBC Texas Rangers, Cactus Mack,
Champion
Director: George Sherman
Associate Producer: William Berke
Story: Luci Ward, Jack Natteford
Screenplay: Betty Burbridge, Stanley Roberts
Camera: William Nobles
Editor: Les Orlebeck

Music Director: Raoul Kraushaar
Songs: "Colorado Sunset" composition by Con Conrad and L. Wolfe Gilbert, "Seven Years with the Wrong Woman," "On Our Merry Old Way Back Home," "Poor Little Dogies," and "Vote for Autry"

35. IN OLD MONTEREY (8-14-39)
Cast: Gene Autry, Smiley Burnette, June Storey, George "Gabby" Hayes, Stuart Hamblen, Billy Lee, Jonathan Lee, Robert Warwick, William Hall, Eddy Conrad, Curley Dresden, Victor Cox, Ken Carson, Robert Wilke, Hal Price, Tom Steele, Jack O'Shea, Rex Lease, Edward Earle, James Mason, Fred Burns, Dan White, Frank Ellis, Jim Corey, Sarie and Sallie, the Ranch Boys, Champion
Director: Joe Kane
Associate Producer: Armand Schaefer
Story: Gerald Geraghty, George Sherman
Screenplay: Gerald Geraghty, Dorrell and Stuart McGowan
Camera: Ernest Miller
Editor: Edward Mann
Music Director: Raoul Kraushaar
Songs: "It Happened in Monterrey," "My Buddy," "Little Pardner," "Tumbling Tumbleweeds," "Born in the Saddle," "Columbia, the Gem of the Ocean," and "The Vacant Chair"

36. ROVIN' TUMBLEWEEDS (11-16-39) originally titled *Washington Cowboy*
Cast: Gene Autry, Smiley Burnette, Mary Carlisle, Douglas Dumbrille, William Farnum, Lee "Lasses" White, Ralph Peters, Gordon Hart, Vic Potel, Sammy McKim, Jack Ingram, Reginald Barlow, Eddie Kane, Guy Usher, Horace Murphy, David Sharpe, Jack Kirk, Rose Plummer, Bob Burns, Art Mix, Horace Carpenter, Frank Ellis, Fred Burns, Ed Cassidy, Forrest Taylor, Tom Chatterton, Crauford Kent, Maurice Costello, Charles K. French, Lee Shumway, Bud Osborne, Harry Semels, Chuch Morrison, the Pals of the Golden West, Champion
Director: George Sherman
Associate Producer: William Berke
Screenplay: Betty Burbridge, Dorrell and Stuart McGowan
Camera: William Nobles
Editor: Tony Martinelli

Music Director: Raoul Kraushaar
Songs: "Old Peaceful River," "Rocky Mountain Express," "Back in the Saddle Again," "Away Up Yonder"

37. SOUTH OF THE BORDER (12-15-39)
Cast: Gene Autry, Smiley Burnette, June Storey, Lupita Tovar, Mary Lee, Duncan Renaldo, Frank Reicher, Alan Edwards, Claire DuBrey, Dick Botiller, William Farnum, Selmer Jackson, Sheila Darcy, Rex Lease, Charles King, Reed Howes, Jack O'Shea, Slim Whitaker, Hal Price, Julian Rivero, Curley Dresden, The Checkerboard Band, Champion
Director: George Sherman
Associate Producer: William Berke
Story: Dorrell and Stuart McGowan
Screenplay: Betty Burbridge, Gerald Geraghty
Camera: William Nobles
Editor: Les Orlebeck
Music Director: Raoul Kraushaar
Songs: "South of the Border" by Jimmy Kennedy and Michael
       Carr; "Come to the Fiesta" by Art Wenzel; "Horse
       Opry" by Fred Rose; "Moon Over Mañana" and "When
       the Cactus Blooms Again" by Gene Autry and Johnny
       Marvin

38. RANCHO GRANDE (3-2-40)
Cast: Gene Autry, Smiley Burnette, June Storey, Mary Lee, Dick Hogan, Ellen Lowe, Roscoe Ates, Rex Lease, Ferris Taylor, Joe De Stefani, Ann Baldwin, Roy Barcroft, Edna Lawrence, Jack Ingram, Bud Osborne, Slim Whitaker, the Brewer Kids, Pals of the Golden West, Champion
Director: Frank McDonald
Associate Producer: William Berke
Story: Pete Milne, Connie Lee
Screenplay: Bradford Ropes, Betty Burbridge, Pete Milne
Camera: William Nobles
Editor: Tony Martinelli
Music Director: Raoul Kraushaar
Songs: "I Don't Belong in Your World" by Gene Autry and
       Johnny Marvin; "You Can't Take the Boy Out of the
       Country" and "Belles of the Bunkhouse" by Walter Sam-
       uels; "Swing of the Range" by Johnny Marvin and Harry

Tobias; "Whistle" by Gene Autry, Johnny Marvin, and
Fred Rose, and *"El Rancho Grande"* and *"El Cucaracha"*

39. SHOOTING HIGH (Twentieth Century-Fox 4-26-40)
Cast: Jane Withers, Gene Autry, Marjorie Weaver, Robert
Lowery, Kay Aldridge, Hobart Cavanaugh, Jack Carson, Tom
London, Charles Middleton, Ed Brady, Eddie Acuff, Frank M.
Thomas, Hamilton MacFadden, Pat O'Malley, George Chandler,
Carl Cotner, Frankie Marvin, Champion
Director: Alfred E. Green
Producer: John Stone
Screenplay: Lou Breslow, Owen Francis
Camera: Ernest Palmer
Editor: Nick De Maggio
Music Director: Samuel Kaylin
Songs: "On the Rancho with My Pancho" by Sidney Claire and
    Harry Akst; "Shanty of Dreams" by Gene Autry and
    Johnny Marvin; "Only One Love in a Lifetime" by Gene
    Autry, Johnny Marvin, and Harry Tobias; "Little Old
    Band of Gold" by Gene Autry, Charles Newman, and
    Fred Glickman

40. GAUCHO SERENADE (5-10-40)
Cast: Gene Autry, Smiley Burnette, June Storey, Duncan Re-
naldo, Mary Lee, Clifford Severn, Jr., Lester Matthews, Smith
Ballew, Joseph Crehan, William Ruhl, Wade Boteler, Ted
Adams, Fred Burns, Julian Rivero, George Lloyd, José Domin-
guez, Olaf Hytten, Fred Toones, Ed Cassidy, Gene Morgan, Jack
Kirk, Harry Strang, Hank Worden, Kernan Cripps, Jim Corey,
Tom London, Walter Miller, Champion
Director: Frank McDonald
Associate Producer: William Berke
Screenplay: Betty Burbridge, Bradford Ropes
Camera: Reggie Lanning
Editor: Tony Martinelli
Music Director; Raoul Kraushaar
Songs: "Keep Rollin'" and "Lazy Longhorns" by Gene Autry
    and Johnny Marvin, "A Song at Sunset" and "Headin' for
    the Wide Open Spaces" by Gene Autry, Johnny Marvin,
    and Harry Tobias

41. CAROLINA MOON (7-16-40)

Cast: Gene Autry, Smiley Burnette, June Storey, Mary Lee, Eddy Waller, Hardie Albright, Frank Dale, Terry Nibert, Robert Fiske, Etta McDaniel, Paul White, Fred Ritter, Ralph Sanford, Texas Jim Lewis and his Texas Cowboys, Champion
Director: Frank McDonald
Associate Producer: William Berke
Story; Connie Lee
Screenplay: Winston Miller
Camera: William Nobles
Editor: Tony Martinelli
Music Director: Raoul Kraushaar
Songs: "At the Rodeo" by Gene Autry and Johnny Marvin; "Dreams That Don't Come True" by Gene Autry, Johnny Marvin, and Harry Tobias; "Carolina Moon" by Burke-Davis

42. RIDE, TENDERFOOT, RIDE (9-6-40)

Cast: Gene Autry, Smiley Burnette, June Storey, Warren Hull, Mary Lee, Si Jenks, Forbes Murray, Joe Frisco, Joe McGuinn, Isobel Randolph, Herbert Clifton, Mildred Shay, Cindy Walker, Patty Saks, Jack Kirk, Slim Whitaker, Fred Burns, Cactus Mack, Hank Worden, Dick Elliott, Franklyn Farnum, Hal Price, Ray Jones, George Morrell, Champion
Director: Frank McDonald
Associate Producer: William Berke
Screenplay: Winston Miller
Story: Betty Burbridge, Connie Lee
Camera: Jack Marta
Editor: Les Orlebeck
Music Director: Raoul Kraushaar
Songs: "Eleven More Months and Ten More Days" by Fred Hall and Arthur Fields; "Ride, Tenderfoot, Ride" by Johnny Mercer and Richard Whiting; "That Was Me By the Sea" by Smiley Burnette; "Leanin' on the Old Top Rail" by Nick and Charles Kenney

43. MELODY RANCH (11-15-40)

Cast: Gene Autry, Jimmy Durante, Ann Miller, Barton Mac-Lane, Barbara Allen (Vera Vague), George "Gabby" Hayes, Jerome Cowan, Mary Lee, Joe Sawyer, Horace MacMahon, Clarence Wilson, Billy Benedict, Ruth Gifford, Maxine Ardell, Vera Ann Borg, George Chandler, Jack Ingram, Horace

Murphy, Lloyd Ingraham, Tom London, John Merton, Edmund
Cobb, Slim Whitaker, Curley Dresden, Dick Elliott, Billy
Bletcher, Art Mix, George Chesebro, Tiny Jones, Herman Hack,
Jack Kirk, Merrill McCormack, Wally West, Bob Wills and His
Texas Playboys, Champion
Director: Joseph Santley
Associate Producer: Sol C. Siegel
Screenplay: Jack Moffitt, F. Hugh Herbert
Special Comedy Sequences: Sid Kuller, Ray Golden
Camera: Joseph August
Editors: Murray Seldeen, Les Orlebeck
Music Director: Raoul Kraushaar
Special Music and Lyrics: Jule Styne and Eddie Cherkose
Songs: "Melody Ranch," "Call of the Canyon," "Same Dream
   Twice," and "Rodeo Rose"

44. RIDIN' ON A RAINBOW (1-24-41)
Cast: Gene Autry, Smiley Burnette, Mary Lee, Carol Adams,
Ferris Taylor, Georgia Caine, Byron Foulger, Ralf Harolde,
Jimmy Conlin, Guy Usher, Anthony Warde, Forrest Taylor,
Burr Caruth, Ed Cassidy, Ben Hall, Tom London, William Long,
Champion
Director: Lew Landers
Associate Producer: Harry Grey
Story: Bradford Ropes
Screenplay: Bradford Ropes, Doris Malloy
Camera: William Nobles
Editor: Tony Martinelli
Music Director: Raoul Kraushaar
Special Music: Jule Styne and Sol Meyer
Songs: "Be Honest with Me" by Gene Autry; "Some Dancin'"
   by Smiley Burnette; "Ridin' on a Rainbow" by Don
   George, Jean Herbert, and Teddy Hall; "Steamboat Bill"
   by Ken Sheilds and the Leighton Brothers; "I'm the Only
   Lonely One" by Jule Styne and Sol Meyer; "Carry Me
   Back to the Lone Prairie" by Carson Robinson; "Sing a
   Song of Laughter," "What's Your Favorite Holiday," and
   "Hunky Dunky Dory"

45. BACK IN THE SADDLE (3-14-41)
Cast: Gene Autry, Smiley Burnette, Mary Lee, Edward Norris,
Jacqueline Wells (aka Julie Bishop), Addison Richards, Arthur
Loft, Edmund Elton, Joe McGuinn, Edmund Cobb, Robert Bar-

ron, Reed Howes, Stanley Blystone, Curley Dresden, Fred Toones, Frank Ellis, Jack O'Shea, Victor Cox, Herman Hack, Bob Burns, Champion
Director: Lew Landers
Associate Producer: Harry Grey
Screenplay: Richard Murphy, Jesse Lasky, Jr.
Camera: Ernest Miller
Editor: Tony Martinelli
Music Director: Raoul Kraushaar
Songs: Included "You Are My Sunshine" by Jimmy Davis and Charles Mitchell; "Where the River Meets the Range" by Sol Meyer and Jule Styne; "I'm an Old Cowhand" (P.D.); "Back in the Saddle Again" by Gene Autry and Ray Whitley

46. THE SINGING HILL (4-26-41)
Cast: Gene Autry, Smiley Burnette, Virginia Dale, Mary Lee, Spencer Charters, Gerald Oliver Smith, George Meeker, Wade Boteler, Harry Stubbs, Cactus Mack, Jack Kirk, Chuck Morrison, Monte Montague, Sam Flint, Hal Price, Fred Burns, Herman Hack, Jack O'Shea, Champion
Director: Lew Landers
Associate Producer: Harry Grey
Story: Jesse Lasky, Jr., Richard Murphy
Screenplay: Olive Cooper
Camera: William Nobles
Editor: Les Orlebeck
Music Director: Raoul Kraushaar
Songs: "The Last Roundup," "Let a Smile Be Your Umbrella," "Patsy's Birthday Routine" and "Blueberry Hill"

47. SUNSET IN WYOMING (7-15-41)
Cast: Gene Autry, Smiley Burnette, Maris Wrizon, George Cleveland, Robert Kent, Sarah Edwards, Monte Blue, Dick Elliott, John Dilson, Stanley Blystone, Eddie Dew, Fred Burns, Reed Howes, Ralph Peters, Syd Saylor, Tex Terry, Lloyd Whitlock, Herman Hack, Champion
Director: William Morgan
Associate Producer: Harry Grey
Story: Joe Blair
Screenplay: Ivan Goff, Anne Morrison Chapin

Camera: Reggie Lanning
Editor: Tony Martinelli
Music Director: Raoul Kraushaar
Songs: "Sing Me a Song of the Saddle" by Gene Autry and
Frank Hartford; "Sign Up for Happy Days" and "Sweet
Patootie Kitty" by Jule Styne and Sol Meyer; "Heebie
Jeebie Blues" by Harry Grey and Oliver Drake; "Casey
Jones," "There's a Home in Wyoming," "Twenty-one
Years" and "Happy Cowboy"

48. UNDER FIESTA STARS (8-25-41)
Cast: Gene Autry, Smiley Burnette, Carol Hughes, Frank
Darien, Joe Strauch, Jr., Pauline Drake, Ivan Miller, Sam Flint,
Elias Camboa, John Merton, Jack Kirk, Inez Palange, Hal
Taliaferro, Curley Dresden, Champion
Director: Frank McDonald
Associate Producer: Harry Grey
Story: Karl Brown
Screenplay: Karl Brown, Eliot Gibbons
Camera: Harry Neumann
Editor: Tony Martinelli
Music Director: Raoul Kraushaar
Songs: "Purple Sage in the Twilight" by Gene Autry, Sol
Meyer and Jule Styne; "When You're Smiling" by Mark
Fisher, Joe Goodwin and Larry Shay; "Under Fiesta Stars"
by Gene Autry and Fred Rose

49. DOWN MEXICO WAY (10-15-41)
Cast: Gene Autry, Smiley Burnette, Fay McKenzie, Harold
Huber, Sidney Blackmer, Duncan Renaldo, Arthur Loft, Murray
Alper, Joe Sawyer, Paul Fix, Julian Rivero, Eddie Dean, Thorn-
ton Edwards, Ruth Robinson, Andrew Tombes, the Herrera
Sisters, Champion
Director: Joseph Santley
Associate Producer: Harry Grey
Story: Dorrell and Stuart McGowan
Screenplay: Olive Cooper, Albert Duff
Camera: Jack Marta
Editor: Howard O'Neill
Songs: "Down Mexico Way," "Maria Elena," "South of the Bor-
der," "Cowboy and the Lady," "Beer Barrel Polka," "*Las
Altanitas*," "*La Cachita*" and "Guadalajara"

50. SIERRA SUE (11-12-41)
    Cast: Gene Autry, Smiley Burnette, Fay McKenzie, Frank M.
    Thomas, Robert Homans, Earle Hodgins, Dorothy Christy, Jack
    Kirk, Eddie Dean, Kermit Maynard, Budd Buster, Rex Lease,
    Hugh Prosser, Vince Barnett, Hal Price, Syd Saylor, Roy Butler,
    Sammy Stein, Eddie Cherkose, Bob McKenzie, Marin Sais, Bud
    Brown, Gene Eblen, Buel Bryant, Ray Davis, Art Dillard,
    Frankie Marvin, Champion
    Director: William Morgan
    Associate Producer: Harry Grey
    Screenplay: Earl Felton, Julian Zimet
    Camera: Jack Marta
    Editor: Les Orlebeck
    Music Director: Raoul Kraushaar
    Songs: "Sierra Sue," "Be Honest with Me," "Ridin' the Range,"
        "Heebie Jeebie Blues," and "I'll Be True While You're
        Gone"

51. COWBOY SERENADE (1-23-42)
    Cast: Gene Autry, Smiley Burnette, Fay McKenzie, Cecil Cun-
    ningham, Addison Richards, Rand Brooks, Tris Coffin, Slim
    Andrews, Melinda Leighton, Johnnie Berkes, Forrest Taylor, Si
    Jenks, Hank Worden, Otto Han, Loren Raker, Bill Wolfe, Bud
    Geary, Forbes Murray, Hal Price, Frankie Marvin, Ethan Laid-
    law, Tom London, Ken Terrell, Ken Cooper, Rich Anderson,
    Roger Kirby, Champion
    Director: William Morgan
    Associate Producer: Harry Grey
    Screenplay: Olive Cooper
    Camera: Jack Marta
    Editor: Les Orlebeck
    Music Director: Raoul Kraushaar
    Songs: "Sweethearts or Strangers," "Cowboy Serenade," "No-
        body Knows," and "Tahiti Honey"

52. HEART OF THE RIO GRANDE (3-11-42)
    Cast: Gene Autry, Smiley Burnette, Fay McKenzie, Edith Fel-
    lows, Pierre Watkin, Joe Strauch, Jr., William Haade, Sarah Pad-
    den, Jean Porter, Milton Kibbee, Edmund Cobb, Budd Buster,
    Frank Mills, Howard Mitchell, Allan Wood, Nora Lane, Mady
    Lawrence, Buck Woods, Harry Depp, George Porter, Frankie
    Marvin, Jeanne Hebers, Kay Frye, Betty Jane Graham, Patsy Fay

Northup, Jan Lester, Gloria and Gladys Gardner, the Jimmy
Wakely Trio (with Jimmy Wakely, Johnny Bond, and Dick
Rinehart), Champion
Director: William Morgan
Associate Producer: Harry Grey
Story: Newlin B. Wildes
Screenplay: Lillie Hayward, Winston Miller
Camera: Harry Neumann
Editor: Les Orlebeck
Music Director: Raoul Kraushaar
Songs: "Deep in the Heart of Texas," "Dusk on the Painted Des-
ert," "Rancho Pillow," "I'll Wait for You," "Cimarron,"
"Rocky Canyon," "Rainbow in the Night," "A Rumble
Seat for Two," and "Oh Woe Is Me"

53. HOME IN WYOMIN' (4-20-42)
Cast: Gene Autry, Smiley Burnette, Fay McKenzie, Olin How-
lin, Chick Chandler, Joe Strauch, Jr., Forrest Taylor, James Seay,
George Douglas, Charles Lane, Hal Price, Bud Geary, Ken
Cooper, James McNamara, Roy Butler, Kermit Maynard, Jean
Porter, Billy Benedict, Cyril Ring, Spade Cooley, Ted Mapes,
Jack Kirk, Rex Lease, William Kellogg, Tom Hanlon, Lee Shum-
way, Betty Farrington, Champion
Director: William Morgan
Associate Producer: Harry Grey
Story: Stuart Palmer
Screenplay: Robert Tasker, M. Coates Webster
Camera: Ernest Miller
Editor: Edward Mann
Music Director: Raoul Kraushaar
Songs: "Any Bonds Today?" by Irving Berlin; "Thinking To-
night of My Blue Eyes," "Modern Design," "Tweedle-o-
Twill," "Twilight in Old Wyomin'," and "Clementine"

54. STARDUST ON THE SAGE (5-25-42)
Cast: Gene Autry, Smiley Burnette, William Henry, Louise
Curry, Edith Fellows, Emmett Vogan, George Ernest, Vince Bar-
nett, Betty Farrington, Roy Barcroft, Tom London, Rex Lease,
Frank Ellis, Ed Cassidy, Franklyn Farnum, Frank LaRue, Fred
Burns, Edmund Cobb, Merrill McCormack, Jerry Jerome, Bert
LeBaron, Monte Montague, George DeNormand, Bill Jamison,
Jimmy Fox, George Sherwood, Bill Nestell, Frank O'Connor,

Griff Barnett, Lee Shumway, Champion
Director: William Morgan
Associate Producer: Harry Grey
Story: Dorrell and Stuart McGowan
Screenplay: Betty Burbridge
Camera: Bud Thackery
Editor: Edward Mann
Music Director: Raoul Kraushaar
Songs: "Home on the Range," "You Are My Sunshine," "Deep
    in the Heart of Texas," "Roll on Little Dogies," "When
    the Roses Bloom Again," "Good Night Sweetheart,"
    "You'll Be Sorry," "I'll Never Let You Go," and
    "Wouldn't You Like to Know?"

55. CALL OF THE CANYON (8-10-42)
Cast: Gene Autry, Smiley Burnette, Joe Strauch, Jr., Ruth
Terry, Thurston Hall, Cliff Nazarro, Dorothea Kent, Bob Nolan,
Pat Brady, Edmund McDonald, Marc Lawrence, John Holland,
Eddy Waller, Budd Buster, Frank Jacquet, Lorin Raker, Johnny
Duncan, Broderick O'Farrell, Ray Bennett, Carey Harrison, An-
thony Marsh, Fred Santley, Frank Ward, Freddie Walburn, Earle
Hodgins, John Harmon, Red Knight, Al Taylor, Jimmy Lucas,
Edna Johnson, Charles Flynn, Bob Burns, Charles Williams, Sons
of the Pioneers, Champion
Director: Joseph Santley
Associate Producer: Harry Grey
Story: Olive Cooper, Maurice Raff
Screenplay: Olive Cooper
Music Director: Raoul Kraushaar
Songs: "Call of the Canyon," "Somebody Else Is Taking My
    Place," and "Boots and Saddles"

56. BELLS OF CAPISTRANO (9-15-42)
Cast: Gene Autry, Smiley Burnette, Virginia Grey, Lucien Lit-
tlefield, Morgan Conway, Claire DuBrey, Charles Caine, Joe
Strauch, Jr., Marla Shelton, Tris Coffin, Jay Novello, Al Bridge,
Terrisita Osta, Eddie Acuff, Jack O'Shea, Julian Rivero, William
Forrest, Bill Telaak, Ken Christy, Dick Wessell, Ed Jauregui,
Guy Usher, Ralph Peters, Joe McGuinn, Howard Hickman, Bill
Kellogg, Carla Ramos, Fernando Ramos, Peggy Satterlee, Ray
Jones, Champion
Director: William Morgan

Associate Producer: Harry Grey
Screenplay: Lawrence Kimble
Camera: Reggie Lanning
Editor: Edward Mann
Music Director: Morton Scott
Songs: "Don't Bite the Hand That's Feeding You," "Forgive
     Me," "At Sundown," "In Old Capistrano," and "Uncle
     Sam Patter"

Bells of Capistrano was the last new Autry film until after he returned from his World War II service. Meanwhile, Republic met the audience and exhibitors Autry demand with reissues of his earlier pictures . . . mostly those of pre-1940 vintage. As far as can be determined, they did not make his first starring film—*Tumbling Tumbleweeds*—available though. Probably because it had been remade as *Carolina Moon*—and *Tumbling Tumbleweeds* wasn't as quite a slick and polished entry as the later films.

57. Sioux City Sue (11-21-46)
    Cast: Gene Autry, Lynne Roberts (formerly Mary Hart), Sterling Holloway, Richard Lane, Ralph Sanford, Ken Lundy, Helen Wallace, Pierre Watkin, Edwin Wills, Minerva Urecal, Frank Marlowe, LeRoy Mason, Harry "Pappy" Cheshire, George Carleton, Sam Flint, Michael Hughes, Tex Terry, Tris Coffin, Frankie Marvin, Forrest Burns, Tommy Coats, Cass County Boys, Champion.
    Director: Frank McDonald
    Associate Producer: Armand Schaefer
    Screenplay: Olive Cooper
    Camera: Reggie Lanning
    Editor: Fred Allen
    Music Director: Morton Scott
    Score: Dale Butts
    Songs: "Sioux City Sue" by Dick Thomas; "Someday You'll
         Want Me to Want You" by Jimmie Hodges; "Yours" by
         Gonzale Roig, Jack Sherr, and A. Rodriguez; "Ridin'
         Double" by John Rox; "You Stole My Heart" by Sosnick
         and Adams; "Chisholm Trail" and "Great-Granddad"

58. Trail to San Antone (1-25-47)
    Cast: Gene Autry, Peggy Stewart, Sterling Holloway, John

Duncan, Tris Coffin, Bill Henry, Dorothy Vaughn, Edward
Keane, Ralph Peters, Cass County Boys, Champion
Director: John English
Associate Producer: Armand Schaefer
Screenplay: Jack Natteford, Luci Ward
Songs: "Down the Trail to San Antone" by Duece Spriggins;
  "That's My Home" by Sid Robbins; "By the River of the
  Roses" by Joe Burke and Marty Symes; "Shame on You"
  by Spade Cooley; "The Cowboy Blues" by Cindy Walker
  and Gene Autry

59. TWILIGHT ON THE RIO GRANDE (4-1-47)
Cast: Gene Autry, Sterling Holloway, Adele Mara, Bob Steele,
Charles Evans, Martin Garralaga, Howard J. Negley, George J.
Lewis, Nacho Galindo, Tex Terry, George Magrill, Bob Burns,
Enrique Acosta, Frankie Marvin, Barry Norten, Gil Perkins,
Nina Campana, Kenne Duncan, Tom London, Alberto Morin,
Keith Richards, Anna Camargo, Donna Martell, Jack O'Shea,
Steve Soldi, Bud Osborne, Frank McCarroll, Bob Wilke, Alex
Montoya, Connie Menard, Joaquin Elizondo, Cass County Boys,
Champion
Director: Frank McDonald
Associate Producer: Armand Schaefer
Screenplay: Dorrell and Stuart McGowan
Camera: William Bradford
Editor: Harry Keller
2nd Unit Director: Yakima Canutt
Music Director: Morton Scott

60. SADDLE PALS (6-15-47)
Cast: Gene Autry, Lynne Roberts, Sterling Holloway, Irving
Bacon, Damian O'Flynn, Charles Arnt, Jean Val, Tom London,
Charles Williams, Francis McDonald, Edward Gargan, Carl
Sepulveda, Paul Burns, Joel Friedkin, LeRoy Mason, Larry Steers,
Edward Keane, Maurice Cass, Nolan Leary, Minerva Urecal,
John S. Roberts, James Carlisle, Sam Adh, Frank O'Connor, Neal
Hart, Frank Henry, Ed Piel, Bob Burns, Joe Yrigoyen, Johnny
Day, Cass County Boys, Champion, Jr.
Director: Lesley Selander
Associate Producer: Sidney Picker
Story: Dorrell and Stuart McGowan
Screenplay: Bob Williams, Jerry Sackheim
Camera: Bud Thackery

Music Director: Morton Scott
Editor: Harry Keller

61. ROBIN HOOD OF TEXAS (7-15-47)
Cast: Gene Autry, Lynne Roberts, Sterling Holloway, Adele
Mara, James Cardwell, John Kellogg, Ray Walker, Michael Bran-
den, Paul Bryar, James Flavin, Dorothy Vaughn, Stanley An-
drews, Al Bridge, Hank Patterson, Edmund Cobb, Lester Dorr,
William Norton Bailey, Irene Mack, Opal Taylor, Eve Novak,
Norma Brown, Frankie Marvin, Billy Wilkerson, Duke Green,
Ken Terrell, Joe Yrigoyen, Cass County Boys, Champion, Jr.
Director: Lesley Selander
Associate Producer: Sidney Picker
Screenplay: John Butler, Earle Snell
Camera: William Bradford
Editor: Harry Keller
Music Director: Morton Scott

(Following are all Gene Autry Productions released by Columbia.)

62. THE LAST ROUNDUP (11-5-47)
Cast: Gene Autry, Jean Heather, Ralph Morgan, Carol Thurs-
ton, Mark Daniels, Bobby Blake, Russ Vincent, Shug Fisher,
Trevor Bardette, Lee Bennett, John Halloran, Sandy Sanders,
Roy Gordon, Silverheels Smith, Francis Rey, Bob Cason, Dale
Van Sickle, Billy Wilkerson, Ed Piel, George Carleton, Don Kay
Reynolds, Nolan Leary, Ted Adams, Jack Baxley, Steve Clark,
Chuck Hamilton, Bud Osborne, Frankie Marvin, Kernan Cripps,
José Alvarado, J. W. Cody, Iron Eyes Cody, Blackie Whiteford,
Robert Walker, Virginia Carroll, Arline Archvletta, Louis
Crosby, Brian O'Hara, Rodd Redwing, Alex Montoya, the Texas
Rangers, Champion
Director: John English
Associate Producer: Armand Schaefer
Story: Jack Townley
Screenplay: Jack Townley, Earle Snell
Camera: William Bradford
Editor: Aaron Stell
Songs: "An Apple for the Teacher," "The Last Roundup," "You
    Can't See the Sun When You're Crying," "One Hundred

and Sixty Acres," and "She'll Be Coming Around the Mountain"

63. THE STRAWBERRY ROAN (August 1948)
Cast: Gene Autry, Gloria Henry, Jack Holt, Dick Jones, Pat Buttram, Rufe Davis, Eddy Waller, John McGuire, Rod Harper, Jack Ingram, Eddie Parker, Ted Mapes, Sam Flint, Champion and Little Champ
Director: John English
Producer: Armand Schaefer
Screenplay: Dwight Cummings, Dorothy Yost
Camera: Fred Jackson
Music Director: Mischa Bakaleinikoff
Filmed in Cinecolor
Songs: "The Strawberry Roan," "When the White Rose Blooms in Red River Valley," "Can't Shake the Sands of Texas from My Shoes," and "Texas Sandman"

64. LOADED PISTOLS (January 1949)
Cast: Gene Autry, Barbara Britton, Chill Wills, Jack Holt, Fred Kohler, Jr., Russell Arms, Robert Shayne, Vince Barnett, Leon Weaver, Clem Bevins, Sandy Sanders, Budd Buster, John R. McKee, Stanley Blystone, Hank Bell, Slim Gaut, Felice Raymond, Dick Alexander, Frank O'Connor, Reed Howes, William Sundholm, Snub Pollard, Heinie Conklin, Champion
Director: John English
Producer: Armand Schaefer
Story/Screenplay: Dwight Cummings, Dorothy Yost
Camera: William Bradford
Editor: Aaron Stell
Music Director: Mischa Bakaleinikoff
Songs: "When the Bloom Is on the Sage," "Loaded Pistols," "A Boy from Texas, A Girl from Tennessee," and "Pretty Mary"

65. THE BIG SOMBRERO (March 1949)
Cast: Gene Autry, Elena Verdugo, Stephen Dunne, George J. Lewis, Vera Marshe, William Edmunds, Martin Garralaga, Gene Stutenroth, Neyle Morrow, Bob Cason, Pierce Lyden, Rian Valente, Antonio Filauri, Sam Bernard, Joseph Palma, José Alvarado, Robert Espinosa, Cosmo Sardo, Alex Montoya, Joe Kirk, Artie Ortego, José Dominguez, Champion
Director: Frank McDonald

Producer: Armand Schaefer
Screenplay: Olive Cooper
Assistant Director: Earl Bellamy
Camera: William Bradford
Editor: Henry Batista
Music Supervisor: Paul Mertz
Music Director: Mischa Bakaleinikoff
Songs: "You Belong to My Heart," "La Golondrina," "Rancho Pillow," "My Adobe Hacienda," "Oh, My Darling Clementine," "Good-by Old Mexico," "Trail to Mexico," and, "I'm Thankful for Small Favors"
Filmed in Cinecolor

66. RIDERS OF THE WHISTLING PINES (May 1949)
Cast: Gene Autry, Patricia White, Jimmy Lloyd, Douglas Dumbrille, Damian O'Flynn, Clayton Moore, Britt Wood, Harry Cheshire, Leon Weaver, Loie Bridge, Jerry Scroggins, Fred Martin, Bert Dodson, Roy Gordon, Jason Robards, Sr., Len Torrey, Lane Chandler, Lynn Farr, Al Thompson, Emmett Vogan, Virginia Carroll, Nolan Leary, Steve Benton, Cass County Boys, Champion
Director: John English
Producer: Armand Schaefer
Screenplay: Jack Townley
Camera: William Bradford
Music: Mischa Bakaleinikoff
Songs: "Hair of Gold," "Let's Go Roaming Around the Range," "It's My Lazy Day," "Little Big Dry," "Every Time I Feel the Spirit," and "Toolie Oolie Doolie"

67. RIM OF THE CANYON (July 1949)
Cast: Gene Autry, Nan Leslie, Thurston Hall, Clem Bevins, Walter Sande, Jock Mahoney, Francis McDonald, Alan Hale, Jr., Amelita Ward, John R. McKee, Denver Pyle, Bobby Clark, Boyd Stockman, Sandy Sanders, Lynn Farr, Rory Mallison, Frankie Marvin, Champion
Director: John English
Producer: Armand Schaefer
Screenplay: John K. Butler
Story: "Phantom 45's Talk Loud" by Joseph Chadwick, published in *Western Aces* magazine
Camera: William Bradford

Editor: Aaron Stell
Music: Mischa Bakaleinikoff
Songs: "Rim of the Canyon" and "You're the Only Star in My Blue Heaven"

68. THE COWBOY AND THE INDIANS (September 1949)
Cast: Gene Autry, Sheila Ryan, Frank Richards, Hank Patterson, Jay Silverheels, Claudia Drake, George Nokes, Charles Stevens, Alex Fraser, Frank Lackteen, Chief Yowlachie, Lee Roberts, Nolan Leary, Maudie Prickett, Harry Mackin, Charles Quigley, Gilbert Alonzo, Roy Gordon, José Alvarado, Ray Beltram, Felipe Gomez, Iron Eyes Cody, Shooting Star, Champion
Director: John English
Producer: Armand Schaefer
Story: Dwight Cummings, Dorothy Yost
Camera: William Bradford
Editor: Henry Batista
Music Supervisor: Paul Mertz
Music Director: Mischa Bakaleinikoff
Songs: "Here Comes Santa Claus," "Silent Night," "America," and "One Little Indian Boy"

69. RIDERS IN THE SKY (November 1949)
Cast: Gene Autry, Gloria Henry, Pat Buttram, Mary Beth Hughes, Robert Livingston, Steve Darrell, Alan Hale, Jr., Tom London, Hank Patterson, Ben Welden, Dennis Moore, Joe Forte, Kenne Duncan, Frank Jacquet, Roy Gordon, Loie Bridge, Boyd Stockman, Vernon Johns, Pat O'Malley, John Parish, Kermit Maynard, Bud Osborne, Lynton Brent, Isabel Waters, Sandy Sanders, Denver Dixon, Robert Walker, Stan Jones, Champion
Director: John English
Producer: Armand Schaefer
Story: Herbert A. Woodbury
Screenplay: Gerald Geraghty
Camera: William Bradford
Editor: Henry Batista
Music Supervisor: Paul Mertz
Music Director: Mischa Bakaleinikoff
Songs: "Riders in the Sky," "It Makes No Difference Now," and "Cowboy's Lament"

70. SONS OF NEW MEXICO (January 1950)
Cast: Gene Autry, Gail Davis, Robert Armstrong, Dick Jones,

Frankie Darro, Clayton Moore, Irvin Bacon, Russell Arms, Marie
Blake, Sandy Sanders, Roy Gordon, Frankie Marvin, Paul Ray-
mond, Pierce Lyden, Kenne Duncan, Harry Mackin, Bobby
Clark, Gaylord Pendleton, Champion
Director: John English
Producer: Armand Schaefer
Story: Paul Gangelin
Camera: William Bradford
Editor: Henry Batista
Music Supervisor: Paul Mertz
Music Director: Mischa Bakaleinikoff
Songs: "Honey, I'm in Love with You," "There's a Rainbow on
the Rio Colorado," "Can't Shake the Sand of Texas from
My Shoes," and "NMMI March"

71. MULE TRAIN (2-22-50)
Cast: Gene Autry, Sheila Ryan, Pat Buttram, Robert Livingston,
Vince Barnett, Syd Saylor, Frank Jacquet, Sandy Sanders, Gregg
Barton, Roy Gordon, Stanley Andrews, Robert Hilton, Bob
Wilke, John Miljan, Robert Carson, Pat O'Malley, Kenne Dun-
can, Eddie Parker, George Morrell, John R. McKee, George
Slocum, Frank O'Connor, Norman Leavitt, Champion
Director: John English
Producer: Armand Schaefer
Story: Alan James
Screenplay: Gerald Geraghty
Camera: William Bradford
Editor: Henry Batista
Music Supervisor: Paul Mertz
Music Director: Mischa Bakaleinikoff
Songs: "Mule Train," "Roomful of Roses," and "Cool Water"

72. COW TOWN (May 1950)
Cast: Gene Autry, Gail Davis, Harry Shannon, Jock Mahoney,
Clark Burroghs, Harry Harvey, Steve Darrell, Sandy Sanders,
Ralph Sanford, Bud Osborne, Robert Hilton, Ted Mapes, Charles
Roberson, House Peters, Jr., Walt LaRue, Herman Hack, Victor
Cox, Ken Cooper, Holly Bane, Felice Raymond, Frank McCar-
roll, Frank O'Connor, Pat O'Malley, Blackie Whiteford, Frankie
Marvin, Champion
Director: John English
Producer: Armand Schaefer
Story: Gerald Geraghty

Camera: William Bradford
Editor: Henry Batista
Music Supervisor: Paul Mertz
Music Director: Mischa Bakaleinikoff
Songs: "Powder Your Face with Sunshine," "Down in the Valley,"
  "Buffalo Gal," and "The Dying Cowboy"

73. BEYOND THE PURPLE HILLS (July 1950)
    Cast: Gene Autry, Pat Buttram, Jo Dennison, Don Beddoe,
    James Millican, Don Kay Reynolds, Hugh O'Brian, Roy Gordon,
    Harry Harvey, Gregg Barton, Bob Wilke, Ralph Peters, Frank
    Ellis, John Cliff, Sandy Sanders, Tex Terry, Merrill McCormack,
    Fenton Jones, Maudie Prickett, Pat O'Malley, Boyd Stockman,
    Lynton Brent, Jerry Ambler, Victor Cox, Champion
    Director: John English
    Producer: Armand Schaefer
    Screenplay: Norman S. Hall
    Camera: William Bradford
    Editor: Richard Fantl
    Music Supervisor: Paul Mertz
    Music Director: Mischa Bakaleinikoff
    Songs: "Dear Hearts and Gentle People," "Beyond the Purple
      Hills," and "The Girl I Left Behind Me"

74. INDIAN TERRITORY (September 1950)
    Cast: Gene Autry, Pat Buttram, Gail Davis, Kirby Grant, James
    Griffith, Phil Van Zandt, Pat Collins, Roy Gordon, Charles
    Stevens, Robert Carson, Chief Thundercloud, Chief Yowlachie,
    Frank Lackteen, Boyd Stockman, Sandy Sanders, Frank Ellis,
    Frankie Marvin, John R. McKee, Bert Dodson, Nick Rodman,
    Wesley Hudman, Robert Hilton, Roy Butler, Kenne Duncan,
    Chief Thundersky, Champion
    Director: John English
    Producer: Armand Schaefer
    Screenplay: Norman S. Hall
    Camera: William Bradford
    Editor: James Sweeney
    Music Supervisor: Paul Mertz
    Music Director: Mischa Bakaleinikoff
    Songs: "Chattanooga Shoe Shine Boy" and "When the Campfire
      Is Low on the Prairie"

75. THE BLAZING SUN (November 1950) originally "The Blazing Hills"
Cast: Gene Autry, Pat Buttram, Lynne Roberts, Anne Gwynne, Edward Norris, Kenne Duncan, Alan Hale, Jr., Gregg Barton, Steve Darrell, Tom London, Sandy Sanders, Frankie Marvin, Bob Woodward, Boyd Stockman, Lewis Murphy, Virginia Carroll, Sam Flint, Chris Allen, Charles Coleman, Pat O'Malley, Almira Sessions, Nolan Leary, Champion
Director: John English
Producer: Armand Schaefer
Screenplay: Jack Townley
Camera: William Bradford
Editor: James Sweeney
Music Supervisor: Paul Mertz
Music Director: Mischa Bakaleinikoff
Songs: "Brush Those Tears from Your Eyes" and "Along the Navajo Trail"

76. GENE AUTRY AND THE MOUNTIES (January 1951)
Cast: Gene Autry, Pat Buttram, Elena Verdugo, Carleton Young, Richard Emory, Herbert Rawlinson, Trevor Bardette, Francis McDonald, Jim Frasher, Gregg Barton, House Peters, Jr., Jody Gilbert, Nolan Leary, Boyd Stockman, Bruce Carruthers, Robert Hilton, Teddy Infuhr, Billy Gray, John R. McKee, Roy Butler, Steven Elliott, Chris Allen, Champion
Director: John English
Producer: Armand Schaefer
Story: Norman S. Hall
Camera: William Bradford
Editor: James Sweeney
Music Director: Mischa Bakaleinikoff
Songs: "The Blue Canadian Rockies" and "Onterro"

77. TEXANS NEVER CRY (March 1951)
Cast: Gene Autry, Pat Buttram, Gail Davis, Mary Castle, Russell Hayden, Richard Powers (Tom Keene), Don Harvey, Roy Gordon, Michael Ragan (Holly Bane), Frank Fenton, Sandy Sanders, John R. McKee, Harry Mackin, Harry Tyler, Minerva Urecal, Richard Flato, I. Stanford Jolley, Duke York, Roy Butler, Champion
Director: Frank McDonald
Producer: Armand Schaefer

Screenplay: Norman S. Hall
Camera: William Bradford
Editor: James Sweeney
Music Supervisor: Paul Mertz
Music Director: Mischa Bakaleinikoff
Songs: "Ride, Rangers, Ride" and "Texans Never Cry"

78. WHIRLWIND (April 1951)
Cast: Gene Autry, Smiley Burnette, Gail Davis, Thurston Hall,
Harry Lauter, Dick Curtis, Harry Harvey, Gregg Barton,
Tommy Ivo, Kenne Duncan, Al Wyatt, Gary Goodwin, Pat
O'Malley, Bud Osborne, Boyd Stockman, Frankie Marvin, Stan
Jones, Leon DeVoe
Director: John English
Producer: Armand Schaefer
Screenplay: Norman S. Hall
Camera: William Bradford
Editor: Paul Borofsky
Music Supervisor: Paul Mertz
Music Director: Mischa Bakaleinikoff
Songs: "Whirlwind," "Tweedle-o-Twill," and "As Long As I
Live"

79. SILVER CANYON (June 1951)
Cast: Gene Autry, Pat Buttram, Gail Davis, Jim Davis, Bob
Steele, Edgar Dearing, Dick Alexander, Terry Frost, Peter Mama-
kos, Stanley Andrews, Duke York, Eugene Borden, Bobby Clark,
Frankie Marvin, Boyd Stockman, Sandy Sanders, Kenne Duncan,
Bill Hale, Jack O'Shea, Frank Matts, Stanley Blystone, John
Merton, Gary Goodwin, Jack Pepper, Pat O'Malley, Martin
Wilkins, Jim Magill, John R. McKee, Champion
Director: John English
Producer: Armand Schaefer
Story: Alan James
Screenplay: Gerald Geraghty
Camera: William Bradford
Editor: James Sweeney
Music Supervisor: Paul Mertz
Music Director: Mischa Bakaleinikoff
Songs: "Ridin' Down the Canyon" and "Fort Worth Jail"

80. HILLS OF UTAH (September 1951)
Cast: Gene Autry, Pat Buttram, Elaine Riley, Onslow Stevens,

Denver Pyle, Donna Martell, William Fawcett, Harry Harvey, Harry Lauter, Tom London, Kenne Duncan, Sandy Sanders, Teddy Infuhr, Lee Morgan, Boyd Stockman, Billy Griffith, Tommy Ivo, Bob Woodward, Stanley Price, Champion
Director: John English
Producer: Armand Schaefer
Camera: William Bradford
Story: Les Savage, Jr.
Screenplay: Gerald Geraghty
Music Supervisor: Paul Mertz
Music Director: Mischa Bakaleinikoff
Songs: "Peter Cottontail" and "Utah"

81. VALLEY OF FIRE (November 1951)
Cast: Gene Autry, Pat Buttram, Gail Davis, Russell Hayden, Christine Larson, Harry Lauter, Bud Osborne, Terry Frost, Barbara Stanley, Riley Hill, Duke York, Teddy Infuhr, Marjorie Liszt, Victor Sen Young, Gregg Barton, Sandy Sanders, Fred Sherman, James Magrill, Frankie Marvin, Pat O'Malley, William Crosby, William Fawcett, Syd Saylor, John Miller, Champion
Director: John English
Producer: Armand Schaefer
Story: Earl Snell
Screenplay: Gerald Geraghty
Camera: William Bradford
Editor: James Sweeney
Music Supervisor: Paul Mertz
Music Director: Mischa Bakaleinikoff
Songs: "On Top of Old Smoky" and "Here's to the Ladies"

82. THE OLD WEST (January 1952)
Cast: Gene Autry, Pat Buttram, Gail Davis, Lyle Talbot, House Peters, Jr., Tom London, House Peters, Sr., Louis Jean Heydt, Dick Jones, Don Harvey, James Craven, Kathy Johnson, Ray Morgan, Frankie Marvin, Dee Pollack, Bob Woodward, Syd Saylor, Buddy Roosevelt, Tex Terry, Pat O'Malley, Bobby Clark, Robert Hilton, John Merton, Frank Ellis, Champion
Director: George Archainbaud
Producer: Armand Schaefer
Screenplay: Gerald Geraghty
Camera: William Bradford
Editor: James Sweeney
Music Supervisor: Paul Mertz

Music Director: Mischa Bakaleinikoff
Songs: "Somebody Bigger Than You and I" and "Music By the Angels"

83. NIGHT STAGE TO GALVESTON (3-18-52)
Cast: Gene Autry, Pat Buttram, Virginia Huston, Thurston Hall, Judy Nugent, Robert Livingston, Harry Cording, Robert Bice, Frank Sully, Clayton Moore, Frank Rawls, Steve Clark, Harry Lauter, Robert Peyton, Lois Austin, Kathleen O'Malley, Riley Hill, Dick Alexander, Boyd Stockman, Bob Woodward, Sandy Sanders, Ben Welden, Gary Goodwin, Champion
Director: George Archainbaud
Producer: Armand Schaefer
Screenplay: Norman S. Hall
Camera: William Bradford
Editor: James Sweeney
Music Supervisor: Paul Mertz
Music Director: Mischa Bakaleinikoff
Songs: "A Heart As Big As Texas," "Down in Slumberland," and "Eyes of Texas"

84. APACHE COUNTRY (May 1952)
Cast: Gene Autry, Pat Buttram, Carolina Cotton, Harry Lauter, Mary Scott, Sidney Mason, Francis X. Bushman, Gregg Barton, Tom London, Byron Foulger, Frank Matts, Mickey Simpson, Iron Eyes Cody, Tony Whitecloud's Jemez Indians, Cass County Boys, Champion
Director: George Archainbaud
Producer: Armand Schaefer
Story/Screenplay: Norman S. Hall
Camera: William Bradford
Editor: James Sweeney
Music Supervisor: Paul Mertz
Music Director: Mischa Bakaleinikoff
Songs: "The Covered Wagon Rolls Right Along," "I Love to Yodel," "Cold, Cold Heart," and "Crime Will Never Pay"

85. BARBED WIRE (July 1952)
Cast: Gene Autry, Pat Buttram, Anne James, William Fawcett, Leonard Penn, Michael Vallon, Clayton Moore, Terry Frost, Eddie Parker, Sandy Sanders, Stuart Whitman, Zon Murray,

Frankie Marvin, Al Bridge, Victor Cox, Bobby Clark, Pat O'Malley, Bud Osborne, Bob Woodward, Wesley Hudman, Duke York, Harry Harvey, Champion
Director: George Archainbaud
Producer: Armand Schaefer
Screenplay: Gerald Geraghty
Camera: William Bradford
Editor: James Sweeney
Music Supervisor: Paul Mertz
Music Director: Mischa Bakaleinikoff
Songs: "Mexicali Rose" by H. Stone and J. B. Tenney; "Old Buckaroo Good-by" by Johnny Marvin and Gene Autry; and "Ezekiel Saw the Wheel" (P.D.)

86. WAGON TEAM (9–8–52)
Cast: Gene Autry, Pat Buttram, Gail Davis, Dick Jones, Harry Harvey, Gordon Jones, Henry Roland, George J. Lewis, John Cason, Gregg Barton, Carlo Tricoli, Pierce Lyden, Syd Saylor, Sandy Sanders, Frankie Marvin, Cass County Boys (Fred Martin, Fred Dodson, and Jerry Scroggins)
Director: George Archainbaud
Producer: Armand Schaefer
Screenplay: Gerald Geraghty
Camera: William Bradford
Editor: James Sweeney
Music Supervisor: Paul Mertz
Music Director: Mischa Bakaleinikoff
Songs: "Back in the Saddle Again," "In and Out of a Jailhouse," and "Howdy Friends and Neighbors"

87. BLUE CANADIAN ROCKIES (November 1952)
Cast: Gene Autry, Pat Buttram, Gail Davis, Carolina Cotton, Russ Ford, Tom London, Maurtiz Hugo, Don Beddoe, Gene Roth, John Merton, David Garcia, Bob Woodward, Billy Wilkerson, Cass County Boys, Champion
Director: George Archainbaud
Producer: Armand Schaefer
Screenplay: Gerald Geraghty
Camera: William Bradford
Editor: James Sweeney
Music Supervisor: Paul Mertz

Music Director: Mischa Bakaleinikoff
Songs: "Mama Don't Like Music," "Froggy Went A-Courtin'," "Old Chisholm Trail," "The Blue Canadian Rockies," "Anytime," and "Yodel, Yodel, Yodel"

88. WINNING OF THE WEST (January 1953)
Cast: Gene Autry, Smiley Burnette, Gail Davis, Richard Crane, Robert Livingston, House Peters, Jr., Gregg Barton, William Fawcett, Ewing Mitchell, Rodd Redwing, George Chesebro, Frank Jacquet, Charles Delaney, Charles Soldani, Eddie Parker, Frankie Marvin, Terry Frost, James Kirkwood, Boyd Morgan, Bob Woodward, Champion
Director: George Archainbaud
Producer: Armand Schaefer
Screenplay: Norman S. Hall
Camera: William Bradford
Editor: James Sweeney
Music Supervisor: Paul Mertz
Music Director: Russ DiMaggio
Songs: "Five Minutes Late and a Dollar Short," "Cowpoke Poking Along," "Cowboy Blues," and "Fetch Me Down My Trusty .45"

89. ON TOP OF OLD SMOKY (March 1953)
Cast: Gene Autry, Smiley Burnette, Gail Davis, Grandon Rhodes, Sheila Ryan, Kenne Duncan, Robert Bice, Zon Murray, Cass County Boys (Fred Martin, Jerry Scroggins, and Bert Dodson), Pat O'Malley, Champion
Director: George Archainbaud
Producer: Armand Schaefer
Camera: William Bradford
Editor: James Sweeney
Music Supervisor: Paul Mertz
Music Director: Mischa Bakaleinikoff
Songs: "On Top of Old Smoky," "I Saw Her First," "Hang My Head and Cry," "If It Wasn't for the Rain," and "Down the Trail to Mexico"

90. GOLDTOWN GHOST RAIDERS (5–20–53)
Cast: Gene Autry, Smiley Burnette, Gail Davis, Kirk Riley, Carleton Young, Neyle Morrow, Denver Pyle, Steve Conte, John Doucette, Champion
Director: George Archainbaud

Producer: Armand Schaefer
Screenplay: Gerald Geraghty
Camera: William Bradford
Editor: James Sweeney
Music Director: Mischa Bakaleinikoff
Songs: "There's a Gold Mine in Your Heart," "The Thieving Burro," and "Pancho's Widow"

91. PACK TRAIN (July 1953)
    Cast: Gene Autry, Smiley Burnette, Gail Davis, Kenne Duncan, Sheila Ryan, Tom London, Harry Lauter, Melinda Plowman, B. G. Norman, Louise Lorimer, Frankie Marvin, Norman Westcott, Tex Terry, Wesley Hudman, Kermit Maynard, Frank Ellis, Frank O'Connor, Dick Alexander, Jill Zeller, Herman Hack, Champion
    Director: George Archainbaud
    Producer: Armand Schaefer
    Screenplay: Norman S. Hall
    Camera: William Bradford
    Editor: James Sweeney
    Music Supervisor: Paul Mertz
    Music Director: Mischa Bakaleinikoff
    Songs: "Hominy Grits," "Wagon Trail," and "God's Little Candles"

92. SAGINAW TRAIL (September 1953)
    Cast: Gene Autry, Smiley Burnette, Connie Marshall, Eugene Borden, Ralph Reed, Henry Blair, Micky Simpson, John War Eagle, Rodd Redwing, Billy Wilkerson, Gregg Barton, John Parrish, John Merton, Charlie Hayes, Champion
    Director: George Archainbaud
    Producer: Armand Schaefer
    Screenplay: Dorothy Yost, Dwight Cummings
    Camera: William Bradford
    Editor: James Sweeney
    Music Director: Mischa Bakaleinikoff
    Songs: "Mam'selle," "When It's Prayer-Meetin' Time in the Hollow," and "Beautiful Dreamer"

93. LAST OF THE PONY RIDERS (November 1953)
    Cast: Gene Autry, Smiley Burnette, Kathleen Case, Dick Jones, Johnny Downs, Howard Wright, Arthur Space, Gregg Barton,

Buzz Henry, Harry Mackin, Harry Hines, Champion
Director: George Archainbaud
Producer: Armand Schaefer
Story/Screenplay: Ruth Woodman
Camera: William Bradford
Editor: James Sweeney
Music Supervisor: Paul Mertz
Music Director: Russ DiMaggio
Songs: "Sing Me a Song of the Saddle" and "Sugar Babe"

Autry appeared briefly in a ninety-fourth feature film, never released, *The Silent Treatment,* by Ralph Andrews Productions, 1968. Done in silent film technique, the cast included: Milton Berle, Marty Ingels, Sherry Jackson, George Raft, Jackie Coogan, Jerry Lewis, Gene Autry. Director: Ralph Andrews.

Gene Autry starred in ninety-one of his own television productions (thirteen filmed in color), and his Flying "A" Productions was responsible for four other series:
"Annie Oakley"—Eighty-one shows with Gail Davis
"The Range Rider"—Seventy-eight shows with Jock Mahoney
"Buffalo Bill, Jr."—Forty-two shows with Dick Jones
"The Adventures of Champion"—Twenty-six shows with the last of the three screen Champions

Index